The Warlords

Nicholas Hagger is a philosopher, cultural historian, poet and former lecturer in Islam and Japan. He is a also a prolific author whose long-term project is to present the universe, world history and human life in terms of the mystic Fire or Light, the metaphysical vision that is central to his work.

By the same author

The Fire and the Stones
A Mystic Way
Overlord
Selected Poems
A Smell of Leaves and Summer
A Spade Fresh With Mud
The Universe and the Light
A White Radiance

The Warlords

From D-Day to Berlin

A Verse Drama

NICHOLAS HAGGER

E L E M E N T
Shaftesbury, Dorset • Rockport, Massachusetts
Brisbane, Queensland

First published in Great Britain in 1995 by
Element Books Ltd
Shaftesbury, Dorset

Published in the USA in 1995 by
Element, Inc.
42 Broadway, Rockport, MA 01966

Published in Australia in 1995 by
Element Books Ltd
for Jacaranda Wiley Ltd
33 Park Road, Milton, Brisbane, 4064

Cover design by Max Fairbrother
Design by Alison Goldsmith
Typeset by Wendy Murdoch
Printed and bound in Great Britain by
Hartnolls, Bodmin, Cornwall

British Library Cataloguing in Publication
data available

Library of Congress Cataloging in Publication
data available

ISBN 1–85230–648–3

CHARACTERS

in order of appearance

A	Gen. Dwight D. Eisenhower, Supreme Commander of the Allied Expeditionary Force
B	Gen. Sir Bernard Montgomery, Commander-in-Chief, British Twenty-First Army Group
B	King George VI
B	Winston Churchill, British Prime Minister and Minister of Defence
SA	Field Marshal Smuts, South African Prime Minister
B	Field Marshal Sir Alan Brooke, Chief of the Imperial General Staff, War Office, and Chairman of the Chiefs of Staff Committee
A	Lt-Gen. Omar N. Bradley, Commanding General, US Twelfth Army Group
A	Lt-Gen. George S. Patton, Commanding General, US Third Army
B	Major Kit Dawnay, Military Assistant to Montgomery
B	Corporal, batman to Montgomery
B	Paul, deputy chef to Montgomery
B	Lt-Gen. Sir Miles Dempsey, General Officer Commanding-in-Chief, British Second Army
C	Lt-Gen. H. D. G. Crerar, General Officer Commanding-in-Chief, First Canadian Army
B	Group Captain J. M. Stagg, RAF, Eisenhower's meteorologist
B	Air Chief Marshal, Sir Arthur Tedder, Deputy Supreme Commander AEF
I	Kay Summersby, Eisenhower's driver and mistress
B	Admiral Sir Bertram Ramsay, Naval Commander-in-Chief, AEF
B	Air Chief Marshal Sir Trafford Leigh-Mallory, Air Commander-in-Chief, AEF
B	Rear Admiral George Creasy, Ramsay's Chief of Staff
B	D-Day soldier
A	Lt-Gen. Walter Bedell Smith, Chief of Staff to Supreme Commander, AEF
A	Lt-Commander Harry Butcher, Eisenhower's Naval Aide
G	Field Marshal Erwin Rommel, Commander of Army Group B
G	Lt-Gen. Hans Speidel, Rommel's Chief of Staff
G	Lucie Rommel, Rommel's wife
FDBe	Chorus of the Occupied
G	Adolf Hitler, Supreme Commander of the Armed Forces and Commander-in-Chief of the Army
G	Martin Bormann, Chief of Nazi Party Chancellery
B	Capt. Johnny Henderson, Montgomery's Aide de Camp
B	Howard Marshall, BBC representative

G Grand Admiral Karl Dönitz, Commander-in-Chief of the Naval High Command (OKM), later President of the Reich (Hitler's successor)

G Reichsmarschall Hermann Göring, Commander-in-Chief, Air High Command (OKL)

G Gen. Burgdorf, Hitler's chief adjutant

B Capt. John Poston, Montgomery's Aide de Camp

F Gen. Charles de Gaulle, leader of the Free French

F French aide

B Chorus of Londoners

A ⋆John Eisenhower, Eisenhower's son

G Gen. Alfred Jodl, Chief of the Operations Staff (OKW)

G Gen. Rudolf Schmundt, Hitler's ADC

G Stenographer

G Field Marshal W. Keitel, Chief, Armed Forces High Command (OKW)

G Field Marshal Gerd von Rundstedt, Commander-in-Chief West (OKW) from 4.9.44

B Air Marshal Sir Arthur Coningham, Air Marshal Commanding RAF Second Tactical Air Force

B John (Jock) Colville, formerly one of Churchill's private secretaries, a fighter pilot

G Chorus of Auschwitz prisoners

G Col. Heinrich Borgmann, one of Hitler's adjutants

B Air Chief Marshal Sir Arthur Harris, Air Officer Commanding-in-Chief, RAF Bomber Command

B Lt-Gen. Frederick Browning, Commander of First Allied Airborne Army (whose daughter later married Montgomery's son)

G Col. Count Claus von Stauffenberg, Chief of Staff to Commander of the Replacement Army, conspirator

G Major John von Freyend, Keitel's adjutant

G ⋆Col. Heinz Brandt, conspirator

G Gen. Erich Fellgiebel, conspirator

G Dr. Joseph Goebbels, Minister of Propaganda, Gauleiter of Berlin

G Albert Speer, Reich Minister of Arms and Munitions

G ⋆Walter Funk, Economics Minister

G Major Otto Remer, Commander of the Guard Battalion Grossdeutschland

G Gen. F. Olbricht, deputy to Col-Gen. Fromm

G Lt Werner von Haeften, Stauffenberg's Aide de Camp, conspirator

G Col.-Gen. F. Fromm, Commander-in-Chief of the Home Army

G ⋆Col. Mertz von Quirnheim, Olbricht's Chief of Staff, conspirator

G Col.-Gen. Ludwig Beck, Head of State designate after July 20th coup

G ★Lt Ewald Heinrich Kleist, conspirator
G Lt-Gen. Erich Hoepner, conspirator
G Hauptmann Bartram, Fromm's adjutant
G ★Lt-Col. Gehrke
G Sergeant
G Firing-squad, including soldier
B Bill Williams Head of Intelligence to Montgomery, ex-Oxford history don
G Heinrich Himmler, SS Reichsführer, Chief of the Gestapo, Chief of Police, Minister of the Interior, Commander of the Reserve Army, Commander of Army Group Vistula
G Ernst Kaltenbrunner, Head of SS Reich Security, Head Office (RSHA)
G Dr. Erwin Giesing, one of Hitler's physicians
G ★Franz von Sonnleithner, Ribbentrop's Foreign Ministry liaison official with Hitler and Hitler's interceptor of foreign messages at Rastenburg
G Dr Roland Freisler, chief judge, the People's Court
G Field Marshal von Witzleben, conspirator
G Count Yorck von Wartenburg, conspirator
G ★Maj-Gen. Helmuth Stieff, conspirator
G ★Gen. Paul von Hase, Commandant of Berlin, conspirator
G ★Lt-Col. Bernadis, conspirator
G ★Capt. Klausing, conspirator
G ★Lt. von Hagen, conspirator
G Dr. Kurt Hanssen, Public Prosecutor
G Cameraman
G Hangman and Executioner
A ★Gen. Humphrey Gale, Chief of Administration, SHAEF
A Gen. Allen, Chief of Staff, 12th US Army Group
B James Gunn, artist
A Lt-Gen. Courtney H. Hodges, Commanding General, US First Army
R Marshal Josef Stalin, Secretary-General of the Communist Party of the Soviet Union and premier of the Soviet state, co-ordinator of First, Second and Third Belorussian and First Ukrainian Fronts
A Maj. Chester Hansen, aide to Bradley
A Maj.-Gen. Sir Francis de Guingand, Chief of Staff to Montgomery
B Gen. Archibald Nye,Vice Chief of the Imperial General Staff, deputy to Brooke
B ★Gen. Freddy Morgan, Eisenhower's Deputy Chief of Staff, SHAEF
B Maj-Gen. K. W. D. Strong, G-2 Division (Intelligence) SHAEF
B Gen. John Whiteley, Chief of Operations, SHAEF

G Gen. Günther Blumentritt, von Rundstedt's Chief of Staff
B Maj.-Gen. R. E. Urquhart, Commander of First British Airborne Division
R Marshal Georgi Konstantinovich Zhukov, Commander on the ground under Stalin of First, Second and Third Belorussian and First Ukrainian Fronts, and direct Commander of First Belorussian Front
R Marshal Konstantine K. Rokossovsky, Commander of First Belorussian Front
R Vyacheslav Mikhailovich Molotov, Soviet Foreign Minister
R Gen. Antonov, Chief of Operations and first deputy Chief of the General Staff
R Paulina Molotov, Molotov's wife and reputedly Stalin's mistress
A Gen. George C. Marshall, Chief of Staff of the US Army
G Gen. Ernst Maisel, chief law officer to Burgdorf
G Manfred Rommel, Rommel's son
G Field Marshal Walter Model, Commander-in-Chief West and Commander of Army Group B
B Dai Rees, golfer
A Brig-Gen. Everett Hughes, a friend of Eisenhower's
A Gen. Kean, Chief of Staff to Hodges
A Lt-Gen. William H. Simpson, Commanding General, US Ninth Army
G Gen. Heinz Guderian, acting Chief of the General Staff of the Army
G Count Helmuth J. von Moltke, conspirator, founder of the Kreisau Circle
G *Father Alfred Delp, Jesuit, conspirator
G *Col. Franz Sperr, conspirator
G Eva Braun, Hitler's mistress and later wife
G Ilse Braun, sister of Eva and Gretl Braun
G Col.-Gen. (later Field Marshal) Ferdinand Schörner, Commander of Army Group Centre
G Chorus of Berliners
R Gen. Vassily Chuikov, Commander of Eighth Guards Army, First Belorussian Front
R Gen. Malinin, Zhukov's Chief of Staff
G SS Guard
G Gen. Walther Wenck, Guderian's Chief of Staff
G Major Bernd Baron Freytag von Loringhoven, Guderian's adjutant
G Capt. Gerhard Boldt, Loringhoven's Aide de Camp
G Gen. Fegelein, Chief of Waffen SS, Himmler's personal representative to Hitler, married to Gretl Braun, Eva Braun's sister
G Chorus of Dresdeners

G Lt-Gen. Helmuth Reymann, Military Commander of Berlin
G Dr. Theodore Morell, one of Hitler's physicians
G Magda Goebbels, Goebbels' wife
G SS Brigadeführer (Brig-Gen) Heinz Lammerding, Himmler's Chief of Staff
A Lt Tex Lee, Eisenhower's office executive
G Col.-Gen. Gotthard Heinrici, Commander of Army Group Vistula after Himmler
G Gen. Theodore Busse, Commander Ninth Army
G Col. Refior, Reymann's Chief of Staff
A Aide to Gen. Marshall
R Gen. S. M. Shtemenko, Chief of Operations
R Lavrenti Beria, Head of the NKVD (state security)
R ★Georgi Malenkov, Secretary of the Central Committee of the Communist Party
R ★Anastas Mikoyan, Minister of Trade and Industry
R ★Marshal Nikolai Bulganin, representative of the Supreme Command for Soviet fronts
R ★Lazar Kagonovich, Transport Minister
R ★Nikolai Voznesensky, in charge of the economy
R Marshal Ivan Stepanovich Koniev, Commander of First Ukrainian Front
G Gen. Hans Krebs, Chief of the General Staff of the Army after Guderian
G Maj-Gen Walter Buhle, organiser of the Reserve Army
R Vassiliev Kokorin, Russian air force officer, nephew of Molotov
G Pastor Dietrich Bonhoeffer, conspirator
G Ex-prisoner
G SS man
G Guard
A Maj-Gen. Alexander Bolling, in charge of 84th Division
G Staff 1 and 2, Ministry of Propaganda
G Rudolf Semmler, assistant to Goebbels
G Joachim von Ribbentrop, German Foreign Minister
G Col. Eismann, Heinrici's Chief of Operations
R Russian soldier
R Lt-Gen. N. K. Popiel, Chief of Staff, First Guards Tank Army
G Traudl Junge, Hitler's secretary
G Gerda Christian, Hitler's secretary, later chief secretary
G Johanna Wolf, Hitler's secretary
G Christa Schröder, Hitler's secretary
G Chorus of Berliners
B Major Peter Earle, Liaision Officer, formerly Military Secretary to the Vice Chief of Imperial General Staff
B Dr. Robert Hunter, Montgomery's physician

G Klaus Bonhoeffer, Dietrich Bonhoeffer's brother-in-law, conspirator
G *Rüdiger Schleicher, also Dietrich Bonhoeffer's brother-in-law, conspirator
G Albrecht Haushofer, poet, conspirator
G *Herbert Kosney, conspirator
G 12 other prisoners, and SS Guards
S Count Folke Bernadotte, Vice-Chairman of Swedish Red Cross and nephew of King Gustav V
G Lt-Gen. Helmuth Weidling, Commander of 56th Panzer Corps, later Commandant of Berlin Defence Region
G Capt. Kafurke, Weidling's Intelligence Officer
G Gen. Hasso von Manteuffel, Commander of Third Panzer Army
G Heinz Lorenz, Hitler's press officer
G Walter Wagner, municipal councillor, registrar of marriages
G *Constanze Manziarly, Hitler's vegetarian dietician
G Major Willi Johannmeier, soldier
G Arter Axmann, Head of the Hitler Youth
B Ernie, a British private
G Belsen men and women
G Lt-Col. Weiss, Burgdorf's adjutant
G Professor Haase, one of Hitler's physicians
G Hans Bauer, Hitler's personal pilot
G Major-Gen. Wilhelm Mohnke, Commander of Waffen SS units near Chancellery
G Major Otto Gunsche, Hitler's SS adjutant and bodyguard
G *Heinz Linge, Hitler's valet
R Lt.-Gen V. A. Glazunov, Commander of 4th corps
G Col. Theodor von Dufving, Weidling's Chief of Staff
G Heidi Goebbels, Goebbels' daughter
G Sgt. Misch, SS guard
R Lt-Col. Matusov, staff officer to Chuikov
R Lt Kiselyov, company commander
R Private Vladimir Abyzov, soldier in Kiselyov's unit
G Heinersdorf, Senior Executive Officer, Ministry of Propaganda
G Gen.-Admiral von Friedeburg, Commander-in-Chief of the German Fleet
G Gen. Kinzel, Chief of Staff, German Army North
G Rear Admiral Wagner, Flag Officer to the Admiral of the Fleet
G Major Friedl, Gestapo
C Lt-Col Trumbell Warren, Montgomery's Personal Assistant
B Col. Joe Ewart, Montgomery's German-speaking Intelligence Officer
G *Col. Pollok, holder of German codes
B Chorus of Londoners

F	*Gen. de Lattre de Tassigny, commander of First French Army
B	*Gen. Sir Harold Alexander, Commander-in-Chief of all Allied Forces in Italy
B	*Clement Attlee, British Prime Minister from July 1945
B	*Anthony Eden, British Foreign Secretary
B	Capt. Pim, in charge of Churchill's Map Room
A	President Harry Truman, US President after Roosevelt
A	Aide to Truman
A	Averell Harriman, US Ambassador to Moscow

*Non-speaking part.

A	American
Be	Belgian
B	British
C	Canadian
D	Dutch
F	French
G	German
I	Irish
R	Russian
SA	South African
S	Swedish

MAIN CAST

An example of how the main speaking parts can be spread between a cast of 33 (based on what is approximately feasible rather than what is desirable in terms of resemblance).

Eisenhower + Bernadotte
Montgomery + Weidling
Churchill + Hunter
Brooke + Hansen + Loringhoven + Wagner
Bradley + firing-squad + Chorus + Lammerding + Fegelein + Pim
Patton + Remer + Gen. Marshall + Guderian + Haase + Matusov
Dawnay + Browning + Olbricht + Model + Buhle + Glazunov
Henderson + Ramsay? + Coningham + Reymann + Kokorin
Chef + Speidel + Fromm + de Guingand + Heinrici + Dufving
Dempsey + Keitel + Kaltenbrunner + Lee + Refior + Lorenz + Beria
Stagg + Howard Marshall + Borgmann + Hanssen + Wenck + Dietrich Bonhoeffer + Kiselyov
Tedder + Rundstedt + Wartenburg + Strong + Himmler
Kay Summersby + Eva Braun + Jean Gordon + Junge
Leigh-Mallory + Colville + Dr. Morell + Urquhart + Hughes + Koniev + Weiss + Sokolovsky
Rommel + Guderian + Stalin + Friedeburg
Bedell Smith + Dönitz + Speer + Allen + Busse + Earle
Butcher + Jodl + Haeften + Freisler + Maisel + Mohnke
D-Day soldier + aide to de Gaulle + stenographer + hangman + Dai Rees + Simpson + Krebs
Bormann + Rokossovsky + Crerar
Williams + Witzleben + Moltke + Bolling + Boldt
Göring + Dr. Giesing + Malinin + Whiteley + Manteuffel + Harriman
Hitler + Truman
Burgdorf + Bomber Harris + Blumentritt + Zhukov
George VI + Poston + Nye + Hodges + Antonov + Semmler + Popiel + Gunsche
De Gaulle + Stauffenberg + Chuikov + Schörner? + Goebbels
Aide + Sergeant + Cameraman + Kean + SS Guard + Shtemenko
Lucie Rommel + Magda Goebbels + Paula + Ilse + Chorus + Marlene Dietrich + Christian
6 Chorus of the Occupied/Londoners/Auschwitz prisoners/Berliners/Dresdeners + Schroder + Wolf + Belsen men and women + SS guards + firing-squad + Heidi + Misch + Kinzel + Wagner + Friedl + Manfred + Klaus Bonhoeffer + Schleicher + Haushofer + Kosney + any other non-speaking parts.

Total 27 cast + 6 chorus, etc. = 33. This can be reduced to 30; it is better if it is increased.

SCENES

PART ONE

1. D-Day 1

2. Normandy: Defeating Rommel 19

3. Stauffenberg's Bomb Plot 41

4. Montgomery's Demotion 58

5. Arnhem 69

6. The Ardennes 83

7. Stalin's Offensive 104

PART TWO

1. Crossing the Rhine: Berlin or Dresden? 133

2. The Defence of Berlin 146

3. The Fall of Hitler 179

4. Unconditional Surrender 196

5. Victory in Europe 205

Plan of the Führer bunker xviii

*Asterisked blocks are candidates for excision if the two Parts are put on as one play.

Recommended intervals: Part One, at the end of Scene 4; Part Two, at the end of the Belsen scene, on p185.

PREFACE
TO THE WARLORDS, PARTS 1 AND 2

The Warlords puts the last year of the war on stage. Its two Parts are therefore necessarily long and rival the length of Goethe's *Faust*, Parts One and Two.

At one level *The Warlords* has been written as a celebration of the 50th anniversary of VE Day (8th May 1995), and besides creating imaginatively realised, living, solid characters who move in and out of known events I have wanted to leave the audience with a clear, historically accurate – and verifiable – picture of the main issues. The Second World War dominated my childhood; I lived in the path of the air raids and the flying bombs. The men in the assault craft were heroes for my generation, and my awe of what they did on D-Day has, if anything, increased over the years. There is still great interest in what happened. After fifty years an event passes into history and people who were once living take on the force of historical characters and appear to represent historical forces. I met both Churchill and Montgomery, and it is with reverence that I now present them in terms of the drives and forces which shaped our lives.

I have found the medium of verse liberating; I have been acutely aware that the sweep of my settings would be impossible in the medium of realistic prose drama. This revival of contemporary verse drama is essentially practical; it gets the job done better than prose could by escaping the constraints of realistic settings and by reviving monologues, soliloquies, asides. As Marlowe and Shakespeare found, and as Goethe also found in *Faust*, Parts One and Two, verse drama can range over battlefields and heaths and get inside the soul of characters.

The verse in *The Warlords* varies the strictness of iambic pentameters (⏑–) by including trochees (–⏑), anapaests (⏑⏑–) and dactyls (–⏑⏑) where feeling requires a loosening, and even tribrachs (⏑⏑⏑), bacchiuses (⏑––), cretics (–⏑–) and sometimes amphibrachs which reverse cretics (⏑–⏑). On rare occasions there may be 4-syllable feet such as paeons (–⏑⏑⏑ or ⏑⏑⏑–) or Aeolic choriambs (–⏑⏑–).

A verse dramatist writing today follows in the footsteps of Marlowe, the inventor of blank verse, and Shakespeare, and their historical plays *Tamburlaine the Great* and *Henry the Fourth* (both in two parts); Webster, whose *The White Devil* draws on the history of Renaissance Italy, and Dryden's *All for Love*; and more recently Fry's *The Lady's not for Burning* and Eliot's *Murder in the Cathedral*.

Every historical dramatist has a source. Marlowe used an English version by P.F. of the German *Historia von D. Iohan Fausten* of 1587; Shakespeare North's Plutarch and Holinshed's *Chronicles*; Webster a German newsletter written from the Fugger banking house in Augsburg; and Dryden used Plutarch's *Life of Antony* as well as Appian's *Civil Wars* and Dio's *Roman History*. I have assembled a library on the Second World War of a couple of hundred books. The British accounts of the last year of the war (such as Nigel Hamilton's) support Montgomery, the American accounts (such as Stephen Ambrose's) Eisenhower. I have tried to be even-handed, and to show both sides. I have gone to some pains (notably visiting Normandy, Berlin, Warsaw, Auschwitz and Munich) to achieve historical accuracy and veracity. Generally speaking, the dialogue reflects established events, while the soliloquies provide imaginative interpretation based on documentation.

My interpretation of the characters has been based on documentary evidence. To focus on some of this, a number of books on the occult influences on Nazism show that Hitler must be seen in relation to the Thule Society and the occult practices of Dietrich Eckart, which included forays into black magic; and that there was at least a suppressed Satanism in the Nazi drive against Jehovah, the Jewish god. Several books show that after the bomb plot Hitler declined into a shuffling, trembling human wreck who was but a shadow of his former dictatorial self. His fascination with the spear of Longinus has been documented in Trevor Ravenscroft's *The Spear of Destiny* and there are several books on the Nazis and the occult, the most sober and academic of which is Nicholas Goodrick-Clarke's *The Occult Roots of Nazism*, the most interesting Nigel Pennick's *Hitler's Secret Sciences*. The first was Pauwels and Bergier's *The Morning of the Magicians*, and the most comprehensive is Francis King's *Satan and Swastika: The Occult and the Nazi Party*. All these books look back to Hermann Rauschning's *Hitler Speaks* (1939) in which the Nazi Governor of Danzig describes his conversations with Hitler between 1932 and 1934, and H.G. Baynes's *Germany Possessed* (1941). Lawyers wanting convictions and executions at the Nuremberg trials suppressed some of the occult material as it might have given the defendants cause to plead diminished responsibility.

That Hitler was shown the *Protocols of the Elders of Zion*, which he mentioned as a Jewish work in *Mein Kampf*, by Rosenberg, to whom Eckart introduced him around 1920, is documented in many books, for example Lucy S. Dawidowicz's *The War Against the Jews, 1933-45*. The Final Solution to kill the Jews was decided on at the Wannsee Conference of January 1942, chaired by Heydrich, but it had its roots in the early 1920s and is heralded in *Mein Kampf.* (For the eschatological connotations in the word "Final", which led Malraux to speak of "le retour de Satan", see Dawidowicz p18.) How Hitler saw the Jews can be found in a number of books, including the chapter "Jehovah as Satan" in Dusty Sklar's *The Nazis and the Occult*. The Allies' knowledge of events in Auschwitz from May 1941, and certainly in March and June 1944, is documented in Martin Gilbert's *Auschwitz and the Allies*.

Montgomery was at heart a very religious man. His father was a clergyman, he always went to church when he could, he wrote of "the Lord mighty in battle" and, according to his deputy chef (who travelled with him from Broomfield House to Lüneburg Heath and with whom I have had a long discussion) he always went to bed at 9 p.m. to pray in his caravan. It was generally known in "A" Mess that Montgomery could not be disturbed on any account after 9 p.m. because he was in prayer, obtaining God's Providential guidance for the huge decisions he faced. For some years he lived simply in a caravan close to Nature, both on North African sand and European grass, and he did not smoke or drink, and thus represented the puritanical tradition.

That the Jewish Paulina Molotov, the Soviet Foreign Minister's wife, became Stalin's mistress after his wife died is suggested in Larisa Vasilyeva's *Kremlin Wives*. Files in the KGB archives show that Niels Bohr gave Stalin nuclear secrets via Beria's agents Vasilevsky and Terletsky, as reported in *The Sunday Times* of 26th June 1994.

Eisenhower's relationship with the Irish driver Kay Summersby is documented in her book (written under her later name, Kay Summersby Morgan), *Past Forgetting: My Love Affair with Dwight D. Eisenhower*. It is not known if she told the whole truth; but if she did then Eisenhower was sexually impotent during the whole war. I have chosen not to believe this entirely.

The conflict between the Christian Montgomery, the occultist Hitler and the materialist Stalin goes deeper than social disquiet and raises metaphysical considerations of good and evil. After fifty years the time has come to present Hitler's racism in its true context, de-demonising Hitler but not hiding his involvement with the occult, without which the Holocaust cannot be understood. (Indeed, failure to address Hitler's occult beliefs about Jehovah is the main reason why the Holocaust has so far not been understood.) Philosophers who study the universe seek to reconcile the opposites of war and peace within the total scheme, as did Tolstoy, and Montgomery's belief in a Providential power for good that orders events in a fallen world offers such a reconciliation.

The Warlords honours the men who delivered us from evil and enslavement by a totalitarian dictatorship and shaped the world we know. The last year of the war threw up so many issues that have dominated the last fifty years: the Russian domination of Eastern Europe; the atomic bomb; the rise of American world power; the decline of British world power, which can be dated back to the demotion of Montgomery on 1st September 1944; the dream of a united Europe; the Final Solution of the Jewish problem which saw five million Jews killed; and the need for a world government. Against a background of conflicting ideologies, philosophies and historical forces, *The Warlords* explores the warlords' leadership, and, I hope, present an eternal image of the relationship between power and good.

The Warlords can be produced as two separate plays or as one play with excisions. Asterisked blocks are candidates for excision.

13th February 1995

LAY-OUT OF THE FÜHRER BUNKER, BERLIN

(Numbers indicate areas referred to in *The Warlords*)

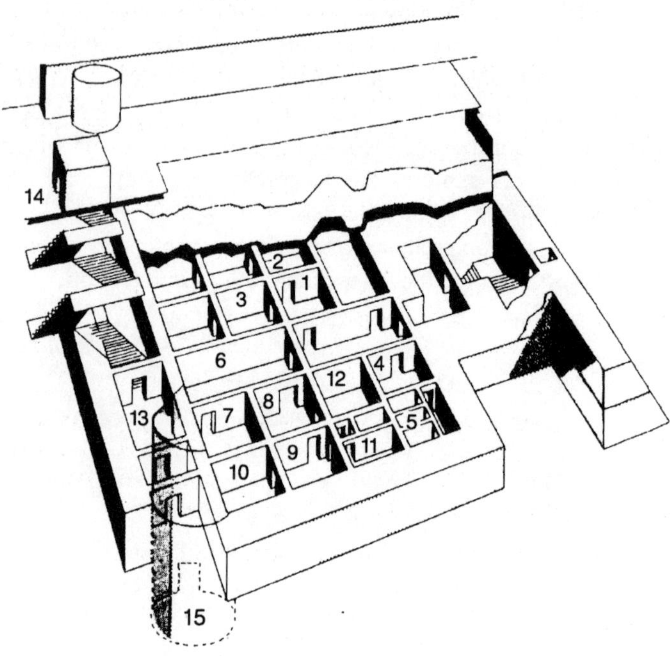

1. Telephone switchboard
2. Dr. Morell's room
3. Orderly officers' social room
4. Blondi's room (Hitler's dog)
5. Toilets
6. Reception room or ante-room in corridor
7. Conference room
8. Refreshment room or ante-room by Hitler's office
9. Hitler's office or study/living room with picture of Frederick the Great
10. Hitler's bedroom
11. Hitler's and Eva's bathroom
12. Eva's bedroom
13. Emergency exit to
14. Garden exit, and
15. Dome-shaped tower

THE WARLORDS, PART ONE

SCENE 1. D-DAY

(15th May 1944, St. Paul's School, lecture theatre. Eisenhower, Montgomery, King George VI, Churchill, Smuts and British Chiefs of Staff sit on chairs in the first row. Generals and their staff sit on wooden benches behind. Several hundred are present. Blackboard, map.)

Eisenhower. Today we present the plan for Operation
Overlord so that every commander has
A last chance to understand the strategy.
It is vital we are honest. It is the duty
Of anyone who sees a flaw to say so.
I now invite General Montgomery,
Allied Land Forces Commander, to come forward.

(Montgomery rises in battledress. He speaks in a tone of quiet emphasis, addressing the audience. As he starts there is a hammering on the door and Patton swaggers in and sits down. Montgomery looks round angrily.)

Montgomery. General Eisenhower has charged me with the
Preparation and conduct of the land battle.
There are four armies under my control.
First American, Second British: assault.
Third American, First Canadian: follow-up.
The enemy. Last February, Rommel took command
From Holland to the Loire. It is now clear
That his intention is to deny any penetration.
Overlord is to be defeated on the beaches.
To this end he has thickened his coastal crust,
Increased his infantry, and redistributed
His armoured reserve. Fortress Europe has
Become more and more formidable. There are
Sixty German divisions stationed in France,
Of which ten are élite Panzer divisions,
And four of these are in the Normandy area,
(Pointing with pointer) At Caen, Lisieux, Rennes and Tours. Rommel
Is an energetic and determined commander,
He has made a world of difference since he took over.
He will try to force us off the beaches
And secure Caen, Bayeux and Carentan.
The Allies *must* seize and hold fast these three
Nodal points, in which case Rommel will revert

To his Alamein tactics of counter-attacks.
Now there are several hundred of you here,
And I want to give you all a clear idea
Of the problem we face, and the solution.

(*Later.*)

Montgomery. So, to sum up, the plan is straight forward
And simple. We hold the enemy at Caen,
Like a boxer holding off his opponent
With his left fist, and then with our right flank
We deliver a terrific surprise blow
From the peninsula around Cherbourg, through Rennes,
To Paris and the Seine, like a boxer
Swinging with his right and hitting his opponent
In his solar plexus, and send him reeling against
The ropes – the river Seine. Is that completely clear?
We're *not* knocking him out at Caen with our left,
We're holding him off with the British and Canadians.
The knock-out comes with our right, the Americans.
I remind you, these phase lines show where we expect
To reach in the ninety days after D-Day.
Now morale is very important. The soldiers
Must go in seeing red. We must get them
Completely on their toes, with absolute
Faith in the plan, infectious optimism
And offensive eagerness. Nothing must stop them.
If we send them into battle in this way
Then we shall succeed, and we'll show Hitler
Who is really Overlord of Europe.

(*Later. Audience standing and chatting. The King, Churchill and Brooke talk.*)

Churchill. It was like Henry the Fifth before Agincourt:
Confident, optimistic, but grave.
Brooke. He
Has pressed me for Overlord since forty-two.
Churchill. He returned to Britain a hero, the conqueror of Rommel.
There's been nothing like the popular acclaim
Since Wellington returned from Waterloo.
When he began going round the country
Speaking to thirty thousand men in a day,
Wearing the beret of a tank soldier
And being cheered for his charisma, I
Thought he really might be after my job.
King. I thought he was after mine.
Eisenhower. I hope not mine.
Churchill. Monty would make a good Prime Minister.
A Prime Minister must be popular,
He must be a showman who can represent

All things to all people, secure support,
Speak simply on many levels at once,
Be understood in factory and office alike,
Be a reconciler who holds together
Conflicting views, coalitions of opinion.
He must appear honest, he must inspire,
He must speak boldly and be identified
With a clear view, and be known for a plan,
Lead from a position well understood
And promise a better tomorrow, over the hill,
For a leader is lost when he stops looking ahead.
A Prime Minister is a General in a beret
Who takes the troops with him by oratory
And the dash he cuts in his battledress.

(*Laughter.*)

A leader is how his people see him.
He is their expectations in terms of which
They may be disappointed. He must strive
To be their dream, even though he is quite other,
And the man within privately scoffs at what
They hang on him, the image they want him to be.
A leader is an actor who plays for applause.

(*Laughter. Eisenhower moves away.*)

Bradley. A brilliant presentation, clear and convincing.
Patton. You were very confident, you radiated confidence.
Eisenhower (*joining them*). Without notes, you were totally in charge,
A very convincing estimate of the situation.
Montgomery. Ike, you handled it well. You said little
But what you said was on a high level.
Bradley. You inspired your King to speak. That was unexpected.
Montgomery. What he said was just right, short but just right.
Patton. Smuts was pessimistic about German ruthlessness,
But Churchill made a stirring speech at the end.
Montgomery. He was more full of life than the last occasion.
Eisenhower. He looked quite dejected then, and when he spoke
He said "I am *now* hardening to the enterprise."
That shocked me, I realised he had not
Believed that Overlord would succeed till then.
Montgomery. He does now. He has faith in the plan now.

(*17th May, Broomfield House study, Montgomery's TAC HQ. Montgomery and Dawnay.*)

Dawnay. A letter from Churchill's military assistant,
General Ismay. Churchill was "much concerned"
By some of the statements made at Monday's
Conference, for example, two thousand clerks
Are to be taken to keep records, and at

D plus twenty there will be one vehicle
To every 4.84 men. Ismay writes:
"The Prime Minister would like to have a discussion
With you and your staff on the whole question
Of the British tail", before dinner on Friday.

Montgomery. It's interference. But I'll have to see him.

(*19th May. Broomfield House study.*)

Montgomery. I understand, sir, that you want to discuss
With my staff the proportion of soldiers to vehicles
Landing on the beaches in the first flights.
I cannot allow you to do so. I took
An unsound operation of war as I
Told you in Marrakesh on New Year's Day,
With the organisation of command and frontage wrong,
And recast it into a clear plan that
Everyone can have faith and confidence in.
Nothing has been left to chance or improvisation.
The staff have done a terrific job preparing
The invasion. After months of meticulous planning
The whole of southern England is an army depot.
There are queues of tanks and lorries and guns
All waiting to be shipped, all checked by SHAEF.
The work is now almost completed. We
Have just enough vehicles, the right number.
All over England troops are moving towards
The assembly areas, prior to embarkation.
To make a change now would cause tremendous
Disruption, and shake their confidence in the plan.
In the last two years I have won battles
At Alamein, Tripoli, Medenine,
Mareth, Wadi Akarit, Sicily,
And Southern Italy. The invasion of Normandy
Has the confidence of the men. Besides commanding
A British army I will command a Canadian
And two American armies. Do you want to come
Between a battlefield General and his men, his staff?
I could never allow it, never. If you think
That is wrong, you have lost confidence in me.
And you must find someone else to lead the expedition.

Churchill. Get the troops ashore, that's the main thing to me.
I will make it an issue of confidence if you don't
Allow me, as Prime Minister, to have my say.
I want the invasion to succeed, I must
Be sure we have made the right preparations.

Montgomery. You cannot talk to my staff. At this stage
For you to address the Twenty-first Army Group
Would be unwarranted interference.
I cannot allow you to do so. My staff

Advise me and I give the final decision.
They then do what I tell them.

(*Churchill breaks down and weeps. Montgomery offers Churchill his handkerchief.*)

Churchill. I'm sorry, Monty.
I'm tired and overstrained, I don't mean
To interfere.

Montgomery. Let's go next door, where I
Will present my staff.

(*Generals, Brigadiers and Colonels are drawn up in a line.*)

Churchill. I'm not allowed to talk
To you gentlemen.

(*Later. Churchill is leaving. Montgomery and Henderson.*)

Churchill. I've signed your Ten Chapters book. Read it out.

Henderson (*reading*). "Chapter Five. On the verge of the greatest
Adventure…I record my confidence
That all will be well and the organisations
And equipment of the army will be worthy
Of the valour of the soldier and the genius
Of their chief, Winston S. Churchill."

(*22nd May. Broomfield House caravan. Montgomery and King walking outside.*)

Montgomery. We only use the House during the day
For meetings and formal dinners. Only the chef
Sleeps in, the rest of us sleep in tents in the field
Round my three caravans which are TAC HQ,
And we eat in the dining marquee. We have
To toughen the minds of the men, and their physique,
Get them used to living in the battlefield.
I'm afraid there are no exceptions. Tonight,
Sir, you will sleep in my caravan, in there.
My batman will bring you water. Corporal
Fetch hot water from the kitchen.

Corporal. Sir. Sir, the new chef
Would like a word. (*Exit.*)

Montgomery. Yes, Paul.

Chef. I'm standing in
For Sergeant Wright. Is tonight's menu to be
Different? I mean, is rationing suspended?

Montgomery. No, we have strict food rationing, this is
The Army, not Windsor where game, fresh fruit,
Vegetables, rabbits, I have heard, are brought
By loyal subjects for your family, sir.
Here like any commoner the King makes do.
There can be no extra rations because

The King has come.

Chef (*embarrassed*). Very good, sir. (*Exit.*)

Montgomery. We eat
At half past six in the House. My bedtime's nine.

King. Can I bath?

Montgomery. No, sir. The water supply was hit
In the Portsmouth bombing raids, it's been off since
We moved here. We receive water from a wagon
That calls, or take jerry cans to an army
Tanker. The men cannot take canvas baths,
Nor we.

King. What are those trenches?

Montgomery. Toilets, sir.
As there is no water, we don't use the house.

(*Dawnay appears.*)

I'll meet you by the cedar, on the lawn.

(*The King goes gingerly into the caravan as the Corporal arrives with water. Montgomery turns away with Dawnay.*)

Kit, I shall want to give the King my *Notes
On High Command in War*, and a photograph
Of myself. Can you get them ready? Wavell,
Auchinleck, Marshall, Mountbatten, Fraser,
Mackenzie-King and Smuts have had copies
And so should the King who, not long ago,
Was in favour of appeasing Hitler
And did not want Churchill to be PM.
It will be educative. You have heard me say,
I have three superiors – God, Churchill, Brooke
In that order – and to none other defer.

(*During the next week. Montgomery speaking to troops. He addresses the audience.*)

Montgomery (*beckoning*). Gather closer, you're too far away. That's better.
Now all of you are soon going to be involved
In D-Day, when we invade France
And deliver the enemy a terrific blow
From which he will not be able to recover.
Now I am travelling about and meeting all
The troops who will be going, and I say to you
We have spent several months perfecting our plan,
Everything is prepared, nothing is left to chance,
And I will only move when I know it's safe.
We have to fight, but I don't want to lose lives.
We have done everything we can on the organisation.
Now it's up to you, and you can do it.
I know you can do it, and I believe in you.

And you have seen me and met me, you've seen
I wear a beret, the same as you, and you
Can now believe in me. I've already
Beaten the Germans in seven battles,
I know how to beat Rommel yet again,
And with your help and the Lord Mighty in Battle
On our side, we will drive the Nazis out of France
And out of Germany and win the war.

(1st June. Broomfield House dining-room. Montgomery at dinner with his four army commanders: Dempsey, Crerar, Bradley, who is shy and quiet,and Patton, who is boastful. A convivial atmosphere.)

Montgomery. It's done, I've written it in my betting book.
Dempsey. And I bet General Bradley five pounds that the war
With Germany will end by November the first.
Bradley. You're on. I'm optimistic, but I'm not
That unrealistic.
Montgomery. That's in my betting book.
And that's *my* target date to end the war
By reaching Berlin by November the first.
(*Rising.*) Commanders, thank you for flying down here
And attending our final conference before D-Day,
Our final look at the plans, and for staying on
For this last supper before the historic invasion.
It has been a very convivial occasion.
And though I only drink water or orange juice,
I want to toast you and the success of
Your four undertakings. To the success
Of Overlord.
Patton. I suppose I should reply
As the oldest army commander present,
And previously Bradley's boss. If everything moves
As planned there will be nothing for me to do
As Bradley will be doing it. I would like to toast
The health of General Montgomery, and declare
Our satisfaction at serving under him.

(The four commanders rise and toast Montgomery.)

(*Aside.*) The lightning did not strike me for my lie.
I have a better impression of Monty
But Dempsey's a yes-man and Crerar doesn't impress.
Montgomery (*aside*). Bradley is diffident and he abhors
The swaggering Patton, who is a sabre-rattler,
Ignorant of battle but good at thrusting.
Dempsey is imperturbable, but I have doubts
About Crerar as a battlefield leader.
(*Aloud.*) Here we are, leading the greatest invasion
In history, and I am reminded of
A scene in *Antony and Cleopatra*

Before Actium when Lepidus is carried out.
Patton. That will be Brad, the quiet ones drink the most.

(2nd June. Broomfield House dining-room. Montgomery dining with Eisenhower.)

Montgomery. A Commander has to be many-sided.
He must assess a situation and
Make a clear plan and communicate it clearly
To all his subordinates. He must have great
Authority and inspire trust. He must make
Men eager to follow his commands. He must take
Account of ever-changing situations
And simplify the complexity so
It is comprehensible. A Commander
Is like an artist who reveals the One
Behind the surface many, in all its forms,
The unity behind multiplicity.
A Commander reveals the aim behind a war
At every twist and turn of a long campaign.
And the men sit in their camp and do not know
How definite the Commander has to be.

(*Silence.*)

Eisenhower. Bushey Park is like an armed camp, canvas
Tents under every tree, GIs sitting
And all round a red wall, sentries at the gate.
Today I wrote my Order of the Day
At Southwick House. It begins: "Soldiers, Sailors
And Airmen of the Allied Expeditionary Force:
You are about to embark on the Great Crusade,
Toward which we have striven these many months,
The eyes of the world are upon you."
Montgomery (*reading*). "You will bring about
The destruction of the German war machine,
The elimination of Marxist tyranny
Over oppressed people of Europe, and
Security for ourselves in a free world."
It's very eloquent. You know, Ike, you're
Just the man for the job.
Eisenhower. I support you
Firmly, Monty.
Montgomery (*aside*). I like him immensely.
He has a generous lovable character,
And I would trust him to the last gasp.
I do like him tremendously. He is
So very genuine and sincere.
(*Aloud.*) Ike,
I'm having trouble with Churchill. Last night
Ismay rang, Churchill wishes to visit

The Portsmouth area this weekend. If he comes
He'll be a bore and may attract attention.
Why in hell doesn't he go and smoke his cigar
At Dover Castle and fix the Germans'
Attention to Calais. He also wants
To go to sea in a cruiser and see the assault
And the bombardment on D-Day. He'll be
An embarrassment and a liability,
And he is too valuable to take such risks.
If anything happens to him we will be
In a bad position. He needs good sense
To control his fighting spirit. Can you stop him?

Eisenhower. I don't know, I can try. Let's go back now
To Southwick House and question the Met men
About the weather for June the fifth.

(*Saturday June 3rd, evening. Southwick House mess room. Eisenhower, his commanders and RAF Group Captain Stagg. Bookcases and French windows, large map.*)

Stagg. Bad news. High pressure is giving way to a low
As a depression over Iceland spreads south.
The weather on June the fifth will be overcast
And stormy with Force Five winds. It's getting worse.

Eisenhower. Thank you. Please leave the room. (*Exit Stagg.*) Well, what do we think?
What do you think, Monty?

Montgomery. I have laid the plan
And prepared the armies. It is for you
As Supreme Commander to say if the armies should go.
A decision to cancel must be made
Twenty-four hours before the landings as
The invasion fleet of five thousand ships
Will assemble then.

Tedder. I don't think we should go.
You can't have an invasion through mountainous seas –
Look what happened to the Spanish Armada –
And low cloud which does not allow air cover.

Montgomery. I am in favour of going. Everything is ready.
A huge operation is co-ordinated.
The morale of the men has been lifted.
If we don't go now, we must wait a month,
And morale will flag, and the Germans may find out.
They think we have an army around Dover,
Operation Fortitude may be discovered.

(*One hour later. Eisenhower with Stagg and the others.*)

Eisenhower. No irrevocable decision has been made.
The American Navy with Bradley's troops
Should leave for Omaha and Utah beaches,

Subject to a possible last-minute cancellation.
I will make the final decision at the weather
Conference at eight tomorrow morning.

(*4th June, 1 a.m. Eisenhower's trailer off Pitymoor Lane, near Southwick House. Eisenhower looking at the sky. Kay Summersby in the doorway.*)

Kay. Dwight, you should sleep.
Eisenhower. No, I'm looking at the sky.
Kay. I don't like to see you so bleakly depressed.
Eisenhower. Not depressed, just with those men on the sea.

(*4th June, 4.30 a.m. Southwick House, mess room. Eisenhower and Stagg.*)

Stagg. Sea conditions will be slightly better than
Expected, but low cloud will ground air forces.
Ramsay. The sky is practically clear, when do
You expect cloud and wind?
Stagg. Five hours from now, sir.
Ramsay. I think we should go.
Eisenhower. Leigh-Mallory?
Leigh-Mallory. I'm against.
Air forces could not carry out the plan.
Montgomery. Some of the air programme would be cancelled,
But most could go ahead. We must go, for
Each hour's delay makes the troops' ordeal worse.
Eisenhower. Tedder?
Tedder. I must disagree with Monty.
We need full, and not partial, air support.
Eisenhower. Overlord is being launched with ground forces
That are not overwhelmingly powerful.
We need the help of air superiority
Or the landings will be far too risky.
If air cover cannot operate we must postpone.
That is my casting vote. Any dissentient voices?
Montgomery (*aside*). The sky is clear, dawn glows, yet we postpone
Because of dissenting meteorologists,
But I have myself revered air supremacy,
And there must be unity of purpose and decision
Under the Supreme Commander. Be silent.

(*Silence.*)

Eisenhower. D-Day is not June fifth.

(*Pause.*)

Monty, perhaps
You and I should walk down to the Golden Lion.
Fruit juice?
Montgomery (*aside*). I must watch Tedder. He and Ike
Swapped houses near Bushey Park. Ike began in
Park House on the golf course, but found it large

And the lane too narrow. Tedder moved out
Of Telegraph Cottage for him. They are
Neighbours, and Ike feels he must reflect his view.

(4th June. La Roche Guyon. Rommel and his Chief of Staff General Hans Speidel.)

Rommel. There won't be an invasion in this weather.
The Straits of Dover are even worse than here.
If they come they won't get off the beaches.
It's my wife's birthday. I'm going to take
A short vacation, I shall drive to Herrlingen
And give Lucie her present, these new shoes,
Then visit the Führer in Berchtesgaden
And press him to move Panzer Group West to
The coast rather than hold it in reserve
As von Schweppenburg and Rundstedt want.
We need three more divisions in all.
Look after the château for me.

(4th June, 7 p.m. Broomfield House. Wind and rain. Eisenhower and Montgomery over dinner in the dining-room. Paul the chef, serving, overhears.)

Montgomery. If we don't go on June the sixth, we can't
Until the nineteenth, and to stand men down
And bring back ships will damage their morale
And blow their secrecy. We have to make it work.
Eisenhower. You're right. If we have air superiority,
We have to go.
Montgomery. Thank God you banned Churchill,
Banished him to a train near Southampton.

(4th June, 9.30 p.m. Southwick House mess room. Wind and rain. Eisenhower, with Montgomery, Tedder, Smith, Ramsay, Leigh-Mallory, Bradley, Gen. Strong, staff officers. Eisenhower at table, the others drinking coffee in easy chairs. Enter Stagg.)

Stagg. This afternoon we saw a break in the weather.
We now agree, the depression in the mid-
Atlantic must slow down, giving a breathing space
Of perhaps a day on June the sixth: little
Cloud, quieter seas. The rain will stop
In two or three hours.

(A cheer goes up. The rain is pouring down.)

Eisenhower (*aside*). Rear Admiral Creasy, Air Marshal Leigh-Mallory,
And Major-General de Guingand are cross-
Examining Stagg. Ramsay is content.
Leigh-Mallory and Tedder are anxious
About the effectiveness of heavy bombers.
But we can call on our fighter bombers.

Ramsay. If Overlord is to happen on June the sixth
The Commander of the American task force
Must be told in the next half hour. If they sail
And are recalled, they cannot sail again
Until the tides are right and must wait till
June the nineteenth.

Eisenhower (*aside*). The lonely isolation
Of making a decision with risk either way.
If Overlord is to happen before the nineteenth
I must decide now.
(*Aloud.*) Smith?

Bedell Smith. It's a helluva gamble,
But it is the best possible gamble.

Eisenhower (*aside*). I must build my decision round Monty.
(*Aloud.*) Monty, do you see any reason why
We should not go on Tuesday?

Montgomery. No, I would say: Go.

Eisenhower (*aloud*). What are the air ramifications of
A decision to go?
(*Aside.*) I mean to go.
(*Aloud.*) Thank you.
I am quite positive that the order must be given.
I order the convoys to put to sea again.
A final irrevocable decision
Will be made at four-thirty tomorrow morning.

*(*5th June, 3.30 a.m. Eisenhower's trailer. Eisenhower outside.*)

Kay. Dwight.

Eisenhower. The wind was shaking the trailer. It's like
A hurricane. The rain is horizontal.
I may have to call the operation off.

(*5th June, 4.30 a.m. Southwick House. Mess room. Eisenhower and commanders all in battledress, Montgomery in fawn-coloured pullover and light corduroy trousers. Coffee.*)

Stagg. The rain will clear within a matter of hours.
Look it's already happening now.

Eisenhower (*pacing, shooting out his chin*).
Who's for go?
Monty. Smith. Ramsay?

Ramsay. I'm concerned about
Spotting for naval gunfire, but will take the risk.

Eisenhower. Tedder?

Tedder. I'm ready.

Leigh-Mallory. Air conditions are
Below the acceptable minimum.

Eisenhower. Thank you, Stagg.

(*Exit Stagg.*)

The ships are sailing into the Channel.
If they have to be called back, we must do so now.
The Supreme Commander is the only man
Who can do that.

(*Eisenhower thinks. Time stops.*)

OK, let's go.

(*A cheer. Everyone rushes to their command posts. Eisenhower, alone, sits on in immense isolation.*)

Eisenhower (*reflecting*). The fate of thousands of men hung on my words,
And the future of nations. I had power
Over the whole world, and was still; but now.
It is too late to change the decision.
The invasion cannot be stopped – even by me.
Overlord now has a life of its own.
It is in the men, not me, that power resides.

*(*5th June, 1 p.m. Eisenhower's trailer. Eisenhower and Butcher playing checkers.*)

Butcher. I'm winning, two kings to one.
Eisenhower. I've jumped a king
And got a draw. It's a good omen.

(*5th June, evening. Newbury. Eisenhower and Kay, who is dressed as his driver. Blackened faces of troops. Sound of planes overhead.*)

Eisenhower. There go the Hundred and First Airborne. Eighty
Per cent casualties Leigh-Mallory reckons.
Well, it's on. (*He chokes back tears.*) Let's go back to the car.

(*5th June, 9 p.m. Broomfield House. Montgomery by his caravan, his batman and Dawnay.*)

Montgomery. Everything possible has been done to ensure the success
Of the landings. We've done everything possible.
It is now in the hands of God. It'll be
All right. I'm turning in at the usual time.
Wake me at the usual time. No, not before.

(*He goes into his caravan.*)

It seems only yesterday that I led, in rain,
My company in a charge at Meteren
At the start of the First World War, and as
I stormed the village was shot through my chest
And knee by a sniper, and the soldier
Dragging me to safety was shot and killed
And fell on top of me. For three hours in
The lashing rain I lay, bleeding. They dug

A grave, and as they picked me up and dumped me
In a greatcoat to sling me and drop me in
An orderly called "Hey, this one's still alive."
If I had died then, who'd have redrawn Overlord?
I feel I was saved by Providence for this moment.
(*Praying.*) O Lord, Eisenhower has entrusted to me
The conduct of Overlord, which is now in my hands.
I have launched the biggest invasion ever,
A hundred and seventy-six thousand men
Are now in the air or on the waves, to land
In Fortress Europe, breach Hitler's Atlantic Wall
Which is in the hands of my old adversary,
Rommel, from whom I captured this caravan.
Lord many will die on both sides, scarring your earth.
Forgive me Lord for destroying your world,
Your hedgerows, wild flowers, chestnut trees and fields,
With tanks, with flamethrowers – forgive me for
Taking part in the killing of men, but if
I don't, what will happen? Hitler will continue
His murderous campaign, his guards will press on
With the Final Solution. I have a just cause,
But Lord, let me not kill unnecessarily.
I will be cautious, to win with minimum loss.
Perception of evil is a point of view,
Lord, let me see within the harmony of the One
That shows this war has meaning in relation to Good.

(*He pauses.*)

O Lord, in this situation I must kill.
You do not want me to. I am like Arjuna
In the *Bhagavadgita*. Let me act without
Interference from my rational, social ego,
Let me act from my soul and I will be in harmony
With your will, and those who die as a result
Of my decision will die at the behest
Of your divine will. O Lord, I am troubled
At the thought of those who will die. I commit them to you,
To the whole, the One. And may you absolve me
From this necessity. For to remove Hitler
And his Final Solution men must die,
And it is worse for them not to die, and for more
To die. O Lord, Overlord.

*(*6th June, 4.00 a.m. Eisenhower's trailer. Eisenhower and Kay.*)

Eisenhower. Well, it's four o'clock, I'm going to bed.

*(*6th June, 6.30 a.m. Rommel's house. Dining-room. Rommel arranges Lucie's presents. The phone rings.*)

Rommel. Speidel. Airborne landings in Normandy?

It can't be the invasion in this weather.
Confirm it and let me know. If it's serious
I'll leave immediately.

(*Chorus of the Occupied.*)

Chorus. The Allies have landed, there is hope again.
No longer shall we walk with sullen faces.
A spring is in our step, liberation
Cannot be far away, freedom from the yoke,
From helmeted Nazis driving by our squares,
From Gestapo questionings and firing-squads,
Freedom from the noose in public places.
Once again we can live without fear – soon.
Come, Montgomery, liberate us, but
Without smashing our towns and killing our men.

*(*6th June, 7 a.m. Eisenhower's trailer. Eisenhower is reading a Western novel.*)

Butcher. Sir, good news from Leigh-Mallory. The air drop
Was a success, casualties were light.

Eisenhower. Good.

(*His face has a huge grin.*)

(*D-Day Soldier.*)

D-Day Soldier. For two nights we tossed on the choppy sea.
It was full of ships and craft, surely the Germans
Would see us and bomb us from the air?
The storm soaked us as we huddled on deck.
No one said much, we waited, seasick. Then
At H-hour a barrage from our Navy ships.
We scrambled down long ropes, packs on our backs,
Clutching rifles near tied gas masks, and jumped
Into assault craft, a ribbon of shore ahead
Gleaming in the early morning sunshine,
With little puffs of smoke from our Navy's shells.
Dipping, swaying, we crouched all tense and looked,
We approached through fire, bullets whipped up the waves
And clanged our sides. We nosed through floating bodies
Towards the smoke. A German plane roared down
And strafed the crowded beach, men and vehicles.
In that moment each one of us was afraid.
Yet we all showed courage. Bang! Down went the flap,
Out, we jumped into three feet of cold waves
And waded through the bullets and corpses
To the sand at the lapping water's edge,
Then dived as the plane whined down and raked our path.
"Mines," someone shouted, "stick to the matting."
We ran doubled-up under sniper fire.

The man beside me on the landing craft
Fell at my side, shot through the head. We gathered
At a muster point at the top of the beach,
And I saw a German soldier dead in a tree.
We were given provisions, and then ran on
Towards a house and fields, we advanced.

(*6th June, 10.30 a.m. Rommel's house. Lucie. Speidel rings.*)

Rommel. Speidel. It *is* the invasion? Are you sure?
I will leave immediately.
(*To Lucie.*) The invasion has come,
It is confirmed, out of high seas and storm,
And I was not at my post. Montgomery,
Who defeated me at Alamein, seems to know
My movements and when I am three divisions short.
The only way to repulse him was to drive
Him off the beaches into the sea. If he now has
A foothold, I fear it may be too late.

(*6th June, later. Broomfield House. Dawnay and Paul, the chef.*)

Dawnay. The great one is amazingly cool. He was woken,
Given the good news, then went back to sleep.
Now he is studying the land we have taken
From the messages sent through to his caravan.
He is sitting quietly, plotting the positions.

(*Montgomery in his caravan. He summons Dawnay.*)

Montgomery. The British and Canadians are ashore,
But the Americans cannot land on Omaha.
The cliffs are defended by Germans who were
Conducting an exercise, we found out too late.
Signal to Dempsey, ask him if he can take
Bradley's troops: "Can you take Five Corps?"

(*Later.*)

Dawnay. Dempsey says: "No, unless you want to leave
Our people out, because it is too crowded
To go in together."

(*6th June, late morning. The Berghof, Hitler's HQ in Berchtesgaden. Hitler and Keitel.*)

Hitler. Again and again I have warned Rommel and Rundstedt
The first invasion will come in Normandy.
In March I several times warned the Generals,
On May the sixth I telephoned Jodl
That I attached particular importance
To Normandy. But Rommel and Rundstedt
Remained convinced the invasion would take place
In the Straits of Dover. Now I can attack

London with my flying bombs. Now the enemy
Is where we can get at them.

(*Silence. Exit Keitel. Enter Bormann.*)

I am not worried.
I do not believe that this "invasion"
Is anything other than a diversion.
I have always said that the main attack will come
In the Pas de Calais. I speak as Will.
The Atlantic Wall will repulse them,
There will be another Dunkirk.
We are invincible, I am a will
To conquer, I have a personal destiny
Within the historical process.

Bormann. Providence
Has saved you to lead Germany
Through this time of trial.

(*Silence.*)

Hitler. There must be no let up
In the solution to the Jewish problem.
By expelling Jews from their privileged positions
I have opened up their positions to the children
Of hundreds of thousands of working class Germans,
And I am depriving the revolutionary movement
Of its Jewish inspiration: Rosenberg,
To whom Eckart introduced me, my mentor,
Brought out of Bolshevik Russia a book,
The Protocols of the Elders of Zion,
The secret plans of the international
Jewish conspiracy for world domination.
I read it shortly after Zionists
Brought America into the First World War.
It shows that the Jewish doctrine of Marxism
Seeks the destruction of all non-Jewish
National states, and plans to hand the world
To the Jews. Russia has been captured by the Jews.

Bormann. Through Bolshevism and the Jewish Trotsky
The Jews seek to achieve world domination.

Hitler. And to spread through Germany as the Thule Society
taught.
The Jews are a race, not a religious persuasion,
They foment revolution with Freemasons
And democrats from Britain and the US.
The Final Solution is the removal
Of Jews altogether. I am the Messiah
Who will save man from the Jewish Antichrist.

Bormann. Zionism has driven the Bolsheviks
To butcher millions in the Soviet Union.

Hitler. And is now driving the Allies' war-efforts.
Hungary is rotten with Jews everywhere,
Right up to the highest level, and a network
Of agents and spies. We must make a clean sweep.
We must do this while we are still able to.
Two days after the Americans entered Rome,
An invasion in Normandy. It is a diversion.
But it is also impudence. Launched from Britain.
Pah, I will pay Britain back with reprisal weapons.
I have eight thousand flying bombs, each one
Twenty-five feet long with a one-ton warhead,
Each pilotless with a jet engine. Prepare
To send the first of these to London.
I will rain destruction from the sky.

(*6th June, early evening. Eisenhower, pacing outside his trailer.*)

Butcher. The landings have been successful. We have now
A hundred and fifty-six thousand ashore,
And two thousand five hundred casualties,
Mostly at Omaha. We have Bayeux,
The seat of William the Conqueror, who
Is the only man besides Caesar, and now you,
To command a successful cross-Channel assault.
Eisenhower. We have not got Caen.

(*7th June, morning. HMS Faulknor. Montgomery and Bradley.*)

Montgomery. Welcome aboard HMS Faulknor. I hope
Your ship is comfortable?
Bradley. Thank you.
Sir, I'm concerned about the operational
Situation on Omaha beach, which is not yet secure.
Montgomery. That is why I am here. The Allied armies
Must link up in view of the German opposition.
Collins' Seven US Corps must fight eastwards
From Utah and join Gerow, not go to Cherbourg.
Bradley. That's a change to the plan.
Montgomery. It is necessary.

(*7th June, mid-morning. HMS Apollo. Eisenhower and Montgomery.*)

Montgomery. Ike, in view of the American difficulty
On Omaha beach, on the whole US Army front
The immediate tactical plan has been altered.
The Utah and Omaha beach troops must link up
Or the Panzer Divisions will obliterate Omaha.
Eisenhower. All right, I will signal the Combined Chiefs of Staff
In Washington to that effect, and will say
That after that adjustment, the original conceptions
Will be pursued.

(*Montgomery rises to move away.*)

Oh, Monty, I'm concerned
That Caen has not been captured.

Montgomery. It's clear the enemy
Intend to hold it strongly and to drive into
My eastern flank. Dempsey will have to envelop it
Rather than take it by a frontal attack,
And then pivot on Caen and swing his right flank
As the plan provides. I am well satisfied
With today's fighting.

(*Montgomery moves away.*)

Eisenhower. I'm not satisfied.

Butcher. I find
Him insufferable. He almost made out that
Americans had messed up his plan on Omaha,
He seemed to derive some satisfaction from
Re-arranging the whole American front.
I find his self-satisfaction irritating.

Eisenhower. He can be self-righteous and rather rigid.

Montgomery (*aside*). I am in theory responsible to Ike
Who is in turn responsible to the Combined
Chiefs of Staff, and beyond them, to two governments,
But I look to Brooke for guidance, I am
The senior British officer in Europe and
I am responsible for my nation's interests.

SCENE 2. NORMANDY: DEFEATING ROMMEL

(*8th June, evening. Creullet. TAC HQ, Montgomery's caravans. Montgomery sitting outside with the BBC rep, Howard Marshall. Beside him, a chamber-pot.*)

Montgomery. Our first location after landing at Sainte Croix-sur-Mer
Was a totally unsuitable place for my TAC HQ.
It was a crossroads between fields with German trenches
And under artillery fire. Colonel Russell
Must have taken it from a map. My Canadian
Assistant, Warren, scouted round and found
Me this lovely château. It was occupied
This morning by fifteen Germans whom he took prisoner.
So here we are. We arrived this afternoon.
I have everything except a chamber-pot.
I tried to gesticulate what I wanted,
And Madame de Druval has produced one,
After bringing vases, and look, you see its crest.
Montgomery. For my ancestors came
From Sainte Foy de Montgomery near Falaise.

Roger de Montgomery was number two
To William the Conqueror. I landed near Dives,
The spot from which William sailed. My family invaded
Britain, and now are liberating the
Conqueror's Norman homeland from the Saxon yoke.
Everything is going well. Rommel's Twenty-first
Panzer Division has arrived at Caen
And half have been destroyed, and half of the rest
Have been sent to retake Bayeux, weakening their thrust.

Marshall. Was it over-optimistic, faulty thinking
To expect troops who landed yesterday morning,
Many seasick, to march on foot to Caen
And capture it by nightfall, without armoured
Troop carriers that follow tanks, of the kind
The Germans have? And why was the British
Tank advance so slow?

Montgomery. Everything is going to plan.

(*Henderson and Dawnay are in the "A" mess tent.*)

Henderson (*to Dawnay*). He's tired and on edge, nothing's gone right
But now he's in the field, all is confidence
And he has time for relaxing anecdotes
About chamber-pots.

(*8th June, later. Montgomery's caravans. Montgomery and Dawnay.*)

Montgomery. Signal to Ike that while the Americans
Concentrate on linking Utah and Omaha
Bridgeheads, Dempsey will strike south of Caen at
Villers-Bocage and then Falaise.
Say I am very satisfied with the situation.

(*9th June, 11.30 a.m. Montgomery's caravans. Dempsey leaving. Henderson. Montgomery.*)

Dempsey (*to Henderson*). The great one's tense and unapproachable.

(*Exit.*)

Montgomery (*to Henderson*). I have written a letter for Ike, it's addressed to
The Chief of Staff at SHAEF. I'd like you to
Catch a motor launch to Portsmouth and take
It to Southwick. Dempsey wants American
Five Corps to go with him. We're going to hold
North and west Caen, where the Germans are counter-attacking,
And push Seventh Armoured Division south of Bayeux
And then swing round left-handed and take Caen
From the rear.

(*10th June. Telegraph Cottage, near Bushey Park. Eisenhower, Butcher and Kay.*)

Butcher. There's no information from Montgomery
Who agreed to cable every night.

Eisenhower. That's too bad.
How can I evaluate what's happening
In Normandy if I don't have any cables?
Monty is slow. Bradley's disappointed,
Taking Caen was supposed to shield his troops,
American troops, and now they're exposed.

Kay. You know,
Montgomery is the only person in
The whole Allied Command whom I dislike.
He's like a desert rat, with his pointed nose
And his quick eyes which dart to either side.
How can you stand not hearing from him? Tell him off.

Eisenhower. I feel angry and frustrated, cut off.
I need to be the field Commander in charge
Of Twenty-first Army Group. Then I'd know
What the situation is.

*(*Later.*)

Butcher. Sir, there was a signal from Monty. SHAEF had it.

(*Butcher waves a cable.*)

(*10th June, 11.30 a.m. Port-en-Bessin. Montgomery, Bradley and Dempsey in a field. Montgomery in hunting jacket.*)

Montgomery. So there are two Panzer divisions dug in
Before Caen, and Dempsey will outflank them
From Bayeux. Could you, Brad, parallel this,
Drive south towards to Caumont? This would confuse
Rommel in Caen and divert enemy troops
From Collins' attack towards Cherbourg.

Bradley. I
Am afraid I cannot, sir. The American
Build-up is twenty-four hours behind schedule.
The Omaha beachhead is only two miles deep.
My priority is to link the two beachheads.

Montgomery (*disappointed*). The Desert Rats will have to fight alone.
They are already advancing through the Eighth
Armoured Brigade's shield near Tilly to seize
Villers-Bocage, the western gateway to Caen.
Fifty-first Highland Division are with them,
My two most experienced divisions, which
Fought under me at Alamein.

(*10th June, early evening. Creullet. Montgomery by his caravan with Dawnay.*)

Montgomery. Signal to Eisenhower that American
Five and Seven Corps have at last joined hands,
And that I have given Bradley the green light
For Collins to race for Cherbourg. Tomorrow
Signal both Ike and Brooke, and say that my
General object is to pull the Germans
On to Second Army so that First Army
Can extend and expand. The British will
Soak punishment so the US can break out.

(*10th June, early evening. Berghof, Hitler's HQ. Hitler, Dönitz and Göring.*)

Dönitz. The invasion has succeeded. The Second Front
Has come.

Göring. The Navy assured us the enemy
Would not risk his best ships in a sea invasion.

Dönitz. Discussion of such matters is not opportune
At present. There should be more air-strikes.
The enemy flew over ten thousand on
Invasion day, our Luftwaffe three hundred.

Hitler. I have warned since March that the first invasion
Would come in Normandy, not the Pas de Calais.
No one would listen to me. Send the 9th
And 10th SS Panzers to the Normandy front.

(*He goes out to his balcony. Bavarian Alps ahead of and below him.*)

(*Alone.*) From this high point in the Bavarian Alps
I look down on the slopes and paths of the world
And think how I have climbed to this great height
From Braunau in Austria, where I was born.
I left school without a certificate,
I lived in a doss-house in imperial Vienna,
I was a corporal in the First World War,
And saw my country humiliated, shrink
And then in Munich, in beer cellars, the Hofbrauhaus,
I stood on tables and spoke and they echoed.
Eckart taught me I had a destiny,
After my rise to Chancellor, it was inevitable
That I would take the Rhineland, Austria
(My home country), and the Sudetenland,
Then Czechoslovakia and finally Poland;
I made my choice and carried out my free act.
I was driven not by personal ambition
But the will to purify the German race
Of all its Jewish blood. I made a pact

With the Bolshevik Devil to take Poland
And cleanse it of its ethnically degenerate past.
Chamberlain was a well-intentioned fool,
He was no match for my diplomacy.
How I despised him when he waved his paper.
I did not seek war with Britain and Russia,
But I blitzkrieged Britain and invaded Russia,
And my Atlantic war drew in Britain's supplier,
The Zionist US. I committed aggression
Against these three powers, beyond good and evil;
Because I sought to impose my vision
Of a pure race of god-men on the world,
And Jews and Bolsheviks were the obstacles.
Now two powers attack me on the west, and I
Am pressed on the east. And this Montgomery,
Who beat Rommel in North Africa and Italy,
Is now poised like some agent of the divine,
To strike and repay me for my cleansing.
But I do not believe in a moral universe,
That aggression leads to destruction, but in power.
I sought like Augustus and Constantine,
Like Charlemagne and Napoleon to rule
Europe and dominate the whole world,
Not for personal ambition, but so that the idea
I embody could find universal expression:
The supremacy of the Aryan race,
The Germanic people's mission to rule the world.
I am a German imperialist, I seek
To destroy the British Empire and inherit it,
To be crowned Kaiser of a world empire
Where German ideas are followed throughout the world,
Where God is dead as Nietzsche said, and where
Beyond good and evil, all is will to power.
I have to become the Christian Antichrist
To reject the *Old Testament* of the Jews
And the Christian code that says "Thou shalt not kill" –
Did not Napoleon reject its good –
In order to combat the Jewish Antichrist
Who seeks to destroy Germany and rule.
I have remade good in a nihilistic world.
Christians see me as the Antichrist, but I am
The Messiah who saves mankind from Jewish rule.
And so Montgomery does not frighten me.
Providence rules by power, not by what is good.
Occult Providence took me to this great height
Because I tapped its secret energy,
Providence is neutral, neither good nor evil.
So I shall continue to fulfil my destiny,
I belong to an idea that will repel

A dying Christendom and the Allies.
European civilisation is not in decline.
There is a union ahead of all its states,
Which I am bringing about. Europe will play
The central role in the coming world order.
Montgomery and I are locked in a tussle of will,
Of power, not of vengeance for evil done;
Between the Allies' world order, and mine.
I live in a universe that is not benign,
That is neutral to the wishes of humans,
In which the strong impose their will, their power,
In which the Superman takes charge for man
And sets up a structure that can survive
A thousand years. Great men with a destiny
Like Napoleon, and me, can kill millions
And remain untouched by any moral law
That was falsely invented by a dying Church.
I am the force of a *new* world order,
An idea that began in Bavaria
With Weishaupt, who was anti-Catholic
And anti-Habsburg, against all religion
And established government through the occult,
A force that Frederick knew before he died,
A force which Zionism later stole.
I will cleanse Weishaupt's power of its Bolshevik grime.
I draw from an occult Bavarian will,
That channels an energy in the universe,
I am its Messiah against both Jew and Christ.
And, with open visionary centres,
With insight that will be known in the new Age,
I will repel the Allies from Normandy,
This little diversion, just as I will repel
The main attack when it comes in the Pas de Calais
And all Zionist power that claims to be "good".

(*10th June, evening. Berchtesgaden. Hitler, Bormann and Burgdorf.*)

Burgdorf. Rommel plans to divert his counter-attack
From the British armour driving on Caen
To the American drive on Cherbourg,
And then return to stop Dempsey's advance
Which is already near Villers-Bocage.

Bormann. Rommel is letting the British advance on Caen.

Hitler. Caen is nearer to Paris than Cherbourg.
I veto Rommel's plan. Army Group B
Will attack the British bridgehead from Caen,
Using the reinforcements we have supplied.
Send Rommel an Enigma signal now.

(*12th June, 9 a.m. Creullet. Montgomery's TAC HQ. Montgomery and Dempsey.*)

Montgomery. The Desert Rats must speed up. We believe
Three more Panzer divisions are on their way
To reinforce Caen. Second Army must
Seize Caen before these Panzer divisions arrive.
Meet Erskine, the Desert Rats' commander,
And Bucknall, and hurry them up.
Now I must cancel my conference with Bradley.
He has the American Chiefs of Staff to lunch,
Marshall, King and Arnold will eat C rations and
Hard TAC biscuits in his new HQ.
O dear, I've got Churchill arriving for lunch,
With Smuts and Brooke. He'll get excited and
Ask dozens of questions when I should be
Concentrating on the task of the Desert Rats.

(*Later, after lunch. Operations trailer. Churchill, Smuts, Brooke, Montgomery, who stands before a map.*)

Churchill (*excitedly*). And the enemy are only three miles away?
Why, German armour may roll through our lunch.

Montgomery. That is unlikely, Prime Minister. But to resume.
My main strategy is to draw the Germans
Onto the British east flank so the Americans
Can break out from Cherbourg and wheel round.
We shall exploit all German mistakes at once.
For example, they've concentrated their
Panzer strength to hold Caen and block what they
Think is a thrust towards Paris and the Seine,
But we have an excellent chance of encircling
Their Panzer corps and capturing prisoners.
The Allied aim is to defeat the German
Armies in the West, not break out towards the Seine.

(*Later. Churchill and Henderson.*)

Churchill (*curious*). So what is Monty's day?

Henderson. Here in "A" Mess
His day is simple. He rises in time
For breakfast at eight and is out by nine
In two jeeps with four redcaps, visiting
Headquarters, front line troops. At four he returns
Takes his uniform off, puts on his grey
Sweater and corduroy trousers. From five
Till six he has his main meal. Then he sits
In the open air with his LOs,
His young Liaison Officers who act as scouts,
His eyes and ears for different parts of the front,

And report what they have seen in the battlefield.
They sit with mugs of tea. Each will have been to
A different battle zone. He took the idea
From the Duke of Wellington – some say Napoleon –
Who had eight Liaison Officers in the field,
And his way of fighting, in caravans near the front,
Is not unlike the method of Waterloo.
From seven he reads and thinks, he goes to bed at nine.
Then he must not be disturbed for
Any reason. I know he prays every night.
In his caravan. I have seen him, heard him.

(*Later. Montgomery and Brooke briefly alone.*)

Montgomery. Thank you for covering my back in London,
With Churchill and Tedder. I wish you could
Do something about Ike. His approach to war
Differs fundamentally from my own.
I am amazed he has commanded the only
Cross-Channel invasion since Julius Caesar
And the Conqueror. Of course it was my doing.

Brooke. For a Caesar he is genial, but behind
The friendly exterior is a ruthless mind
That balances conflicting national interests
And appears to lead by compromise, but may
Favour his masters' interests, not blatantly
But indirectly, at one remove, so that
At surface level all seems reasonable
And there are sound military reasons
For what may at heart be political.
Beware of him. He has a restlessness
That latches on to any new idea
And seeks to integrate it within the scheme,
Always for a military reason, you follow.
There is something in him that reminds me of a fox.
He is a great man, and a simple one,
Both at the same time. I find it hard to understand
How a great man who leads like William the Conqueror
Can while away his time with Western novels.
There's a disparity between his decisions, what he gives out,
And his tastes, what he imbibes. Perhaps his mind
Is more advanced than his culture, or perhaps
He is quite simply, just an American.

Montgomery. He is pulling against me the whole time.

Brooke. You must remember how you were appointed.
He was made Supreme Commander because Roosevelt
Would not release Marshall, his Army Chief
Of Staff, just as Churchill did not wish to
Release me, his Chief of Staff. Eisenhower

Hoped for Alexander, but his easy-
Going nature alarmed our War Cabinet
Who, as you know, on my recommendation
Vetoed his preference and gave him you,
And you then ripped to pieces the COSSAC plan.

Montgomery. It was a bad plan.

Brooke. But he had accepted it.
He will continue to be difficult,
But under a surface friendliness. You see.

(*Later. Montgomery and Henderson.*)

Montgomery. Now I've got Churchill out of the way I can deal
With Leigh-Mallory. We need his paratroop drop
Near Caen. Urquhart is keen to do it, but,
Sitting in his office, he says it must be at night
And our navy might fire at his planes in the dark.
Signal de Guingand. LM is a gutless
Bugger who refuses to take a chance
And plays for safety on all occasions. I have
No use for him.

(*13th June, later. Montgomery and Poston.*)

Montgomery (*thinly*). What happened at Villers-Bocage?

Poston. The Desert Rats
Entered the cheering village and some tank crews
Got out. Some Cromwells pushed on. Just outside
Five Tiger tanks of I SS Panzer Corps
Lay in wait, commanded by Michael Wittmann,
The ace who destroyed a hundred and thirty-eight
Tanks on the Russian front. He set off alone
And destroyed four of our tanks in the village
With eighty-eight millimetre shells, blocking
Retreat. He returned and attacked our column.
He destroyed the first tank, then went down the line.
By mid-morning his one Tiger destroyed
Twenty-seven tanks and twenty-eight armoured
Vehicles and killed eighty infantrymen.
His own tank was disabled but he escaped.
Bucknall then withdrew. Dempsey was not consulted.

Montgomery. Rommel has given us a bloody nose.
My Desert Rats. I will see that Bucknall
And Erskine are sacked.

Poston. And his counter-attack
Has taken Carentan, the junction between
The two American armies. He ignored Hitler.

(*Later. Montgomery and Henderson.*)

Montgomery. Now, Rommel has ignored Hitler and sent
His Second Panzer Division defiantly

Westwards and taken Carentan and mauled
The Desert Rats. The weather is getting worse,
And threatens our naval resupply, our troop
Reinforcements. Bradley is overstretched
And should delay his southern offensive.
We need to hold the Caen-Bayeux road and
Lure Rommel into counter-attacking us
So we can destroy his armour as at Alamein.
We have four hundred tanks there, and should not
Attack yet. We should postpone Dempsey's pincer
Movement to encircle the Panzer divisions.

(*14th June, morning. London. Eisenhower's HQ at 20 Grosvenor Square.*)

Eisenhower. What's the matter with Monty? Why won't he attack?
The Germans should be kept off balance, but he
Needs supplies, and doesn't make any gains,
And even retreats. He hasn't taken the airfields
South of Caen, as he promised Leigh-Mallory,
And the air commanders at this morning's meeting
Spoke of "a state of crisis". Even Tedder says
The present situation has the makings of
A dangerous crisis. Leigh-Mallory's
Going to visit Monty today.

(*14th June, late morning. Montgomery's TAC HQ. Montgomery. Enter de Gaulle with a French aide.*)

Henderson. An unexpected visitor.
Aide. General de Gaulle.
De Gaulle. I landed at Courseulles today, on the beach
Juno of the Canadians, with the Free French
And now that I 'ave returned to France, as
Leader of the Free French, I am in charge
Of all territory liberated by
Your Operation Overlord.
Montgomery. No you're not,
I'm in charge as Land Commander of the Allied
Expeditionary Force, which does not include the French.
France collaborated with Hitler, I remind you.
De Gaulle. That is not right –
Montgomery. I'm in charge.

(*Later. Montgomery and Henderson.*)

Henderson. I've found de Gaulle. He's in Bayeux, he made
A speech to the locals and caused a traffic jam.
His staff kept shouting "General de Gaulle"
And pointing at him to create interest.
He said the Free French are reconquering
France "with the aid of the Allies". Wait till Ike hears.
Military vehicles were unable to get through.

Montgomery (*furiously*). Who does he think he is? He signed "France"
In my visitors book. He's interfering in
My running of the war. Stop him. Send him
Back to England.
(*Aside.*) He's a poor fish who gives
Out no inspiration.

(*Later.*)

Henderson. An order from Churchill. He has vetoed
Your instructions. You are "to leave de Gaulle in peace".
Montgomery (*angrily*). It's all very well for a politician in London
To say that, but we're running a war here,
And if de Gaulle is stopping our tanks getting through
Then "leaving him in peace" will be costly.
Henderson. The Resistance does look to him.

(*Chorus of Londoners.*)

Chorus. What is that whine that suddenly cuts out?
What is that crash, that devastation as
Houses crumble, bodies are strewn in the street?
What weapon has been unleashed upon us?
What are these flying bombs, that without pilots
Can be fired across the Channel at random,
To fall anywhere, any time, with no more warning
Than a stopped whine? We are all terrified.
Death hovers in the air and we do not know
Where it will strike. May it not be us. Not us.

(*15th June, 4 p.m. Creullet, Montgomery's TAC HQ. Eisenhower, his son and Tedder waiting. Enter Montgomery.*)

Montgomery. Ike, I'm sorry, I didn't know you were coming.
I've been visiting Bradley.
Eisenhower. It's my fault. My son.

(*Montgomery shakes hands with Ike's son and greets Tedder.*)

John can you leave us? Perhaps find something to eat?

(*Exit Eisenhower's son.*)

The first flying bomb has fallen on London,
And we've come to see if there really is a crisis.
Montgomery. Leigh-Mallory was here yesterday, he offered me
An air bombardment along five thousand yards
So that the army can advance behind it,
A most encouraging development.
Eisenhower. We arrived this morning, and, finding you gone,
We visited Dempsey's headquarters and found
An Army/Air conference in session.
Tedder. I was concerned as neither Spaatz nor Coningham

Was represented.

Montgomery. Yesterday I asked
Leigh-Mallory to send his planning staff.
It came out of yesterday's meeting.

Eisenhower. Leigh-Mallory
Has not told anyone else that he would support
An infantry attack with Bomber Command
And 8 USAF.

Tedder. Coningham and I
Are sure this cannot be done effectively.
I have sent the airmen home, the idea is dropped.

(*Montgomery stares at Tedder.*)

Montgomery. You disapprove of air support to armies
By heavy bombers.

Tedder. It just will not work.

Montgomery. Then the armies will have to fight Rommel
Without the support of SHAEF's heavy bombers
And without *all* weapons in our arsenal.
Come to the operations caravan
And I will put you both in the picture.

(*Later, in the caravan. Eisenhower is taking notes.*)

Montgomery. The conduct of war is like a game of chess.
Both players must think ahead and have a plan,
A strategy, to feint on the left and slice
Through on the right. To play by simply reacting
To the other player's moves is ragged, chaotic,
Suicidal, and yet some would have us do that.
War is fought in the mind, and the victor
Is the one who is the more mentally tenacious.
I must stress, Caen is the key to Cherbourg.
Rommel, and Hitler, must be made to believe
That the British are attempting to break out
In the east towards the Seine, so they dare not
Release the four Panzer divisions to block
The American thrust to Cherbourg. Villers-
Bocage has helped to create that belief,
It has not imperilled Bradley's drive at all,
It is the key to his success.

Eisenhower. Monty,
We're impressed. There is no crisis.

Tedder. The idea of a crisis was over-stressed.

Montgomery. My Normandy strategy is succeeding.

(*16th June. Montgomery's TAC HQ. Montgomery and Dawnay.*)

Montgomery. The PM said he is very anxious
The King should come over here, just to land,
Have lunch with me, and go away. I agreed

But told Simbo to keep anyone else away,
To warn Eisenhower off. I can't deal with
More than one VIP. I've told Churchill
He must not come again just yet. Anyhow,
Having agreed, I now learn Eisenhower
Wants to resurrect Anvil round Bordeaux.
Signal to Brooke, it is a gross distraction
From the critical battle of Normandy. Bordeaux
Will be difficult to supply and cover from the air.
The Supreme Commander should use his supreme
  command
To prosecute the battle in Normandy
With all available weapons.

(*Enter Henderson.*)

Henderson. His Majesty the King, sir.

Montgomery. Glad you could come,
Sir, and see the liberation of Normandy.
I don't think the people of Normandy wish
To be liberated, as that means heavy fighting
And their towns destroyed and many killed.
When they chucked their hand in they thought they could
  escape
All this, but now they find they can't. The French
Are now paying, and don't like liberation.
They want to end the German occupation
And expel the Germans without dirtying their hands.
I was saying to Churchill and Brooke –

(*Dawnay has taken a phone call in the caravan and is gesturing.*)

Excuse me.

King. He is polite to me, but his eyes have
An insolence, an independence that says
"I honour Churchill for what he has done,
And Brooke because he was at Sandhurst too,
But you are in truth a Hanoverian
Who did not get where you are by merit –
Have not dirtied your hands as others have –
But merely took the trouble to be born.
And your brother is a known pro-German."
Much of being a King a find tedious.
All need to bow at, cheer, salute something,
The crown I wear, and so they bow to me.
I am like a cardboard cut-out and they hang
Their wishes, dreams, aspirations round my neck
Like a Hawaiian garland, and I must pass
From place to place and smile, for them, not me.
How much I sacrifice for their wishes.

But this war I am involved in, and I want
To share the discomforts and fate of my people:
We are all at risk from these new flying bombs,
From the sudden roar from the sky and explosion
That can leave Buckingham Palace a pile of stone.

(*16th June. London. Tedder and Coningham.*)

Tedder. Power has gone to his head. He tells the great
Who he will see and who he will not, and when.
He keeps the Supreme Commander waiting all day
Who has just been escorted by thirteen fighters.
We sent him a message before we arrived,
He could have come back early from Bradley,
Indeed, cancelled his visit. He tells the PM
Not to come, he speaks to the King with a cold contempt.
He tells Liddell Hart he is "too busy"
To see him, he offers a Napoleonic image.
He is on a pinnacle, and it is hubris,
It will surely tempt the gods to fling him down,
To cause him to fall.

Coningham. We shall see the consequences
Of what we have started.

(*17th June, morning. Margival, near Soissons, Hitler's reserve HQ, Wolfschlucht 2. Hitler, Rommel and Runstedt. Jodl, Schmundt and others. Stenographers.*)

Stenographer. This man is the terror of the world. Four Focke-
Wulf Condors flew him and his staff to France,
The entire fighter force along the route
Was grounded, anti-aircraft batteries
Shut down. As he drove from Metz airport to here,
Luftwaffe fighter planes patrolled the highway.
He has come to boost the Field Marshals' confidence
After the reverses in the battlefield.
All men tremble at the power his conquests brought.
I look forward to seeing what the man is like.
I am sure he will have Rommel quaking too.

Hitler. Soissons is near the battlefield where I
As a corporal won my Iron Cross.
Rommel and Rundstedt have asked for an urgent
Conference on the situation in France.

Rommel. The situation does not improve. The troops,
Both Army and SS, fight like tigers,
But the balance of strength tips against us.
Reinforcements are not getting through,
The Allied Airforce and warships bombard us
Every day. The British are trying to break out
Towards the Seine, the Americans –

Hitler (*radiating confidence*). Are you losing your nerve?

Rommel. I know Montgomery from the desert.
He will press relentlessly till our cordon breaks,
Then nothing will stop him. It is only days
Before the front caves in. Rundstedt agrees.

Rundstedt. I asked permission to withdraw my forces
From the peninsula to Cherbourg port
And fortress.

Hitler. Yes. The fortress should hold out
As long as possible and until mid-July
To hinder the enemy's sea-supply.
The withdrawal is part deception, as there will be
A winter attack by four Panzer divisions.

Aide. Air-raid warning.

(*The stenographers leave. Rommel and Hitler stand together in the air-raid shelter with Rundstedt, Schmundt and Chiefs of Staff.*)

Rommel. My Führer, please believe
Politics will soon have to play a part,
Or the situation will deteriorate
Too far to be salvaged.

Hitler (*snapping*). The time is not ripe
For a political decision. One sues for peace from strength.
To do so now would be to admit defeat
In Normandy. I have often spoken
Of my "secret weapons", and already London
Has been bombarded by V-1 rocket bombs
And is reeling as under the blitz. Britain will now
Sue for peace.

Aide. False alarm.

(*The stenographers return.*)

Hitler. If you can contain the enemy
Diversion in Normandy, if we can defeat
The expected landing in the Pas de Calais
On the beaches, as at Dieppe, then the German
Position will be one of strength.

Rommel. To regroup,
I need to withdraw my Panzers, but can't
While the British press round Caen.

(*Hitler shrugs.*)

*(*17th June. Montgomery's HQ. Dempsey and Montgomery.*)

Montgomery. We'll change our plan. You launch a mock
Attack on our right near Caumont, and then,
When Rommel is looking the wrong way, unleash
8 Corps in a blitz attack and envelop Caen
From the north-east. That is Operation Epsom.

*(*18th June. Dempsey's HQ. Dempsey and Montgomery.*)*

Montgomery. So you don't like the new plan?
Dempsey. For 8 Corps
To attack Caen east of the two rivers is a risk.
There's too little room for our troops and artillery,
As I've said. I think we should go back to the first
Plan: attack on the right and not the left.
Montgomery. Very well. Your left flank will be defensive.

(*20th June. Eisenhower in an air-raid shelter with Butcher.*)

Eisenhower. I'm cooped up in these cramped conditions because
Hitler still has the buzz-bomb rocket sites.
Monty should be hurrying to reach them, but no,
He's postponed an offensive yet again. He's slow.
I'm ordering Anvil in Bordeaux, I know
There will be no landings till mid-August,
But at least we're doing something. He's like a snail.

(*A whine cuts out, a crash of a doodlebug.*)

*(*22nd June. Creullet. Montgomery's TAC HQ. Meeting for all corps and divisional commanders. Montgomery.*)

Montgomery. The weather has been very stormy, but don't lose heart.
I say to all you corps and divisional commanders,
We have been successful in pulling the German reserves
To the Caen, or eastern, sector of our lodgement area,
And I congratulate you. This has relieved
Pressure in the American sector,
And as a result we now own the whole
Of the Cherbourg peninsula except the port
Of Cherbourg itself.

(*22nd June, later. Creullet. Montgomery's TAC HQ. Montgomery and Poston.*)

Poston. The storm has destroyed the American Mulberries,
But only damaged ours. But nothing can be unloaded.
All that we need to resume our offensive
Is tossing on ships near the floating harbours.
Montgomery. We are five days behind in our build-up,
This delay is what Rommel needs, for he can
Get more Panzer divisions into Normandy.
Arrange for a signal that Dempsey's blitz attack
Is postponed still further.

(*Enter Dawnay.*)

Dawnay. A signal. Eisenhower
Has ordered Wilson to start Anvil quickly,
As part of the Overlord strategy.
Montgomery. It will ruin the Allied Offensive in Italy

And will not help me a jot. He has not consulted
Me, the Overlord Commander. It's outrageous.
And then on top of everything we have to move
Our TAC HQ because the BBC
Reported the King had met me in my HQ
"In the grounds of a château", as good as told
The Germans where we are. Marlborough
And Wellington didn't have the whereabouts
Of their HQ broadcast for the enemy to hear.

*(*25th June. Eisenhower's HQ. Eisenhower and Butcher.*)

Butcher. A signal from Monty. The blitz attack
On Caen starts tomorrow. He says "If we
Can pull the enemy on to Second Army
It will make it easier for the First Army
When it attacks southwards."

Eisenhower. At last. Signal back, "I am hopeful that
Bradley can quickly clean up the Cherbourg mess."

*(*26th June. Eisenhower's HQ.*)

Butcher. A signal from Monty: "It can be accepted
That Cherbourg is now in First Army hands
And the enemy commander has been captured."
Cherbourg was the priority in the Overlord plan.

(*Eisenhower grins.*)

*(*27th June. Blay, Montgomery's new HQ. Montgomery and Dawnay.*)

Montgomery. I am sending you to England with a letter
To Brooke which assesses the situation.
Bradley is cautious, but the worst problem,
Churchill apart, is the jealousies that have lost
Us air support, I mean Tedder and Coningham,
Who are in league against Leigh-Mallory.
I will keep out of it, but we need air cover.
It's a sensitive letter, I hope he can help.

(*29th June. Berchtesgaden. Hitler, Rommel and Rundstedt.*)

Hitler. I have Rommel's figures: thirty enemy
Divisions have landed, sixty-seven more
Are waiting to cross the sea. I have accepted
We are now on the defensive in France.
I blame our Luftwaffe, and the women
And cooking of France, which have softened our troops.
I have said there must be attacks on ships,
Requisitioning of trucks and convoy highways
Protected by aircraft to supply Normandy.

Rommel. Field Marshal Rundstedt speaks for me. Rundstedt.

Rundstedt. In my view no counter-attack can be made

And we should give up our position at Caen
And withdraw out of range of the ships' artillery.
General Schweppenburg feels the same,
His assessment is here.

Jodl. That is the first step
To the catastrophic evacuation of France.
It is better to fight the decisive battle
Where we stand.

(29th June. London underground war rooms. Churchill's office. Churchill and Colville.)

Churchill. A memorandum to Anthony Eden.
"The Foreign Office have copied a telegram
For immediate distribution to the War Cabinet,
Which makes it clear that eight hundred thousand
Hungarian Jews have been deported and sent
To Birkenau near Oswiecim, where it says
A million and a half Jews from Europe
Have already been killed. What can be done? Or said?"

(He ponders.)

Colville. Sir, a signal from Monty. Bradley is
Delaying his thrust until July the third
Because the storm has delayed reinforcements.
Dempsey now faces eight Panzer divisions
Round Caen. An Ultra signal shows
Rommel is about to attack Cheux. Monty
Welcomes the attack as part of his strategy
To hold Rommel's armour while Bradley breaks
To Rennes and St. Malo, and also Paris.

Churchill. Stalin has said that the crossing of the Channel
And landings in Normandy are "an unheard
Of achievement, the magnitude of which
Has never been undertaken in military history".

(Chorus of Auschwitz prisoners.)

Chorus. What will become of us? Who will help us.
We hear that Montgomery has landed,
Normandy is a long, long way away.
How many months will it be before his troops
Have captured Berlin and reached here? Where are
Zhukov's men? Last month, eight thousand were killed.
This month, some two hundred and twenty-five
Thousand, mostly Jews sent from Hungary.
We know, we've seen them, we drag the bodies
From the gas chamber into the crematorium
Next door, we burn them and bury the surplus.
Each day prisoners are taken out and shot
Before the killing wall next to block eleven,

And more are hanged on the portable gallows.
Montgomery, make haste, help us, help us.
We cannot wait more than a few more weeks.
It will be our turn soon. Help us, help us.

(*1st July. Churchill's office.*)

Churchill. Send a message to Stalin: "The first week
Of the Soviet summer offensive in Belorussia
Has been outstandingly successful.
This is the moment for me to tell you
How immensely we are all here impressed
With the magnificent advances of the Russian armies,
Which seem, as they grow in momentum, to be
Pulverising the German armies which
Stand between you and Warsaw, and afterwards Berlin."

(*1st July. Rundstedt on phone.*)

Rundstedt. Keitel? Rundstedt. While Rommel and I were away
The British 11th Armoured crossed the Odon.
When General Dollmann heard this, he poisoned himself.
Officially he died of a heart attack.
Caen is now undefendable. You say
"What should we do?" Make peace, you idiots.
That's what I will be advising Hitler.

(*1st July. France. Rommel and Rundstedt. Enter Col. Heinrich Borgmann.*)

Rundstedt. You are one of Hitler's army adjutants.
Borgmann. The Führer has sent me to decorate you
With the Oak Leaves.

(*He decorates Rundstedt.*)

And to give you a blue envelope.
(*To Rommel.*) The Führer has sent a signal, that you must hold
The present lines.
Rommel (*to Rundstedt*). What does it say?
Rundstedt. Kluge
Has taken my place. I am no longer
Commander-in-Chief, West.

(*2nd July, morning. Blay, TAC HQ. Church bells and guns, yapping from two puppies. Eisenhower and Bradley outside the map caravan. Enter Montgomery.*)

Montgomery. Ike, Brad, what a pleasant surprise. I've been to church.
Eisenhower. I'm over here for a five-day visit
To send a first hand report to the Combined
Chiefs of Staff, and I'm glad to escape London.
The V-1 raids mean we're living underground.
We've evacuated SHAEF. From our viewpoint

As we shelter, it looks like stalemate here.
Montgomery. Come and see the German Panther and Tiger
Tanks we've knocked out and captured,
And then I'll brief you on my strategy.

(*Later. Eisenhower and Bradley outside the map caravan. Montgomery still inside.*)

Eisenhower. I am stunned by the clarity and logic
Of his plan. In London he seems too slow,
Over-cautious, but here, I've fallen under
His conviction, his professionalism, his
Physical presence, his spell. He has a certain
Charisma, and I can see you and Dempsey
Cannot go any faster. This bocage
Is not tank country.
Bradley. Collins told me,
The British were in the war nearly three years
Before us, and took heavy casualties in
North Africa. It's natural that they're cautious.
Eisenhower. But the fact remains, the British have failed to expand.
I still want, nay demand, an offensive.
I wonder why he's not mentioned Anvil.

(*8th July. Blay, Montgomery's HQ. Montgomery and Dawnay.*)

Montgomery. I am perplexed. Ike seemed to understand
When he was here, but now he urges haste,
Expresses concern at our lack of progress
Because Bradley failed to break out on the third,
With the Germans defending every yard of ground.
He wants a major attack on the left. But I've just
Launched Charnwood, a direct assault from the north,
As I briefed him I would when he was here.
He doesn't understand the battle, nor
Does anyone at SHAEF. And he's losing his nerve.
Dawnay. Perhaps there are political pressures
For a swift advance to the Pas de Calais
To capture the V-1 rocket launch-sites.
Montgomery. He's lost his nerve, just as we're taking Caen.
I shall write to him now and say that we
Must be quite clear as to what is vital or,
Our sense of values wrong, we may go astray.
Dawnay. The city of Caen, save for its southern suburb,
Is now in British and Canadian hands.

(*10th July. Blay. Montgomery's caravan. Bradley, Dempsey, Crerar and Patton.*)

Bradley (*depressed*). I've failed in my effort to break out.
Montgomery (*quietly*). Never mind.
Take all the time you need, Brad. If I were you

I think I should concentrate my forces more.

Dempsey. And what should I do now? What is my role?

Montgomery (*to Dempsey*). Go on hitting, draw the German armour
On to yourself to ease the way for Brad.

Patton. I can't wait to smash into Brittany,
I don't want to wait till August, I want there now.

(*14th July. London. Bushey Park Eisenhower's HQ. Eisenhower. Bedell Smith shows in Bomber Harris.*)

Bedell Smith. Air Marshal Harris.

Eisenhower. Monty needs you to provide
Heavy bomber assistance. Now I know
There have been reservations about supporting infantry
From the air, but we're going on the offensive
All along the line, we're going to gain ground and
Kill Germans. I've explained this to Churchill.
We're all excited by the prospect of an attack
That will be decisive. At one stroke we will
Knock loose our shackles.

Harris. So the new operation
On the seventeenth, Goodwood, will break out? You're on.

(*16th July. Blay. Montgomery's HQ. Montgomery and Henderson.*)

Montgomery. I'm alarmed that Ike's signal is euphoric.
No commander can have done more to avoid raising
Expectations. I've sent Kit to the War Office,
Written seven pages to Brooke, and sent
De Guingand to brief Ike, to simplify
The complex issues, to stress with simplicity
We are making the *enemy*, not the British or SHAEF,
Believe that we are breaking out to Paris;
And that our true aim is to dent Rommel's armour,
To muck up his plans and kill enemy troops.
Rommel is the objective.

(*Enter General Browning.*)

Browning, sit down.

Browning. As commander of all airborne divisions
I have dropped parachutists, and we have found
Rommel's HQ, and know where he goes to fish
And shoot pigeons. Would you like us to kill him?

Montgomery (*aside*). How strange that what I have heard in my deepest thoughts
And do not allow to surface should now be
Externalised in this proposal. What is right?
To say Yes and help the British break out
Or say No with the Christian code? He is
My old adversary at Alamein and elsewhere,
I would rather beat him face to face, fairly

As in a duel with pistols. But fair play
Has no place in war. War is war.
(*Aloud.*) Yes, I would.

(*17th July, morning. La Roche Guyon. Rommel and Speidel.*)

Rommel. The German front in France will collapse
In a few weeks. We have tried to convince Hitler
To surrender. He will not. Yesterday
I warned him in my dispatch of a grave crisis
And told him the proper conclusion must be drawn,
That I must speak plainly. We must now surrender
On our own responsibility and open
Independent peace negotiations with the Allies
As soon as possible.

Speidel. I agree. But will you now
Join the movement against Hitler?

Rommel (*shocked*). No, no.
I have my soldier's oath, which is ancient
And holy in the German tradition.
I am a professional. I disapprove
Of any movement against our Head of State.
To make a change in Berlin is not the way.
The Commander-in-Chief, West, who is now Kluge,
Should negotiate for the Allies to march,
Unopposed, across the Seine and into Germany.
We will talk further when I return tonight.

(*17th July, 9 p.m. Blay. Montgomery's HQ. Montgomery and Henderson.*)

Henderson. A report that will interest you. Rommel
Was in his staff car on a country road.
Two of Broadhurst's fighter bombers strafed it.
The driver lost an arm, Rommel was thrown
Out of his car and is now in hospital
With a severely fractured skull and splinters
In his face. Your enemy is out of the war.
The village near where the attack took place
Was Sainte Foy de Montgomery.

Montgomery. My ancestor's.
If I am Achilles, he was my Hector.

(*Montgomery turns away and goes to his caravan.*)

(*Praying.*) Lord, my enemy has been removed from the war,
And if that is your will, then I thank you.
But if I am responsible – if he was targeted
By Browning's men, and the name of the village
Suggests this, or else it is an amazing coincidence –
Then I am sad, for he is a noble man
And deserved a better end to his career.

Lord, be with him now, help him to recover,
Remove his pain, support his family.
And now, Lord, I put him out of mind for good.

(*Silence.*)

I feel it may have been better for the war
If Rommel were still in charge, but I don't know why.

(*He rises and slowly takes Rommel's picture off the caravan wall.*)

SCENE 3. STAUFFENBERG'S BOMB PLOT

(*18th July. Blay. Montgomery's HQ. Montgomery and Poston.*)

Montgomery. How has the Goodwood battle gone?
Poston. A day
Of awe-inspiring power. Four and a half
Thousand aircraft pummelled German positions
East of the Orne on the southern outskirts of Caen.
I saw Tiger tanks buried, set ablaze,
Flung upside down. Then our armour went in –
Not our infantry because the War Office warned
Dempsey casualties could not be replaced –
And seemed to break through, but the German defences
Were over six miles deep, and our tanks caught fire,
We lost four hundred in all. The Desert Rats
Were slow, the infantry lagged behind – Crerar
Is no commander and a poor soldier – and the day
Ended with only yards gained, and no breakthrough,
And Dempsey, with five thousand casualties
And no headway despite three armoured divisions,
Has withdrawn. Goodwood has been a disaster.
Montgomery (*quietly*). I shall claim it was a tactical success.
I like a picador, have paralysed
The bull's neck muscles with my twisting lance.
(*Depressed.*) But Bradley has delayed his pass again.

(*19th July evening. London, Bushey Park, SHAEF's HQ. Butcher on the phone.*)

Butcher. Ike's lying down. His blood pressure's up,
He's had ringing in his ears, it's the mental strain
Of being frustrated at Monty's slowness.
He's been in bed all day.

(*Eisenhower appears.*)

It's Tedder, sir.
Eisenhower (*taking phone*). The British armoured units have withdrawn.

You say Monty stopped the armour going further?
How dare he.

Butcher (*nervously*). Your blood pressure, sir, let me –

Eisenhower (*waving him aside*). The British air commanders are disgusted.
You are now telling me "I told you so".
You say the British Chiefs of Staff would support
Any recommendation I make. The sack?
Huh huh. Let me make sure I've got that now.
I take over field command, Alexander
Replaces Monty in charge of Twenty-first,
Chief Big Wind, you say, will be made a peer,
And you take Leigh-Mallory's place and command
The air forces. I'll have to think about that.
I'll call you.

(*19th July, late evening. London, underground war rooms. Churchill in blue and gold dressing-gown in bed, a canary on his head. Brooke.*)

Churchill (*furiously*). Goodwood has failed, and now Ike says General
Montgomery banned all the VIP visits
During the battle. Who is he to dictate
To me? To stop me? When I was Minister of Munitions
In the First World War, Haig always allowed me
To visit. I have written to Ike that I
Have no intention of visiting General
Montgomery's headquarters and that Ike
Should provide a Staff Officer to show me about.
If General Montgomery disputes my visit
In any way, the matter will be taken up
Because I have a right and a duty
To acquaint myself with the facts on the spot.

Brooke. I will visit Monty tomorrow morning.

*(*20th July. London, Bushey Park, Eisenhower's HQ. Butcher on phone.*)

Butcher. Bedell Smith? Butcher here, sir. Ike has asked
Me to let you know, he's been to see Monty
In response to that signalled invitation
To visit him alone – that meant without Tedder.
Monty's given him a logical explanation,
And although Ike pointed out that there will soon
Be more American troops than British in France,
He says there's to be no hint of what he discussed
With you last night. Sir, I don't know what Monty
Has done, but he sure worked some magic. Ike is now
A changed man. He's gone fishing, he's thrown away
His blood pressure pills, he's more happy with
Monty's conduct of the war in Normandy.

(20th July, 12.35 p.m. Von Stauffenberg with a briefcase, in Keitel's sitting-room in Hitler's headquarters in Rastenburg, Wolfsschanze, the Wolf's Lair.)

Stauffenberg (*alone*). Now is the moment of my destiny.
For nine months I have plotted to restore
Germany's greatness from a tarnished regime.
Ever since I became Olbricht's Chief of Staff,
And Olbricht promoted me to be Chief of Staff
To Fromm so I could activate his Reserve Army
And impose martial law when the Führer dies.
All my life has led up to this moment,
To kill the man who has shamed Germany
And operate Valkyrie; and I have been
The leader of the plotters – politicians, Generals.
Though I am crippled and have no right hand
And only three fingers on my left hand, yet still
I can carry a briefcase and prime a bomb.
Twice I marched the troops of the Reserve Army
To take Berlin, and twice I aborted the plan,
The first time because Göring was not there,
The second time because Hitler left early.
Now I have the best opportunity of all
As Hitler wants me to attend a staff conference.
It should be in the underground concrete bunker
But has been transferred to a wooden hut.
I have a wife and children. If I fail
I will put them at risk, and many others.
But I must act, this tyranny cannot go on.
Hitler's atrocities shame all mankind.

(Stauffenberg moves to disclose von Haeften, sitting.)

(To Haeften.) Two two-lb packages of explosive.
Haeften. They're here.

(Stauffenberg stoops and breaks the fuse capsule of one of the packages with pliers held in his three fingers. The door opens. Stauffenberg starts.)

Orderly. Keitel wants you to hurry up.
Stauffenberg. Coming.

(Major John von Freyend, Keitel's adjutant, appears.)

Freyend. Stauffenberg, do come along now.
Haeften. You've only primed one of the packages.
Stauffenberg. One will have to do. It should be enough.

(Exit Stauffenberg, leaving Haeften holding one of the packages. Stauffenberg reappears.)

Stauffenberg. Now I will put the briefcase close to Hitler.

I will lay the bomb under his conference table,
Then the Wehrmacht will have a putsch, and then
We will arrange to surrender to the Allies
And stop the senseless conduct of the war.

(*He enters the hut and puts the briefcase under a heavy oak table near Hitler. Col. Brandt moves it to the other side of the table's leg.*)

Haeften. Colonel Stauffenberg, phone call from Berlin.
Stauffenberg. Excuse me.

(*He goes out and waits with Gen. Erich Fellgiebel. They watch. The hut explodes in smoke and flame. Two bodies fly out of the open windows. One is Brandt's.*)

No one could have survived that.
I will telephone Berlin to activate Valkyrie.
Then von Haeften and I will bluff our way
Out of the compound and drive to the airfield
Where our Heinkel is waiting.

(*They leave. Hitler staggers out, his trousers and hair on fire. He beats out the flames.*)

(*20th July, 12.45 p.m. Rastenburg, Wolf's Lair, a corridor in the Guest Bunker. Hitler and Keitel. Hitler's face is smoke-blackened.*)

Hitler. I thought it might be a paratroop attack
So I avoided the windows for the corridor.
Keitel. That must have been one of the Todt workmen.
Hitler. A German workman would never lift his hand
Against me. I always sensed this opposition
To me in the General Staff. Stalin knew what
He was doing when he rubbed out Marshal Tukhachevsky.
Now, I shall make a clean sweep. Send for Dr. Morell.

(*He sits unsteadily, and takes his own pulse. His secretaries appear.*)

(*Grinning.*) Well ladies, things turned out well again. Ah, Dr. Morell.

(*A few minutes later.*)

Hitler. I am invulnerable, immortal.
My survival is a great miracle.
Dr. Morell. You have some badly torn skin on your legs
And a hundred splinters from the oak table. Your face
Has been cut by splinters, a timber has bruised
Your forehead. Your eardrums are perforated.
Hitler. This was the work of cowards. If they had drawn a gun
On me I might respect them, but they didn't dare
Risk their own lives. I shall make an example of them

That will make anyone else think twice before betraying
The German people. My own life is not
Important, but anyone who lifts a hand
Against the German State during a war
Must be destroyed, must be executed.
Guards, search for hidden fuse cable and for
Additional bombs. Now I shall have lunch.
Call in the secretaries or I will be late. I meet
The Duce from his train at two-thirty.

Dr. Morell. You can't possibly meet the Duce now.

Hitler. I must. What would the world's press say if I didn't?

(*20th July, mid-afternoon. Goebbels in his office with Speer and Walter Funk, Economics Minister. The telephone rings.*)

Goebbels. My Führer. A failed assassination attempt?
That is scandalous, treasonous, criminal.
You are safe. That is Providential. A coup?

(*He looks out of the window.*)

Yes, my Ministry is being surrounded now.
I will deal with it.

(*He puts poison capsules in his pocket.*)

There is an attempted coup,
Please excuse me. Send in Major Remer.

(*Enter Major Otto Remer almost immediately.*)

Remer, what is going on?

Remer. Sir, the commandant
Of the Berlin garrison, General von Hase,
Has told me the Führer has been assassinated
And the SS are attempting a putsch. I have orders,
Which I must obey, to seal the Wilhelmstrasse
And arrest some ministers, including you.

Goebbels. But you have an oath of personal loyalty
To the Führer.

Remer. The Führer is dead.

Goebbels. He's alive.
An ambitious group of Generals has begun
A military putsch, the dirtiest in history.
I am going to speak to the Führer now.
You will speak with him.

(*Goebbels telephones on his direct line.*)

My Führer, it's Goebbels again.
I have *Major* Remer here.

Remer. Jawohl, mein Führer.
Jawohl, mein Führer.

(*He hands the phone back to Goebbels who listens.*)

Goebbels. I understand, my Führer.
Colonel Remer is to crush the rebellion in Berlin.
He is to obey my orders or those of Himmler
Who is Commander of Reserve Army in place of Fromm.
And General Reinecke. I will broadcast
That the coup has failed.

(*He turns to Remer.*)

Arrest the plotters.

(*20th July, 4.45 p.m. Bendlerstrasse, upstairs now, 2nd floor. Colonel-General Fromm in his office. Stauffenberg, Olbricht, Haeften, Kleist.*)

Stauffenberg. Why didn't you activate Valkyrie
At once, as soon as I telephoned?
Olbricht. I was at lunch.
But that aside, the Führer is alive.
He is entertaining Mussolini to tea.
As soon as Fromm heard Hitler is alive
He refused to go along with us.
Stauffenberg. Hitler
Is dead. As usual Field Marshal Keitel's
Lying. I saw his body carried out.
Olbricht. Orders for Valkyrie have now been given.
Fromm (*raging, banging fists on desk*). I am in command, I will not allow
Subordinates to do such things. You are
All guilty of insubordination,
Revolution, treason. The penalty
For all of you is death. Who ordered this?
Olbricht. Colonel Mertz von Quirnheim.
Fromm. Bring von Quirnheim.

(*Enter Colonel von Quirnheim, Olbricht's Chief of Staff.*)

I want to confirm, did you give orders
For Valkyrie?
Quirnheim. I did.
Fromm (*raging*). You, all of you,
Are under arrest. (*To Quirnheim.*) Cancel the orders.
Quirnheim (*sitting down*). Colonel-General, since I am under
Arrest, my freedom to move's restricted.
Fromm (*to Stauffenberg*). The assassination attempt has failed.
Stauffenberg, you will have to shoot yourself.
Stauffenberg. No, we are in control. It is you who's
Under arrest. Take his pistol. Guard him.

(*Fromm rises and lurches forward, lunging with his fists towards Stauffenberg.*)

Fromm (*shouting*). You haven't been my Chief of Staff three weeks
And now you've got me into trouble with –

(*Haeften and Kleist draw their pistols. Fromm sits back.*)

Stauufenberg. Put him in his adjutant's room next door.

(*Nearly midnight. Pro-Nazis let Fromm out of his room. There is an exchange of gunfire. Stauffenberg is hit in his good left arm in a corridor. Stauffenberg is brought into Fromm's room by Beck, Olbricht, von Quirnheim, Haeften and Hoepner. Enter Fromm with his adjutant Hauptmann Bartram. Haeften points his pistol at Fromm, who cowers. Stauffenberg, bleeding from his shoulder, indicates that Haeften should lower his pistol. He looks at Fromm with contempt. Enter Lt-Col. Gehrke and staff officers. They observe.*)

Fromm. All of you, over there. We have you covered.
You have plotted against the Führer, you
Have caused him pain. This is a court martial.

Stauffenberg. He has known of the plot for weeks and has
Done nothing to prevent it and he wants
To kill us so we can't reveal that he
Is one of us. And now he is our judge
And jury. Some trial.

Fromm. Quiet. You will not speak
Unless addressed. I pronounce you guilty
Of conspiring to assassinate our
Beloved Führer, high treason. Sentence:
Colonel-General Beck, General Olbricht, Colonel-
General Mertz, this Colonel whose name I will
Not speak, Lieutenant-General Hoepner and
Lieutenant von Haeften are condemned to
Death. Sentence will be carried out at once.
Have you any last wishes?

Stauffenberg. I alone
Am responsible for everything. These
Men are just soldiers who obeyed orders
I gave. They are guiltless.

Fromm. No, they are guilty.

Beck. I wish to keep my pistol for private use.

Fromm (*nodding*). You must do it now. Here.

Beck (*stunned at the speed*). Goodbye, my friends.

(*Standing, he points his Luger at his temple, flinches as he pulls the trigger. Loud report. He falls back into Stauffenberg's bloodstained arms with blood trickling from his head wound.*)

(*moaning*). Another gun. Quickly.

Staff Officer. Try this Mauser.

(*Standing, Beck tries again. Loud report. He falls to the floor, moaning.*)

Sergeant. Beck is not dead.
Fromm (*contemptuously*). He has even bungled that.
Help the old gentleman.

(*The sergeant bends over Beck, whose head is bleeding, and administers the coup de grâce in front of the conspirators, who wince.*)

Take his leather
Overcoat as your reward. Any more
Last wishes?
Hoepner. I had nothing to do with
The plot, I wish to compose a defence.
Olbricht. I wish to write a statement.
Fromm (*thinking*). Very well.
Hoepner. Please can I see you in private.

(*Half an hour later. Fromm emerges from the room next door. Hoepner is led away under guard. Olbricht stops his writing. Stauffenberg is sitting apparently in prayer, clutching his shoulder.*)

Fromm. Further investigations are required.

(*Enter a soldier.*)

Soldier. General, the Grossdeutschland Guard Battalion
Has arrived under Lieutenant Schady.
Fromm (*starting*). Thank you. Hauptmann.
Bartram. General.
Fromm. Go down and pick
Ten Unteroffizieren from Schady's
Men and line them in the courtyard in front
Of the pile of sand the builders have left,
And line his army trucks with headlights on. (*Exit Bartram.*)

(*Only a little later. Stauffenberg seems in another world.*)

Fromm (*to Olbricht*). You've written enough now.
(*To guards.*) Take these four down
To the courtyard.
Stauffenberg. Goodbye my loyal friends.
We will rise above their guns and hold ourselves
Erect, for our idea was right, to stand
Against atrocities. What we thought we
Will act, our self-control will show we still
Hold our beliefs, our self-mastery in
The face of wrong. We will call others to
Complete our task. Our Germany thanks you.

(*Stauffenberg, Olbricht, Haeften and Quirnheim are marched under guard and stood against a mound of sand. Dim light from a row of army lorries with hooded headlights. The firing-squad appears.*)

Fromm. Execute them. They shame our Fatherland.
Stauffenberg (*standing straight, shouting*). Long live our sacred Germany.
Haeften (*shouting*). Not him.

(*Haeften dives in front of Stauffenberg and takes his bullets. The crash of the firing-squad reverberates. Three fall. Stauffenberg is still standing. Perplexed, the firing-squad reloads. The crash of the firing-squad again. Stauffenberg falls back on the sand.*)

Soldier. Did he shout "sacred" or "secret" Germany?
Fromm. Send a teleprinter message to the Führer:
"Attempted putsch by irresponsible Generals
Bloodily crushed. All ringleaders shot."
Take their bodies to the local churchyard.

(*Later. Enter Speer and Remer.*)

Fromm. I've just had some criminals executed.
Remer. I am not pleased, we wanted to question
These men. You must come to the Propaganda
Ministry, and be questioned by Goebbels
And Himmler.
Speer. A very hasty end. Say what
You will, these men, if wrong, were very brave.

(*21st July, 1 a.m. Martial music on radio, then Hitler's voice.*)

Hitler. I am speaking to you, first, so you may know
I am unhurt and well, and second so that
You may hear details of a crime unparalleled
In German history. A conspiracy
To eliminate me has been hatched by
A tiny clique of ambitious, irresponsible,
Stupid and criminal officers. I was spared
A fate which holds no terror for me, but would
Have had terrible consequences for
The German people. I regard this as a sign
That I should continue the task imposed
Upon me by Providence. The criminals
Will all be ruthlessly exterminated.

*(*A little later. Rastenburg, Hitler's room. Hitler and Bormann.*)

Hitler. I will have blood, I will have sacrifice.
Just as in Warsaw, Stroop gave me the gift
Of the Ghetto for my birthday, so now

I will see the conspirators on meat hooks.
They must be hanged like cattle. On thin wire.

Bormann. I will attend to it. They will be filmed.
I have the idea of using piano wire. (*Exit.*)

Hitler (*alone*). I must watch them suffer, with you my dear.
We will receive the sacrifice of blood
Of thousands who made me suffer like this.
Oh Eva, you have written from Bavaria,
I wish you were here. My spear, I will spear them.

**(21st July, 3.40 a.m. Hitler's HQ. Hitler and Bormann.)*

Bormann. General Fromm has just been arrested, and
The traitors' action is now at an end.
(*Wheedling.*) A letter from von Kluge about Rommel.
"The view of the Field Marshal is unfortunately right.
I have spoken with the commanders around Caen
And the regrettable evidence is that in the face
Of the enemy air forces' complete command,
There is no way we can counterbalance
Its annihilating effect without giving up
The field of battle."

Hitler. They are defeatist,
All my Generals.

(21st July, morning. Blay. Montgomery's HQ. The dining marquee. Montgomery alone.)

Montgomery (*aside*). Brooke has told me Churchill has an order
In his pocket, dismissing me. All TAC HQ
Know this rumour. I will meet fire with fire. Brooke
Says Ike told him I am keeping him from France,
Which made him furious. I will welcome him
Although I regard his visit as meddlesome.
He likes canaries, I will charm him with mine.
A General must be confident to all.
I will radiate optimism and boost his nerve.

(Enter Henderson and Churchill wearing blue coat and cap. There is a frosty atmosphere. Paul the chef is listening behind a tent-flap.)

(*Aloud, shaking hands.*) Prime Minister, I'm delighted and honoured
To welcome you to near the Cerisy forest,
And I'm greatly looking forward to briefing you.
Have you seen my dogs and canaries, sir?

Churchill (*sitting*). I have
A canary that sits on my head. Henderson,
Would you mind leaving us?

(Exit Henderson to the kitchen tent, with Paul. They listen.)

Monty, SHAEF – Ike and
Tedder – want you dismissed. We've had setbacks –

Montgomery. Setbacks? What setbacks? The battle is going
Excellently.

Churchill. They say we're losing the war
And you're panicking, they want Alexander
To take over. And I'm Defence Minister
And Prime Minister, and I've a right to be here,
Monty.

Montgomery. It's dangerous, sir.

Churchill. Let me be the judge
Of that.

Montgomery. There's no panic here, come into
The operations caravan and I'll show you a map.
The Germans are doing exactly what we want.
Tedder doesn't understand my plan, I don't want
To take Caen but to keep pressing on it
To bring the Germans to me, then Patton can
Swing round.

Henderson (*to Paul*). You should not be hearing this.

Paul. Nor you.

(*Montgomery and Churchill walk to the caravan.*)

Montgomery. I am not fighting the Germans and the Italians
Alone, but the Americans and British as well,
The only people I'm not fighting are
The Russians.

Churchill. Monty, I know the feeling well.

Montgomery. In four to five weeks you will have all France
In your pocket.

(*They enter the caravan.*)

(*Later. Enter Brigadier Bill Williams, Intelligence Officer. He knocks on the caravan door. Montgomery opens.*)

Williams. Sir, we have gleaned from scraps of Ultra there's
Been a sort of revolution in Berlin.

Montgomery. How intriguing. Sir, do you know anything
About this?

(*Churchill holds keys on a long chain and opens two red boxes.*)

Churchill. There's something about it in here.
See what you can find.

(*Montgomery and Williams rifle through the dispatch-boxes.*)

Williams. These are Ultra signals. Sir, have you read this?

Churchill. No.

Williams. This could mean a sudden end to the war.

Montgomery. There could be a surrender this morning.
The American Cobra attack may not be needed.
We've got the Germans on the run.

(*They emerge from the caravan, Churchill beaming.*)

Churchill. Monty,
I must be off.

(*Exit Williams.*)

Montgomery. Whenever you get angry
In the future, sir, you're to send me a telegram
And find out the truth.

Churchill. I promise I will.

Montgomery. And this bottle of cognac is a peace offering.

(*They shake hands. Exit Churchill. Enter Henderson.*)

He is volatile, he's up and down, and love
Can turn to rage, but that was very friendly.

Henderson. You've bought yourself another month, I would say.

Montgomery. Things will have improved by then.

(*21st July Berlin, Prinz Albrechtstrasse, Gestapo HQ. Himmler visits the cellars with Ernst Kaltenbrunner.*)

Himmler. The Special Commission you set up yesterday
Already has four hundred officials who
Interrogate day and night the ever-widening circle
Of those implicated in this shameful plot.
Each day Kielpinski will write a summary
Of what has developed and send it to Bormann.
I would like to see your methods, how you extract
Confessions, so I am knowledgeable
If Bormann asks. Take me to a cell where I
Can see an interrogator at work.

Kaltenbrunner. Hundreds of officers have been arrested,
Including General Fromm. We are getting names.
Generals include von Tresckow and Wagner
And Field Marshals Rommel and von Kluge.
Also von Stulpnagel. We suspect Canaris,
Moltke, Dohnanyi, and Bonhoeffer.
There will be thousands of names. This is how they talk.

(*He opens a door. There is a muffled shriek, a groan.*)

His legs are in metal tubes with sharp spikes,
That are screwed into his flesh. There are more spikes
In his fingertips. A helmet and blanket
Muffle the screams. He will talk, they all do.

Himmler. (*nodding and turning back*). The Army has been purged.
Guderian,
The new Chief of Staff, has pledged its allegiance

To the Führer. The army salute will be
Abolished for the party raised arm. All
Chiefs of Staff will be party men, and teach
The tenets of Hitler. This will be announced.

(24th July. Rastenburg, Hitler's room. Hitler and Dr. Giesing. Bormann and Sonnleithner nearby.)

Hitler. My right ear is bleeding, my eyes flick to
The right, I keep thinking I am falling
To my right. But the shock has got rid of my nerve
Complaint, my left leg does not tremble now
But my hearing....Cauterise my ear again,
Ignore my pain. I stopped feeling pain long
Ago, pain exists to make a man of you.
(*To Sonnleithner.*) I had *both* eardrums perforated, yet
I did not feel a thing, it happened so fast.
That's probably how it is when you shoot yourself.
Even if you shoot yourself in the mouth, not the brain,
I now know you don't feel a thing.

Dr. Giesing. It's amazing you were not more badly hurt.

Hitler. Providence protected me. I am immortal
Until I have completed my Providential task.
(*To Bormann.*) Exhume Stauffenberg and the three others.
They were buried in their uniforms with their medals.
I want proof that they died, I do not trust Fromm,
Or the Army, who may have invented
The execution to put me off their track.

Bormann. I will attend to it. Rest assured, it will be done. (*Exit.*)

*(*24th July. London, Bushey Park. SHAEF HQ, Eisenhower on phone.*)

Eisenhower. Winston, you're just back from Normandy. What
Do you people think about the slowness
Of the situation over there? You are
Supremely happy with the situation?
Tedder said Monty deliberately
Restricted Dempsey's break-out, and that he did
Not have the slightest intention of a clean breakthrough
To Paris. A diversion? You support him.
(*Aside.*) He's obviously sold Winston a bill of goods.

(25th July. Blay. Montgomery's HQ. Montgomery and Eisenhower.)

Montgomery. How are you?

Eisenhower. Still suffering from high blood pressure.
I think it's been caused by all the sleep I've lost
As a result of the buzz-bombs. I've come to see
The start of Cobra but did not expect
American planes to bomb American troops
Two days running with over seven hundred
And fifty casualties. The lesson is,

Heavy bombers can't give tactical support.

Montgomery. We're still trying to find out why this happened.

Eisenhower. Monty, you should know there's a strong feeling in the US
That American troops are doing more than British
As Americans have suffered more casualties
And captured more prisoners.

Montgomery. Your bigger casualties –
Ten thousand to the British and Canadian six –
Are due to American lack of skill in fighting,
For example, bombing their own side.

Eisenhower. That's not right.
I'm under pressure from General Marshall.
There's a feeling that there will soon be more
American troops than British, that they're doing more,
And if Cobra fails – and the battle is touch and go –
Then there may be criticism of your command.

(*25th July. Rastenburg. Hitler and Goebbels in his office, on phone.*)

Hitler. Goebbels, I am indebted to you for crushing
The army putsch by the officer corps.
You are now to be Reich commissioner
For total mobilisation of resources for war.
You are to have power over all civilians
And party authorities.

Goebbels. My Führer, I am honoured.
And pleased to serve you.

(*He leaves Hitler's room. Outside, to his assistant.*)

If I had had these powers
Earlier, when I wanted them, the war would now
Be finished. It takes a bomb under his arse
To make Hitler see reason.

(*27th July. London. Churchill's underground HQ. Dinner. Eisenhower, Bedell Smith, Brooke, Churchill.*)

Churchill. Over lunch yesterday, you expressed dissatisfaction
With Montgomery, and I have asked you to repeat
These criticisms in the presence of my Chief of Staff,
And now I would like to hear his reply.

Brooke. The criticisms which the Supreme Commander
And his Chief of Staff have again expressed
To the Prime Minister are defeatist and
Do not accord with the picture I have received
From General Montgomery today. He is fighting hard
On the eastern flank to assist the Americans
On the western side. I am quite certain that
Montgomery's strategy is about to pay off,
And anyone who doubts that knows nothing about strategy.
If the Supreme Commander has any criticisms

Of the way his Land Forces Commander-in-Chief
Is directing the battle, he should return
To Normandy and put them to his face
And not complain to others behind his back.

Eisenhower. I am shy of doing that in a sensitive matter.
I want to maintain the best relations between
The British and Americans and win the war.

Churchill. We cannot make a public statement about
Our strategy in making the Germans believe
The British are trying to break out when they're not,
As this would be read by the enemy. Silence is best.

(*29th July. Bradley's HQ in France. Montgomery and Henderson.*)

Henderson. Ike's with Kay, his Irish driver.

Montgomery (*scathingly*). You mean,
His floozie.

Henderson. It's her first time in Normandy.

(*Enter Eisenhower, Kay Summersby and Bradley. Montgomery ignores Kay, who talks aside with Bradley.*)

Eisenhower. It's excellent news that Brad's armoured divisions
Have caused the German front to disintegrate.

Montgomery. Yesterday I took Dempsey to Brad's headquarters,
Dempsey's launching his next armoured attack
From Caumont and Kluge will be out of position
As he expects us to thrust towards Paris.
We all agreed the plan is working well.

Eisenhower. Did you get my signal, that I am delighted
That your basic plan has begun to unfold
Brilliantly with Brad's success?

Montgomery (*nodding*). Yes, I did.

Eisenhower (*elated*). I've told the American censor, General Surles,
That I am responsible for strategy
And major activity in Normandy
And that any criticism of you
Is criticism of me.

(*Eisenhower and Bradley turn away.*)

Montgomery (*to Henderson*). O-o-oh, did you hear that?
Now he smells triumph, he's taking the credit.

Henderson. It's time to meet Bradley, sir.

*(*1st August Churchill's office. Churchill and Brooke.*)

Churchill. Rokossovsky is ten miles from Warsaw,
Having advanced four hundred miles in six
Weeks, and today the Polish Home Army,
At the direction of the Polish Government
In Exile in London, have risen against
The Germans in their city, the Warsaw Uprising.

Koniev has taken Lvov, and other Russians
Are in North Poland and Lithuania.
I want to know what Stalin will do. Will he help
The Free Poles?

(*2nd August Stalin's Kremlin Office. Stalin on phone.*)

Stalin. Rokossovsky? Your report? You have lost
A hundred and twenty-three thousand men
On the way to Warsaw, your troops are exhausted.
You fear a German attack from the south.
You are still outside Warsaw. Stay where you are,
Don't move on Warsaw. The Uprising is led
By a General Bór, real name Komorowski,
Who wants a pro-British democratic Poland,
He is against the Red Army and will fight you
If you go in. Sit tight and let him fight
The Germans, and when they are both worn out,
And street-fighting is no longer a danger,
Then you may go in.

*(*3rd August, 10 a.m. Dempsey's HQ in France. Map. Montgomery and Dempsey.*)

Montgomery. Now that the plan is working, and we have Rennes,
And Patton is going to make an eastward wheel
While you, Crerar and Bradley tie Kluge down
Between Caen and Mortain, and swing his right
Flank round towards Paris, outflanking the enemy
And forcing some back to the Seine; it will be
Possible for you and Hodges to outflank
The Germans to the north in this Falaise gap.
And if Crerar strikes south towards Falaise
We can surround the enemy in a pocket.
This is the consequence of sticking to the plan
For two months, making the struggle for Normandy
The longest ever battle in the West,
Surpassing the three-week battle for France
And the twelve-day battle of Alamein.

*(*7th August. Forêt de Cerisy, Montgomery's new TAC HQ. Montgomery and Bradley.*)

Montgomery. I would like a full encirclement to the Seine.
Bradley. Sir, time is critical, that would take too long.
I advise a short encirclement at Falaise.
I can't believe that Hitler has sent in
Four Panzer divisions, right into our trap.
Kluge doesn't seem to know what we're about.
We should spring it as soon as we can. It will be
A present to Ike, who's setting up SHAEF HQ
In Tournières today.

(*8th August, eight conspirators before Freisler's People's Court: von Witzleben, Hoepner, Stieff, von Hase, Bernadis, Klausing, Hagen and von Wartenburg, all army men, ranks ranging from Field Marshal to Lieutenant. Freisler is in a blood-red robe. Swastika flags.*)

Freisler (*shouting*). Witzleben, you were a Field Marshal, why
Are you fiddling with your trousers? You dirty old man.

Witzleben. My belt has been taken away.

Freisler. Can't you speak?

Witzleben. My teeth have also been taken away.

Freisler. Wartenburg, you wanted to tell the Court something?

Wartenburg. Of my contempt for National Socialism.
Man has a moral and religious duty
To oppose any regime which lacks respect
For the sacredness of human life.

Freisler. Enough.

(*He has signalled to the cameras behind a swastika to stop filming.*)

I won't have any more of these irrelevant
Speeches.

(*He signals to the cameras to resume.*)

You say you are guilty. The Court
Accepts your confession. We have now heard
The evidence. This is the last day of this trial.
The Court finds all the defendants guilty.
It denies them the honour of beheading
And sentences them to death by hanging.
Sentences to be carried out at Plotzensee
This afternoon, film to be sent to the Führer.

(*8th August. Later. The Plotzensee execution building, two windows under eight meat hooks on a roof beam. A black curtain. A camera, two cameramen. Film lights. The Public Prosecutor Hanssen, sitting. Von Witzleben is led in.*)

Hanssen. Accused, the People's Court has sentenced you
To death by hanging. Hangman do your duty.

(*Von Witzleben is led to under the first meat hook by two executioners. The grinning hangman, one of the two, puts piano wire round his neck.*)

Witzleben. Piano wire. And meat hooks. (*Scathingly.*) For a human being.

Hangman (*grinning, leering*). A slow hanging.

(*The wire is shaped in a figure of 8. They lift him and throw the upper noose over the meat hook. They let him drop. The wire bites into his neck, causing a ring of blood. As his feet move they draw a curtain but leave a gap for the camera to watch. Hoepner is led in, the General who escaped Fromm's firing-squad.*)

Hanssen. Accused, the People's Court has sentenced you
To death by hanging. Hangman do your duty.

(*Hoepner is led to under the second meat hook by the two executioners. The same process is repeated. The black curtain half drawn.*)

Cameraman 1. Sir, we can't face any more.
Hanssen. The Führer has said
"They must be hanged like cattle." It must be filmed.
The Führer wants to watch them die tonight.
A plane is standing by to fly your film
To Rastenburg.

SCENE 4. MONTGOMERY'S DEMOTION

*(*13th August, 12.15 p.m. Forêt de Cerisy, Montgomery's HQ. Montgomery, Bradley and Dempsey.*)

Montgomery. Thank you for flying up here, Brad. Now, Patton
Has raced away and could reach Paris, the Seine,
But you still favour the short encirclement
At Falaise?
Bradley. Yes sir. Once Patton starts racing,
He can find he's going in the wrong direction
As at Palermo. We have Germans in a trap.
It's wiser to spring it now, rather than let
Them out.
Montgomery. In that case, none must cross the Seine
Without being mauled. The plan is as follows:
The Canadians will attack, supported by
Heavy bombers; Dempsey will seize Falaise
To allow the Canadians to push towards
Trun and Argentan, where Collins will
Arrive from the southern flank, and Patton will
Act as long stop east of L'Aigle.

*(*15th August, 7.30 p.m. Rastenburg, Wolf's Lair, Hitler's HQ. Hitler bent, with cotton wool in his ears. Bormann.*)

Hitler. Patton is rampaging through Brittany,
The Americans have attacked us near Falaise
All day, and still no sign of Field Marshal
Von Kluge, and now we learn his radio truck
Has been silent all day, and he is mentioned
In an enemy radio signal. Either he is dead,
Or he is surrendering to the British and
Joining forces with Russia, an idiotic

Notion. SS General Hausser will now
Take over Army Group B and stop the enemy.

*(*16th August. Later.*)

Hitler. The worst day of my life. I have not slept,
The sedatives don't work, send my doctor.
Now Eberbach's headquarters report that
Kluge arrived last night in the middle of the trap,
With no explanation for where he was yesterday.
There are reports he has contacted the British.
Signal he is to leave the area at once.
I can no longer trust him. Contact Field Marshal
Model and appoint him Kluge's successor.
Oh my headache. Damn Stauffenberg.

(*16th August. London, Churchill's underground HQ. Churchill and Brooke.*)

Brooke. In the BBC news yesterday there was a report
That Eisenhower has taken personal command
In France with Bradley's and Monty's army groups
Under him. This was retracted today.
It is clear to me that Eisenhower now wants
To be Field Commander of the Allied army groups
In France once he's set up battlefield HQ.
He's now in Normandy, but Monty is
Treating him like a VIP, he's forbidden
Him to attend meetings with Bradley, Patton,
Dempsey and Crerar. He's inviting trouble.
Listen to this disturbing letter I've had:
"Ike is apt to get very excited and talk
Wildly at the top of his voice. He is now here,
Which is a very great pity. His ignorance
As to how to run a war is absolute
And complete....He is such a decent chap that it is
Difficult to be angry with him for long.
One thing I am firm about; he is never allowed
To attend a meeting between me and my
Army Commanders and Bradley."

Churchill. He's digging his grave.
He is self-willed and convinced of his mastery
Of modern battlefield warfare, and scorns
The "lesser" talents of his fellow Generals.
He has no sense of tact or diplomacy.
Someone should tell him that Eisenhower is
In charge of over a million American troops.
It is not for us to say this to him now.
It has been said already. The Anvil
Landings near Marseilles will affect Italy.
We have the Pacific to think of. We must

Visit the Italian front, and Monty will
Have to fend for himself, and it is up to him
Whether his character strengths or flaws will
Gain the upper hand, whether he has learned
From the advice you have given him, and his treatment of me.

(*17th August. Fougères, Bradley's HQ. Montgomery and Bradley.*)

Montgomery. We must keep a grip on the battle and not be
Carried away. Patton has charged towards Paris
Like a bull – Palermo again – and the Canadians
And the Poles are trying to close the jaws of our trap
Without Patton. We have taken a hundred and fifty
Thousand prisoners in Normandy, and another hundred
Thousand troops are in the Falaise bag. Meanwhile
Leclerc has raced off to beat Patton to Paris:
Another hole. Gerow has pulled him back.
We need to think ahead beyond the Seine,
Which we will reach tomorrow. As I see it
Twelve and Twenty-one Army Groups should keep
Together as a solid mass that need
Fear nothing. The British and Canadians
Should hug the coast and go for Antwerp and
Capture the rocket sites that threaten England.
You should form a right flank towards Aachen,
Cologne and then the Ruhr. Together we will form
A single, narrow thrust.

Bradley. I agree entirely.

Montgomery. I have not yet discussed the plan with Ike.
I want to put to him that the US Seventh
Army, driving up from the south of France,
Should target the Saar. Ike is not likely
To have any great objections, and he will,
I think, undoubtedly accept what we say.

Bradley (*aside*). Does he really believe that? Wishful thinking.
He is deluding himself.

(*17th August, later. Bradley's HQ. Eisenhower and Bradley; Hansen, Bradley's aide.*)

Hansen. (*to Eisenhower*). Sir, a communication from General Marshall.

(*Eisenhower takes it and reads.*)

Eisenhower. Hey, Brad, listen to this: "The Secretary",
That's Stimson, "and I and apparently all Americans
Are strongly of the opinion that the time has come
For you to assume direct exercise of command
Of the American Contingent." He says that
"The astonishing success of the campaign"
Has evoked "emphatic expressions of confidence

In you and Bradley". He doesn't say the same
About Monty. I'm taken aback.

Bradley. Me too.

(20th August Rastenburg. Hitler's HQ. Hitler and Bormann.)

Bormann. My Führer, Kluge is dead. Army doctors
Say it was a cerebral haemorrhage.
He was still shocked by the failure of his
Counterattack on Avranches, and then Falaise.

Hitler. It is scandalous that the Canadians have
Taken Falaise. This was largely Kluge's fault.
He was defeatist and pessimistic.
But could he not have committed suicide?
He was linked to the putsch, along with Speidel.
I want a second army autopsy.
Model is to be congratulated on
Saving the German forces from encirclement.
He does not know the meaning of surrender.

(21st August. Tournières. Eisenhower's HQ. Eisenhower and Butcher.)

Eisenhower. Marshall wants me to command, and I have here
A letter from Monty to Brooke, which arrived after
Brooke left for Italy, saying the two
Army Groups should keep together. However Brad
Favours an eastward drive to Germany,
Not north via the Lowlands, and the Red Army
Yesterday launched its offensive to Romania.
The balance of Allied troops has changed.
On D-Day America had fewer troops than Britain.
Now America has twice as many,
No three-quarters of all forces. It is
Impossible not to change the command structure.
I have now decided to change the system of command
On September 1st. I will take command
Of the two Army Groups, and Bradley's Twelve Group
Will drive for Metz and Saar. The British can
Go north to destroy V-bomb rocket sites
While the Americans go into Germany.
The Army Groups will separate. Send a cable
To the Combined Chiefs of Staff, and a directive
To Monty.

(21st August, evening. Condé, Montgomery's new TAC HQ. Montgomery and de Guingand.)

Montgomery (*devastated*). Tomorrow the battle of Normandy will be won.
I do not agree with the decisions reached.
I am sending you back to General Eisenhower
With some *Notes on Future Operations*.
You are to tell General Eisenhower that

These *Notes* represent my views and that Bradley
Has expressed his agreement with them.
Ask the Supreme Commander to lunch with me
The day after tomorrow. He should come and see me.
(*Aside.*) Eisenhower will read in the *Notes* that I want him
To abdicate command over both Army Groups.

(*Exit De Guingand. Enter Henderson.*)

Henderson (*gently*). I said you'd bought a month.
Montgomery. But when I've just won.
Eisenhower wants to scoop the reward.
I thought he was too decent to do this.
I was wrong. This, in the hour of my greatest triumph.
It is dangerous to swap horses in mid-stream.
And when the Germans are on the run, and the war….
(*Aside.*) O Brooke, would that you were in the War Office
And not on a long visit to Alexander.

(*22nd August. Condé, Montgomery's HQ. Montgomery and de Guingand, who has returned from Eisenhower, and Nye, Brooke's deputy.*)

De Guingand. I spent two hours with him in an apple orchard.
He wouldn't budge. The Allied Forces must split,
The British to the north, the Americans perhaps to the east.
He says the British can't count on any Americans
In the north.
Montgomery. Procrastination. "Perhaps to the east."
I disagree with any plan which splits
The Allied force.
Nye. Sir, as Brooke's deputy,
I beg you not to split the Allied command
While Churchill and Brooke are out of England.
The Alliance must come first.

(*23rd August. Laval, Bradley's new HQ. Montgomery and Bradley.*)

Montgomery. On August the seventeenth you agreed with me
That both Armies should go north.
Bradley (*dropping the "sir"*). No, I did not.
I see that the British should go north because
Of the V-1 sites, but I have always wanted
To go east to Germany.
Montgomery (*thinly*). You have been got at.
Yesterday, when you went to visit Ike.
Bradley. No. The American army has put behind it
The poor performance at Kasserine Pass,
Salerno and Anzio, and has a new confidence.
We're pouring fifty divisions into Europe
While fighting in the Pacific, we've come of age.
We have double the troops, we want to go east
To Germany. We can do it on our own.

Montgomery (*sadly*). I trained you, and now you want to race off
Like Patton. It's a mistake to split the Armies.
It will not shorten the war but prolong it.

Bradley. We don't see it that way. And as regards training,
I'm "the military Lincoln" in the press back home. Good day.

(*23rd August, 12 noon. Condé, Montgomery's HQ. As Montgomery returns, Eisenhower arrives with Bedell Smith and General Gale.*)

Montgomery (*to Eisenhower*). I must see you alone and get your decision
On certain points of principle. The staff
Should not be present.

(*Eisenhower and Montgomery go alone into the map caravan. Montgomery stands before the map, feet apart, hands behind his back, eyes darting.*)

You know I want a northward
Thrust of both Armies, who would be so strong
They need fear nothing. The immediate need
Is for a firm plan. I think it's a mistake
To split the Armies, and for you to take command
In the field. The Supreme Commander should be on high,
On a perch with a detached view of land, sea, air,
Civil control, political problems. He should
Not descend into the intricacies of
The land battle, someone else should do that.
And it is a whole time job for one man.
Today the Falaise trap is closed, we are now
Bombing the Germans caught inside. We have won
A great victory because of land control,
Not in spite of it. If American public opinion
Is the problem, let Bradley control the battle,
Put me under Bradley.

Eisenhower. No, that's not my intention.
I don't favour a single thrust to the Ruhr.
The Germans are in confusion, I want two thrusts
With the flexibility to reinforce either,
Depending on which is succeeding the most.

Montgomery. I don't think either will be strong enough, alone.
The British, alone, need additional forces
For the northern thrust to the V-1 sites.

Eisenhower (*deliberately*). They can have American assistance, but
It should be kept to a minimum.

Montgomery. Who should command
The northern thrust?

Eisenhower. There must be one commander. You.

Montgomery. Twenty-first Army Group only has fourteen divisions.

Eisenhower. How many American divisions would you need
For your thrust to the north?

Montgomery. An American Army
Of at least twelve divisions on our right flank.

Eisenhower (*speechless*). If that happened the Americans would only have
One Army, and public opinion would object.

Montgomery. Why should public opinion make you want to take
Military decisions which are definitely unsound?

Eisenhower. You must understand, it's election year in the States.
I can take no action which may sway public
Opinion against the President, and lose
Him the election. And so we must now separate
The two Army Groups, I must take command
Of the ground forces and send the two Army
Groups in different directions so there is
No question of the Americans being under
The operational control of a British General.

Montgomery. Military logic does not base itself
On public opinion.

Eisenhower. The American Army Group
Will become two armies, so we have three
In all: an Army Group of the North, of the Centre
And of the South. And I will be Generalissimo
In the field.
(*Aside.*) He takes a narrow military view
And lacks the diplomatic sense to grasp
That I must do what Marshall and Roosevelt want,
And how they perceive public opinion is
A pressure on me I cannot ignore.
He puts my blood pressure up. I want rid of him.
The only way I'll agree to a single thrust
In the north, is if it accords with the separation
Between Americans and British my masters want.

Montgomery (*aside*). SHAEF are behind this mess, and Bedell Smith,
Not the American election, that's an excuse.
In his heart of hearts he knows it's wrong.
(*Aloud.*) So the British are on their own in the north, but are not
Strong enough to thrust without American help,
Which must be commanded by an American.
(*Shaking his head.*) We have split the Allied effort on the day
It achieved its greatest victory in World War Two,
At its highest point when it could shorten the war.
I speak from the highest summit the Allies reached.
This is a mistake and will lengthen the war.

Eisenhower. Bedell Smith and I will go off and draft
A directive I will show you before it goes out.

(*Eisenhower leaves the caravan.*)

Montgomery (*alone*). This is the reality of war. Meetings,
Signals, modifications of the plan,
Developments, bickerings, and the Generals
Are all isolated from the main action.
They are like instruments in an orchestra.
Each has its own position, plays its own note,
But together they sound a great symphony
Like the *1812* with cannon and mortar fire
That ends in triumph to cheers and applause.
But each remains quite separate, alone,
And only the score - the plan - holds them together;
And if that is changed, there is cacophany.

(*Later. General Allen, 12th US Army Group's Chief of Staff. Enter Patton.*)

Patton. Where is everybody?
Allen. Gone, sir. You've just missed them.
Generals Eisenhower, Bradley and Montgomery.
Patton. Say, I've just thought up the best strategical idea
I've ever had. Write it down. The Third Army
Will cross the Seine at Melun, and the Yonne at Sens,
And swivel north across the Marne and the Oise
And cut off German troops fleeing from Dempsey
And Hodges at Beauvais. In other words,
Third Army abandons Saar and takes part in
Monty's northern thrust.
Allen (*thinly*). Sounds fine to me, General.
Patton. Tell it to Brad when he comes back. I want
To start this tomorrow. (*Exit.*)
Allen. I think you're too late,
General, by just an hour.

(*Later in August. Falaise, the battlefield. Eisenhower stands apart from Kay.*)

Eisenhower. Now I, the Supreme Commander, am confronted with
The reality to which my plans have led:
The Falaise battlefield, covered with tanks,
Guns, vehicles, horses and thousands of dead
German soldiers in uniform, overhung
Like a morning mist with the foul stench of death
That gets in my throat and chokes and sickens me;
A field of decaying flesh, as if the top
Had been taken from a burial ground, exposing
The rotting corpses of the hidden dead.
This is an inferno, this is infernal.
I loathe war, I despise what my plans have done,
This victory I have won over these humans.
I am disgusted with myself for being
Involved in this slaughter, this massacre,

Which falls below the standards I uphold.
War is like a cesspit that must be cleared out,
There is nothing for it but to wade in muck
And inhale the sickening stench and finish the job.
But while I do it, I hate what I am doing
And want to keep casualties to a minimum.
The odour of war nauseates me, Kay,
And I feel ashamed to have ordered that these young men
Should be bombed and strafed into lifelessness like this.
Civilisation is not pretty when
It resorts to war and deeds of barbarism.

(29th August. Avernes, Montgomery's new TAC HQ. Montgomery and Brooke.)

Brooke. It's a pity this all happened while I was away.
It will add three to six months to the war.
But you can look back on a staggering victory,
Perhaps the most outstanding military victory
In the whole of human history, and all through your plan.
Our political chief, Grigg, thinks the same.

Montgomery (*tiredly*). We killed ten thousand Germans in the Falaise pocket
And took fifty thousand prisoners. You
Could walk for hundreds of yards stepping on dead flesh.
The stench was awful, and many horses died.
The men who got out were stragglers without vehicles
Or equipment. It was a terrific blow.
Paris has fallen – I declined Eisenhower's
Invitation to go there – and Dieppe will soon fall.
Overlord has reached a successful end.
But what now? I go north with six or eight
American divisions under Hodges,
In all less than half what I have had. Patton
Says it's a mistake for Hodges to turn north,
That he could end the war in a few days
By driving eastwards. I am now out of
Telephone communication with Bradley.
And the Germans are not finished by any means.
I have isolated myself to perfect the art
Of field command from the front, keeping TAC HQ
Separate from Main, and I see with military
Eyes, not political or national antennae.

Brooke. We are seeing the rise as a great power
Of the United States, to whom events now pass.
I fear we shall see the decline of the British Empire.

Montgomery (*depressed*). War happens when nations' interests conflict.
Either through misunderstanding or aggressive greed,
Which must be checked; and rightness is settled
By a challenge of strength as in a tournament

Two knights jousted with lances while kings watched
And territory was ceded by the fallen
Giant in armour. So jousted Rommel and I.
Such a contest is primitive, and unless
Providence is with the winner, not always just.
Councils and conferences are better, but
Words must be enforced. If national interests are
Behind war, it is better that there should be
Large regional blocks or a world government.
And I dream of a world in harmony,
In which my battlefield skills are not required,
In which men and women go about their lives
Without seeing their homes and families knocked to bits
By tanks and heavy bombers and artillery.
I deploy fire-power, but the great need is
For a new system of international law
And universal harmony under
A benevolent, benign authority,
And a single, decent, humane, good World Lord
Who represents all regions of the world.
Then greed and territorial dispute
And racial or historical aspiration
Can be sorted out without recourse to all this
Planned carnage, chaos and destruction
Which when I stop and think fills me with disgust.

Brooke. It doesn't do to stop and think like that.

Montgomery. Right now, I can see into the depth of things
And I am filled with horror and despair.
I know that all the wars and leaders' plans
And all the territorial gains they made
Are not worth one sentence of a philosopher
Who has seen truth and reflects the hidden One,
Or one memorable line of an epic poet
That reveals how the universe really is,
And all my skill in battles is as worthless
As tantrum fisticuffs in a school playground.

Brooke. You need a good night's sleep. You'll look on things
Differently in the morning when you're less tired.

*(*30th August. Churchill's underground HQ. Churchill in bed in blue and yellow dressing-gown. Brooke.*)

Churchill. I've got a temperature of a hundred and three.
Pneumonia. Did you see Monty?

Brooke. I did.
He's bearing up, but pretty devastated.

Churchill. I want to make him a Field Marshal on
September the first, to mark the approval
Of the British people for his leadership.

(*31st August. Same scene. Churchill in bed and George VI.*)

Churchill. I have the submission ready, sir. Could you
Sign it now, using my pillow as a table.

(*The King signs.*)

It is the highest rank in the British Army.
It puts him on a par with Wellington,
Haig, Kitchener – and Brooke. He is paying
The penalty for being unable to
Communicate with his superiors.

(*1st September, evening. Dangu, Montgomery's new HQ. Montgomery sitting alone on a canvas chair, being painted by James Gunn. They are observed by Henderson.*)

Henderson. He looks like a medieval English king
Surveying his lands at Crécy or Agincourt.

(*The session is over. Montgomery rises and goes into his caravan.*)

Montgomery. Demoted. Elevated to Field Marshal
But demoted as Commander, from Land Forces
To Twenty-first Army Group. And by a man
Who had not seen a shot fired in his life
Before Overlord, does not understand strategy,
Has failed to impose a clear strategic plan
On the battlefield, squandering all our gains,
And is therefore useless as a field commander.
He's completely and utterly useless.
Demoted after the greatest invasion ever
And a three-month battle resulted in victory,
And me, across the Seine, heading for Brussels.
Where is the justice in that? What is the meaning?
(*Praying.*) O Lord, I asked for your help for Overlord.
You gave it, and we were victorious,
But the task is only half-done, and now the command
Is in the hands of a man who will lengthen the war.
Is this what you want? Is this part of your purpose?
If it is, I am content, though I cannot see
The benefit to the Allies, the troops, or
The German people of prolonging the war.
Is it time for America's Grand Design?
Is it time for the British to hand over
Their imperial rule and their world role?
O Lord of Light, I accept my demotion
If it is a part of your greater plan.
We warlords tussle for power but over all,
Our Overlord, is your Providential Light
Which knows the whole tapestry of history,

The past, the future, why events happen,
When one power rises and another declines,
Why one General rises and another is demoted.
What is baffling in nineteen forty-four
May be clear fifty years later, part of a pattern.
Shine into my soul, for I do not understand.

SCENE 5. ARNHEM

(3rd September. Dempsey's HQ at Lailly, near Amiens. Dempsey, Bradley, Hodges, Montgomery.)

Bradley. It's a pity General Eisenhower can't be here.
The American commanders met yesterday –
Ike, Patton, Hodges and me, it was going on
When you rang me, Monty, to fix this council –
And he flew back to Granville yesterday in high winds
And injured his knee trying to pull his plane
To safety. What emerged from our meeting was,
That the main American effort will be to Frankfurt
Through Metz and Nancy. Monty, we strongly felt
That Hodges' 5 US Corps should be switched
From you to cover Patton's left flank as
He thrusts into Saar south of the Ardennes. We felt
You don't need help with your effort north of the Ruhr
As you won't find much opposition up there,
And that the First US Army on your flank
Should be depleted. The Americans don't
Need British help with an airborne drop near Liège,
But thank you for offering.

Montgomery (*thinly*). We are getting away
From the original plan of one big thrust
Of forty divisions who need fear nothing.
I have not seen General Eisenhower for nearly
Two weeks, and have had no orders from him, so
I am drawing up plans to advance to the Ruhr
And I need your help, Brad. Brussels is falling,
The Canadians are stuck on the Seine and the Somme,
Now Dempsey has to approach Antwerp and attack
The whole of the Ruhr without significant
American help, and Hodges is going east.
It isn't going to work.

Bradley. I'll tell you what.
I will make two simultaneous thrusts to the Rhine,
One south, one north of the Ardennes. That will help
You, Monty, in place of Hodges. There can be
A pincer attack on the Ruhr.

Montgomery. The British must still cross
The Meuse and Rhine. We will need an airborne drop

To secure the bridges ahead of my thrust.
Given the withdrawal of American support,
And that I have no orders, an airborne drop
Seems essential in the region of Arnhem.

(*4th September. Granville, Eisenhower's Forward HQ. Meeting with Bedell Smith, Freddy Morgan, Humphrey Gale, Strong, Jock Whiteley. Bedell Smith is talking as he is handed a telegram.*)

Bedell Smith. The German army is retreating along the coast.
Antwerp has fallen, but not the approaches
To Antwerp harbour from the North Sea. Should you
Give the order for these to be taken?
(*Reading telegram.*) Telegram from Montgomery. He says
One thrust to Berlin can now end the war,
And it should go through the Ruhr rather than Saar
As the American plan states. I'll pass it round.
He wants to meet you, sir. He wants a decision
By tomorrow.

Eisenhower (*sighing in exasperation*). He hasn't spoken to me
For nearly three weeks, and now he wants a decision
By yesterday. No, I've got too much on:
My broadcast to the peoples of North West Europe,
Linking the Italian campaign with Overlord,
A conference with General Devers on control
Of the Franco-American forces. And there's Greece.
He's four hundred miles away, and my knee….
What should we do?

Strong. Speaking for Intelligence,
I vote for one strong thrust through Belgium to
The Rhine.

(*Eisenhower looks at Strong.*)

Eisenhower. Can we go outside?

(*They go out, Eisenhower limping, in pain.*)

Read this telegram.
It's from Stimson, our Secretary of State for War,
Urging me to take control. What can I do
In the face of this? I have to take account
Of the political ramifications. If I put
Monty in charge of the British and Americans,
Stimson will be angry, besides Brad and Patton.
There must be two thrusts, for political
If not military reasons.

(*They return to the meeting.*)

(*To Bedell Smith.*) Draft a written reply
To Montgomery. Say I like his idea
Of a powerful and full-bloodied thrust towards

Berlin, but that I do not agree it should be
Initiated at this time to the exclusion
Of all other manoeuvres. There can be
No question of a thrust to Berlin until
Le Havre and Antwerp harbours are operating.
The Allies will advance to both the Ruhr
And the Saar. I believe Montgomery's thrust
To the Ruhr will be via Aachen, and this can be tied
To Patton's thrust via Metz.

Strong. Sir, shouldn't you
Meet Montgomery?

Eisenhower. And be insulted by
The new Field Marshal? No, the telegram will do.

(*4th September. Rastenburg. Hitler's HQ. Hitler is in bed with jaundice. Hitler and Goebbels.*)

Hitler. Why have my Generals withdrawn from France
In defiance of my orders that they fight on?
My telegram to the German HQ in Paris
Said "Paris must only fall into the hands
Of the enemy as a field of rubble."
Although the Eiffel Tower, the Elysée Palace
And forty-five bridges were wired with charges
That would cause a firestorm and burn the city down,
Choltitz did not act, and the Allies are in Paris
And all its cultural treasures are intact.
I do not trust the officer corps. They withdraw.
I want more party men who will observe
My orders to the letter.

Goebbels. My Führer you are
A thousand miles away from the action,
And cannot appreciate that the German force
Is short of fuel and ammunition.
The British and Canadians under Montgomery
Have covered two hundred miles in four days
And are in Belgium, have taken Brussels
And Antwerp. Hodges has moved as far
And is in South-East Belgium, and has Liège.
Patton has reached the Moselle and has linked
With the French American Army from the Riviera.
We need to prepare the defence of the Fatherland.
The Siegfried Line is largely unmanned,
The West Wall, and many guns have been stripped.
The British and Americans are four hundred miles
From Berlin. The Russians a mere three hundred.
In three months since D-Day we have lost
A million and a quarter men, dead, wounded,
Missing – fifty divisions in the east,
Twenty-eight in the west. We have no guns,

Tanks, lorries, our allies have deserted us.
Germany now stands alone. The Allies have
Two million men in Europe, the Soviets have
Five hundred and fifty-five divisions.
We need a defensive plan. I will raise
A new army of a million men, and all
German industry will produce the arms
And equipment we need to repulse our enemies.

Hitler. No withdrawal. We must keep on fighting
Until, as Frederick the Great said, one
Of our enemies tires and gives up.

Goebbels (*aside*). Hitler's very name is terror, he is seen
As a wolf who has gobbled up the countries round him,
But somehow he's acting that part, calling
His headquarters "the Wolf's Lair", for the man within
Is really quite gentle, awkward, hesitant
Even, and watching him fumble his way
To his decisions I marvel that so uncertain
A man should have thousands of helmets, planes,
Tanks, ships hanging on his slightest word.
Of course he is not now, since Stauffenberg's bomb,
As he was before, when his hand did not tremble
And he rode, standing in his car, his right arm out,
Through hundreds of thousands of soldiers in miles of ranks
On both sides of Berlin's East-West Boulevard,
On his fiftieth birthday, in the most awesome
Display of power mankind has ever seen,
But even then in his quieter moments he
Was not the tyrant the world dreads. But he
Is able to open to a current of energy,
Which fills him and radiates conviction, faith.
It is not a good energy, it cannot be
Seeing where it has led him and his people.
He thinks it's a demonic energy,
An evil power that has come from Lucifer.
But he's not possessed by this for much of the time.
When he is possessed by it, even I fear him.
But the more vulnerable he becomes, the more
I know I must follow him to the end.

(*5th September. Granville, Eisenhower's HQ. Eisenhower alone.*)

Eisenhower. Stalin has personal rivalries to endure.
Zhukov and Koniev hate each other, I have heard
And Rokossovsky is not easy. How is it
That when he sets them to compete, they do.
Whereas when I do the same, Monty, Patton
And Bradley demand priority over each other?
Monty is the worst. He thinks he is a better
Commander in the field and planner than me.

His overweening egotism and self-esteem,
His vanity and brashness and arrogance
Make him insubordinate. He writes,
"One really powerful and full-blooded thrust
Towards Berlin is likely to get there and thus
End the German war." He demands all the
Funds and transport, and says Bradley
Can do the best he can with what is left.
I know I try to keep everyone happy
And tend to compromise, but I bristle
When he weighs the Ruhr and Saar and writes, "If we
Attempt a compromise solution and split
Our maintenance resources so that neither
Thrust is full-blooded we will prolong the war.
I shall reply that a thrust to Berlin
Should not be initiated at this moment
To the exclusion of all other manoeuvres.
There will have to be a compromise: a broad front,
Resources split between Monty and Bradley.
We must take the ports of Antwerp and Le Havre
Before we go to Berlin. All SHAEF agrees.

(*9th September. Everberg, Montgomery's HQ. Montgomery and Dawnay.*)

Montgomery (*angrily*). I have received Ike's reply in two parts,
The second part two days *before* the first part.
Now, four days after my message, signal:
"Providing we can have the ports of Dieppe,
Boulogne, Dunkirk and Calais, and in addition
Three thousand tons per day through Le Havre
We can advance to Berlin." Tell Ike I
Must see him in Brussels tomorrow, please
After my 9 a.m. conference with Dempsey.

(*10th September. Brussels airport. Eisenhower's aeroplane. Eisenhower, Tedder, Montgomery in the cabin with others.*)

Eisenhower. I hurt my knee last week when we landed
On a beach in a high wind, and we had to push
The plane away from the sea. I can't move. It's
Been as much as I can do to fly to Brussels.

Montgomery. I want everyone to leave the cabin including
Tedder.

(*Eisenhower gestures, all leave. Tedder is still in the plane but out of earshot.*)

Ike, I have your signal here.
It arrived in two parts, the second part first.
The first part two days later, so I didn't get
The drift till yesterday. How can we run
A war if we can't communicate where we're

Going? I had no orders from you for a fortnight.
There's no communication apart from telegrams
Written four hundred miles away from the front line.
There's no plan, we in the field don't know what we're
Doing, we're making it up as we go along.
It seems that Patton, not you, is running the war.
The double thrust will end in certain failure.
You've dispersed the Allied war effort, there's no
Field command or grip –

(*Eisenhower puts his hand on Montgomery's knee.*)

Eisenhower. Steady Monty. You can't
Talk to me like that. I'm your boss.
Montgomery (*humbly*). I'm sorry, Ike.
A new weapon hit London yesterday,
The V-2 rocket, which is silent and
Arrives without warning. It came from Holland.
We need to go through Holland to capture the sites.
The British Government wants me to find and destroy
The V-2 sites near Rotterdam and Utrecht
And that means I need to get to Arnhem.
If I can do that I must have priority
Of supplies over Patton and command in the north
Over American supplies and troops. I think you're wrong,
But I'm not insisting on a thrust to Berlin.
Arnhem is the gateway to the Ruhr as well
As to the V-2s, and after that Berlin.
But I need fuel and tanks. Give me these now
And I can get there.
Eisenhower. Monty, you must understand
There are certain things that I cannot change.
The Allied armies must be kept separate;
You cannot command American troops in the north;
Your Ruhr thrust cannot have priority
Over Patton's Saar thrust as regards supplies.
I am now running the war, and that's my view.
And as I said in my signal, we cannot start
A thrust to Berlin now. But we can look
At your bold plan for a bridgehead over the Rhine
At Arnhem, which I wholeheartedly support.
If you can achieve that, you can cut off the Ruhr
And advance into northern Germany.
There can be a combined Anglo-American
Airborne drop. I'll wire you. Now if you'll call
Tedder, my knee is hurting.
Montgomery. (*aside*). This man is no
Commander. He's a genial fellow,
He talks to everyone and is popular
And then works out a compromise all like

That pleases everyone. He has no plan.
He finds out what his subordinates think,
Collects their ideas and then reconciles them.
He visibly flinches from bold moves, he is
Timid and fearful in the teeth of pain, like a boy
Who winces at the whine of a dentist's drill.
He holds conferences in order to liaise,
I to give orders.

(11th September, Tournières Eisenhower's HQ. Eisenhower and Bedell Smith. Kay Summersby, going.)

Bedell Smith. There are now three armies, and the Germans,
Fighting on three fronts, are far from beaten.
The way to the Saar is blocked by good divisions.
I can see a drop to seize Walcheren would
Control the approach to Antwerp the Navy want,
And help open the port. Montgomery's
Arnhem thrust would secure a Rhine bridgehead
And be most useful to our present cause.

Eisenhower (*aside*). I am torn this way and that. It is not easy
To be a Supreme and a land Commander.

(*Smith receives a paper.*)

Bedell Smith. A signal from Montgomery. He has postponed
The Allied airborne drop across the Rhine
For twelve days, because he lacks supplies.

(*Eisenhower buries his head in his hands.*)

Eisenhower. Do I accept it? Or do I keep the drop?

Bedell Smith. It will be useful.

Eisenhower. Go and see Monty,
And give him all he needs. We will stop the thrust
To Saar in view of the German opposition.
Give priority to the Ruhr and the Arnhem drop:
Operation Market Garden on the seventeenth.
(*Aside.*) I am giving Montgomery what he has urged.
I hope I am not making a strategic blunder.
If Arnhem fails, I should have said No.

**(15th September. Granville, Eisenhower's HQ. Eisenhower and Bedell Smith.)*

Eisenhower. A signal to Monty: "Berlin is the main prize,
In defense of which the enemy is likely
To concentrate the bulk of his forces.
There is no doubt whatsoever in my mind
That we should concentrate all our energies
On a rapid thrust to Berlin. But this should
Not be concentrated but spread across
The whole front, with combined US-British forces."

*(15th September. Rundstedt's HQ. Rundstedt and his Chief of Staff, General Gunther Blumentritt.)

Blumentritt. Why have the Allies not gone for Berlin?
There were no German forces behind the Rhine
At the end of August, the front was wide open.
Berlin was the Allies' target, Germany's strength
Is in the north. Berlin and Prague were there
For the taking. Why did the Allies not take them?

*(15th September. Speer listening to radio.)

Goebbels' voice. Germans, you know my total mobilisation
Is to find a million men for our war effort.
I warn you what to expect if we lose this war.
Roosevelt and Churchill, meeting in Quebec,
Have discussed the US Treasury's plan, which
Secretary Morgenthau has drawn up. Germany
Will be dismembered, our heavy industry
Destroyed, much of our territory will be transferred
To Poland, the Soviet Union, Denmark, France.
Germans, we will be a pastoral economy
Existing at subsistence level under this plan.
You must strengthen your will, work with the Führer
And repulse the enemy before these things happen.

Speer. He did not say that Churchill opposed the plan,
And that the plan is dead. Propaganda,
And taking my skilled men from my industry.

(27th September, 11 a.m. Eindhoven, Montgomery's HQ. Montgomery, depressed and deep in thought. Williams.)

Williams. You were very close to victory at Arnhem.
The largest airborne landing in history,
And the road for our troops was wide open.
There's an Ultra message from the German
Commander-in-Chief on the twenty-fourth, asking
Hitler for permission to withdraw all forces
In Holland to the Meuse (or Maas) and Waal.
Hitler refused and ordered von Rundstedt
To counterattack.

Montgomery (*philosophically*). The target was not Arnhem,
But the Ruhr. Urquhart was to threaten to seize Arnhem
While O'Connor's 8 Corps turned eastwards towards
The Ruhr. We have advanced our Ruhr campaign.
Here we are now in Eindhoven, we have
A bridgehead across the Waal at Nijmegen,
Enough life was lost across the Neder Rijn.
We did the best we could, given the lack
Of American support, which made it
A British effort; given that Eisenhower

Reinstated the Saar's equal priority.
There are many ifs – those two German armoured
Divisions, the rain – but we must put a brave face
On Arnhem, and consider what we gained.

(*Enter General Urquhart, exhausted and downcast, with Henderson.*)

(*Gently.*) My good fellow.

Urquhart. I'm sorry. I failed.

Montgomery. You're
Worn out, you've had no sleep, you're exhausted,
You'll spend tonight in my caravan. I only move out
For Winston Churchill and the King, but tonight it's yours.
Tomorrow I'll ask you what went wrong at Arnhem,
But tonight, you sleep in there. Where's my batman?

(*Exit Montgomery, looking for his batman.*)

Urquhart. (*to Henderson*). I'm overwhelmed. Such a gentle reception.

Henderson. He calls "A" Mess here his family, and he's like
A caring father concerned for his children.

(*5th October. Bradley's HQ. Eisenhower, Montgomery, Brooke, Ramsay, Bradley, Patton, Dempsey, Crerar, Hodges. A conference for all commanders.*)

Ramsay. We are an Allied force, as for Overlord,
I don't defend operations on national grounds.
Arnhem was a British undertaking. Perhaps
There could have been more American support,
But the plan was Field Marshal Montgomery's
And any criticism he should accept.
I am concerned that he didn't choose to secure
The approaches and port of Antwerp, rather than
Undertake this risky drop behind enemy lines.

Montgomery. (*thinly*). There were no orders from the Supreme Commander
To take the approaches and port of Antwerp.
What does the CIGS think?

Brooke. I have to say
I feel that for once Field Marshal Montgomery's
Strategy was at fault. Instead of advancing
On Arnhem, he should have made certain of Antwerp.
I have been a supporter of the Field Marshal,
Who won a brilliant victory in Normandy,
But on Arnhem I have to agree with
Admiral Ramsay. The port of Antwerp first.

Eisenhower. To conclude, we have had a reverse at Arnhem.
For this the blame is entirely mine as I
Approved Field Marshal Montgomery's plea

To operate an airborne drop at Arnhem.
Any blame belongs to me alone and is
My responsibility, and no one else's.
Now we need to get on with the war, and our thrusts
Into the Ruhr and the Saar against an enemy
That is not as defeated as we thought a month ago.

(*The conference breaks up into talking groups. Brooke and Ramsay stand together. Montgomery stands alone, isolated.*)

Ramsay. That was spoken like a military statesman.
Brooke. Whatever his shortcomings as a battlefield
Commander, he has great personal stature.
Ramsay. He has a nobility that I admire.
And Montgomery has now been marginalised.
Brooke (*sadly*). He has been the victim of an American coup,
But he has also contributed to his undoing
And has to some extent marginalised himself.
After Arnhem, and with only a quarter of
The Allied troops, Britain has a junior role.

(*6th October. Eindhoven, Montgomery's TAC HQ. Montgomery alone.*)

Montgomery. I am in gloom. I know I could have ended
The war in three weeks from my Normandy victory,
Which left me invincible in the German mind
If not in SHAEF's. And now, in this vacuum,
Without my single thrust I have been defeated
By the Germans at Arnhem, and the Americans.
I will open the port of Antwerp, but
I am full of scorn at the useless Eisenhower
And Bradley, who want to show the world the power
Of American might, and blunder in their decisions,
Dispersing the Allied effort on too wide a front.
And I am powerless to alter the course
Of the shambles they have created, and so the war
Will last through winter till next spring. My men
Visit mistresses in Brussels. I turn a blind
Eye. Not much happens. It's cold and damp.

(*Enter Dawnay.*)

Oh Kit.
I am sending you to England, to Phyllis Reynolds.
You will take my summer wear – vests, pants and shirts –
And bring me my winter clothes: thick vests and pants,
Woollen pyjamas and my dressing-gown.
You wouldn't have had to do this if I'd been in charge.

(*About 6th October. Stalin's office in the Kremlin. Zhukov standing by a map on a table with green baize in front of Stalin's desk. Rokossovsky, Molotov and Antonov. Stalin pacing, smoking his pipe.*)

Zhukov. My site meeting with Rokossovsky confirms,
The Forty-Seventh Army has many casualties.
The Seventeenth Army is in a bad way.
Supply lines are affected by our Russian winter.
The First Belorussian Front is worn out.
It needs time to recover and reinforce.

(*Stalin has looked at the map, and has then resumed pacing. He puts down his pipe.*)

Molotov. Germany is virtually defeated.
It is mad to ease up now.

Zhukov. The Red Army
Has suffered huge losses, if we do not have time
The situation on the Vistula will deteriorate.

Stalin. Do you agree with Zhukov?

Rokossovsky. I do.

Stalin. Both of you,
Go out to the ante-room with your maps
And think a little more.

(*8th October. Eindhoven, Montgomery's HQ. Montgomery and Gen. Marshall, Bradley and Hodges.*)

Bradley. General Marshall, Chief of Staff of the US
Army.

Montgomery. General, could you spare me a few moments
In my office caravan? Would you mind Generals?

(*Marshall looks at Bradley and Hodges, shrugs and follows Montgomery into his caravan.*)

I feel you should know that since the Supreme Commander
Took personal command of the land battle
As well as forces on the sea and in the air,
The armies have become separated
Nationally, not geographically.
There is a lack of grip, of operational
Direction and control. Our operations
Have become ragged, disjointed, and we
Have now got ourselves into a real mess.

Marshall. Field Marshal, I have listened.

Montgomery. And?

Marshall. There is
More than one view in such complex matters.

Montgomery. I can see that you entirely disagree.

Marshall. There has to be a balance of national effort.
General Eisenhower is the Supreme Commander.

(*Silence.*)

(*12th October. Eindhoven, Montgomery's HQ. Montgomery and Dawnay.*)

Dawnay. A reply from Eisenhower. He's threatening you
With dismissal.

(*Montgomery reads the signal.*)

Montgomery. On October the ninth
He urged me to take Antwerp or Allied
Operations would reach a standstill. I
Replied reminding him that at Versailles
He had made the attack in Holland the main effort.
He replied it was now Antwerp, and Beetle Smith
Rang and demanded when there would be action
And threatened through Morgan I would lose my supplies.
I wrote back blaming the failure at Arnhem
On lack of co-ordination between Bradley's troops
And mine, and I asked to be given sole control
Of the land battle. Now he threatens to go
To the CCS, and he will win. I have pushed
Him as far as I can and must now promise
A hundred per cent support, and give Antwerp
Top priority, when I can wind down Holland.

(*13th October. Rastenburg, Hitler's HQ. Hitler and Bormann.*)

Bormann. My Führer, I have a report on Rommel.
You recall, Speidel testified on October the fourth
He knew of the plot against you from Hofacker
And passed the information on to Rommel.
You arranged for Keitel to summon him here.
Rommel pleaded his head injury. He
Has recovered from the crash, the Gestapo report
He goes for walks "leaning on his son", and I have
Reports from local party officials who say
He is still making mutinous remarks.
He should be told to see you if he's innocent,
Or behave like a Prussian officer
And gentleman, or face the People's Court.

Hitler. Send Burgdorf and his chief law officer
To Rommel's villa with such a request.

(*14th October, lunchtime. Rommel's villa near Ulm. Rommel in his study and voices. Lucie.*)

Lucie (*nervously*). Two men to see you. They're from the Führer.

(*Exit.*)

(*Gen. Burgdorf and Gen. Ernst Maisel appear.*)

Burgdorf. Field Marshal. A letter from the Führer.

(*Rommel reads it.*)

Rommel. Does Hitler know about the two statements,
By Speidel and Hofacker?

Burgdorf. Yes, he does.
If you don't go to Rastenburg to contest
The evidence of Speidel and Hofacker,
The choice is the People's Court and execution –

Maisel. Sequestration of your house –

Rommel. Or?

Burgdorf. Poison,
Not pistol, and a State funeral with full
Honours, your reputation still intact.
No one will know. You will have died of your injuries.
And there will be a guarantee of safety
For your family, which will be revoked
If you choose the other way, the People's Court.

Rommel. It is "die now" and save my family
Or "die later" and put them both at risk.

(*Burgdorf nods.*)

I need time to think.

Burgdorf. We'll wait downstairs. Ten minutes.
We will leave in your staff car. You will say
Goodbye to all who wait downstairs, then go.

Rommel. Send up my wife.

(*Exeunt Burgdorf and Maisel.*)

The moment I have expected,
For three months has arrived. There is no choice.
Disgrace and poverty for my family,
Or this, oblivion, and my family keep
This house and all I have mustered for them.
I knew of the plot, was shocked and would not join,
But I wanted our surrender and an honourable peace.
Speidel's testimony has done for me.
He was trying to save himself. I am innocent,
But cannot disprove the evidence, and I
Will not stoop to plead or beg for mercy.
There is no choice. Just the furtherance of
A legend. Montgomery, you wanted my end
But you never dreamt it would be at Hitler's command.
I think you will be sorry. And I hope
That one day, there can be reconciliation.
Perhaps our sons will be friends.

(*Enter Lucie. He holds her.*)

My dearest Lucie,
You must be strong and look after Manfred.

I have to say goodbye.

(*He gives her the letter.*)

Lucie. But it's not true,
What Speidel has said. You can deny it, and prove –
Rommel. No, it will be execution, and you will lose
Everything and Manfred.
Lucie. There's no other way?
Rommel. The choice is clear. They are waiting for my cap,
My Field Marshal's cap and baton.

(*Enter Manfred.*)

Manfred. Papa.

(*Rommel hugs Manfred.*)

Rommel. You must be very strong. I have to say goodbye.
Manfred. Those men?
Rommel (*nodding*). I have to go with them. It is for the best.
My first thoughts are of you, and of the life you will have.
Remember me as an honourable officer
Who fought well but couldn't stand the casualties,
Who when he knew we had lost the war, sought peace,
And pulled the front line further and further back.
I love you both very much.
Manfred. You're going
With those two men?
Rommel. Yes. They are waiting for me.
I will be going in my staff car. But you
Will remember.
Manfred. Yes, Papa.
Rommel. I love you both.
Now, goodbye. Be strong.

(*Rommel embraces both. Lucie escorts Manfred out. Rommel is briefly alone. He puts on his greatcoat and cap and picks up his baton.*)

Montgomery, a Prussian officer's salute.

(*Burgdorf and Maisel return.*)

Rommel. Where?
Burgdorf (*holding a packet*). On the back seat of your staff car. You
Died from your injuries. There will be no pain.
Burgdorf. Believe me, this is the best way. I am sick
At what has happened to our culture. (*Exeunt.*)

(*Later in October. Goebbels' office. Goebbels and Speer.*)

Goebbels. Germany is now under siege. Last month
The Führer announced a scorched earth policy.
Any land conquered must be reduced to a desert.

No German wheat must feed the invaders,
All industrial plant and food supplies must be
Blown up. I am now cutting food rations.
The youth are digging trenches, and today
Himmler has set up the People's Storm, so each
Male of active years can be drafted to defend
The Fatherland. The Führer has ordered
The building of a bombproof bunker beneath
The Chancellery, and when it is ready
He will move back to Berlin. The company that
Are building it are Hochtief.

SCENE 6. THE ARDENNES

(*Later in October. Rastenburg. Hitler and his Generals. Rundstedt, Model, Göring.*)

Hitler. While I was in bed with jaundice in September
And recovering from the bungling Stauffenberg's bomb,
I studied maps and have found the weak point
In the American front line. The Ardennes!
Where Manstein and I struck in May 1940.
The Americans have three weak divisions there,
If all goes well, my offensive can annihilate
Twenty or thirty divisions, and drive them back.
I shall amass twenty-eight divisions.
My Panzers will cross the Meuse and take Antwerp,
Drive a wedge between the British and Canadians,
And the Americans. It will be another Dunkirk.

(*The Generals protest.*)

Hitler. No, I will have no objections. I have drawn up my plans
With Jodl, and I have given Rundstedt instructions
That they must not be altered. The British
Are worn out, the Americans will collapse. We can defeat
Them in the west and then turn our forces to the east
And attack the Red Army on the Vistula.

(*The Generals protest.*)

Generals. But sir –
Hitler. I will hear no more. I have two Panzer
Armies, six hundred thousand men. I shall wait
For bad weather when Allied planes cannot fly.

*(*End of October. Churchill's underground HQ. Churchill and Brooke.*)

Churchill. I am exhausted. I have been twice to Moscow,
Travelling like a wandering minstrel
In the cause of Allied unity, and of the Poles.
They are unspeakable. I told Stalin

I reaffirmed the Curzon Line as Russia's
Eastern frontier, as we agreed at Teheran.
I raised the Balkans, I told him Britain
Has an interest in Greece, but Romania
Is a Russian affair. He said he didn't want
To use the phrase "dividing into spheres" because
"The Americans might be shocked". I wrote
Some percentages on a piece of paper,
Suggesting proportional interest in five countries:
Romania, Greece, Yugoslavia, Hungary
And Bulgaria. He studied the list and ticked
It with a blue pencil and gave it back.
There was a silence, he said I should keep it.
I wrote Stalin a letter saying no ideology
Should be imposed on any state. I showed it
To Harriman, the US Ambassador. He said
He was certain Roosevelt would repudiate it
So I did not send it. That evening the Free Poles
From London joined us. They refused to accept
The Curzon Line as it gave Eastern Galicia
And Lvov to the Soviet Union. Stalin said
They must accept the Curzon Line without conditions.
I had a further talk with the Poles the next day,
And proposed to Stalin that they would accept
The Curzon Line in return for fifty-fifty participation
In the new government. Stalin agreed –
But the Poles stuck out for Lvov. I lost my temper
With them, told them, "I will have nothing more to do with you,
I don't care where you go, you deserve to be
In your Pripet Marshes." Then I offered
To appeal to Stalin to throw in Lvov.
But they still wouldn't accept the Curzon Line.
Eden proposed we saw the Curzon Line
As a demarcation line, not a frontier.
Stalin refused to accept anything less than a frontier
And stayed with the Lublin Communist Poles.
I made one more appeal to the Poles.
They said No. I've had the Poles, they're the end.

(*12th November, evening. Nancy, Patton's HQ. Marlene Dietrich sings Lily Marlene for Patton, who wears his pearl-handled pistols, on his 59th birthday, and his "niece" Jean Gordon. A notice says 59.*)

Patton (*drunk*). Thank you Marlene, and thank you everyone
For wishing me a happy thirty-ninth birthday.
(*A chorus of "Thirty-ninth?"*)
Now we Americans are showing how
To win this war, and if you look at my headquarters
Here, you'll understand why we still haven't reached the Saar,

And with gals like Marlene around, and my niece Jean,
(*A chorus of "Niece?"*)
You'll understand why we ain't too worried about that
And why we think this is a better way
Of running the war than Montgomery's way,
Cooped up in his poky little caravans.
Bring me the maps of the Saar.

(*Burlesque map is produced: a pair of knickers.*)

Dietrich (*suggestively*). Did you say S.A.?

(*Patton draws his pearl-handled pistols, fires them in the air, and collapses back, paralytically drunk.*)

(*Mid-November Moscow. Stalin's Kremlin office. Stalin and Rokossovsky.*)

Stalin. The Soviet general staff have now drawn up
A plan for the greatest campaign in history,
An offensive that will take the Red Army
Forty-five days, and start between the fifteenth
And twentieth of January. It will cover
The entire eastern front from Barents
To the Black Sea, eight countries, and its aim
Is the lair of the Fascist beast, Berlin.
There will be three fronts to Operation Berlin,
It is vital that you, Rokossovsky,
Zhukov and Koniev should put aside
Rivalries and work together, co-ordinate.
Your three fronts will end the war in the west.
If you and Koniev don't advance, Zhukov
Will not either. You will approach from the north,
Koniev from the south, Zhukov from the east.
I attach such importance to the drive
That I will direct it, not my Supreme
Command staff, the Stavka, or army general
Staff – I will co-ordinate the three fronts,
First and Second Belorussian and First
Ukrainian and a fourth front, the Third
Belorussian, which will help the northern flank.
The commander in the field will be Marshal Zhukov,
Who stopped the Germans at Moscow and then
Defeated them at Stalingrad and Kursk.
He will spearhead the offensive, and take Berlin.
I want no arguments, no defiance.
You were sentenced to death seven years ago,
Though still under sentence I made you a Marshal.
And I look to you to co-operate
In our great undertaking as we kill the beast.

(*7th December. Maastricht. Conference of commanders. Bradley and others. Montgomery.*)

Montgomery. First Army is struggling forward, but there are no reserves,
Everybody is attacking everywhere,
With no reserves anywhere. I propose Patton's
Third Army should be moved north for the Ruhr
Offensive, and that Brad should be Commander-
In-Chief of Land Forces, as General Eisenhower
Is simply not doing the job. Or at the least,
That Brad should command all Allied forces north
Of the Ardennes, so that the Allies can fight
With one effort, under one unified command.

Bradley. That is not a good idea. There should be separate
National armies, with me as Commander
Of the American forces, and they should fight
In separate places.

Montgomery. Then how do we deal
With the Sixth SS Panzer Army, which is now
Strengthening German lines according to reports?

Bradley. Those Panzers are to plug holes that will be made
When Hodges and Patton attack the Ruhr and Saar.
Patton's new drive will start December nineteen.

Montgomery. So although the present plan has failed, we must
Consider it has not failed and stick with it?

(*Mid-December. Rastenburg. Hitler and Burgdorf.*)

Hitler. What is the weather in the Ardennes?

Burgdorf. Sir, misty. The clouds are in the treetops.

Hitler. Treetop cloud? Good. I have prayed for such weather
Since September. The sun always shines for my parades
But now I want mist, Providence gives me mist.
The time has come to strike without warning!

*(*16th December, 8 a.m. Luxembourg, Bradley's HQ. Bradley having breakfast with his aide Major Hansen, who takes a call.*)

Hanson. Sir, Hodges on the line.

Bradley. An attack at dawn
On 8 Corps? A spoiling attack, I agree.
Can you handle it, I'm about to leave for Paris
To meet the Supreme Commander.

(*16th December, 11.30 a.m. Hitler has woken up. Burgdorf has a report from Model.*)

Hitler. What is the news from the Ardennes? The Allies?

Burgdorf. Taken totally by surprise. An artillery
Bombardment rained down on the American line,
So fast it seemed it hailed mortars and shells.
Then came the tanks out of mist over forty miles.

The American First and Ninth Armies were
Driven back.

Hitler. Providence be praised!

(16th December, morning, Eindhoven. Golf course. Williams arrives.)

Williams. Field Marshal Montgomery? Is he here?
Club Official. He is playing golf with Dai Rees over there.

(*Montgomery and Dai Rees.*)

Montgomery. Ah, Bill. Have you met Broadhurst's driver?
Williams. Who's winning?
Dai Rees. The Field Marshal.
Montgomery. Oh, I'm having a lesson.
Trouble? Excuse me.
Williams (*to Montgomery*). Sir, the Germans have attacked
Hodges' First Army in the Ardennes, in force.
Montgomery. This is no ordinary move. LOs must scout.
(*To Dai Rees.*) I'm afraid I must fly back to Zonhoven.

(*16th December Zonhoven, Montgomery's HQ. Montgomery and Henderson.*)

Montgomery. Signal to General Eisenhower's *deputy*
Chief of Staff that we have no reserves to block
Enemy penetration, that we have no plan,
That our attacks are unco-ordinated,
That the Supreme Commander's last directive
Was on the twenty-eighth of October, eight weeks ago.
Unless he makes up his mind and issues orders
We will drift into difficulties with the enemy.

(*16th December, 6 p.m. Versailles, Hotel Trianon Paris, Eisenhower's HQ. Eisenhower playing bridge with Bradley, Bedell Smith and his friend Everett Hughes. Kay. Champagne. Bradley's aide Chester Hansen, leaving.*)

Eisenhower. Yes, von Rundstedt lived here until recently.
A staff wedding, and my fifth star, come on,
Stay and celebrate with us.
Kay. Yes, we don't want
Anyone to go. Stay and have something to eat.
Hansen. Brad and I had a huge lunch at the Ritz,
I couldn't. Besides, Ernest Hemingway's waiting
For me at the Lido –
Kay. That's where bare-breasted girls
Do the hootchy-kootchie most of the night. Stay here.
Bedell Smith. Sir, a call for General Bradley from Hodges
In the Ardennes. He says it's more than a spoiling attack.
Bradley (*more interested in his cards*). I stand by what I told
Strong: it's a spoiler.
Bedell Smith. Strong did say there's German radio silence.
Bradley. Tell him the two most senior American
Commanders, having discussed infantry

Replacement, can't be disturbed till they've finished
Five rubbers of bridge.

Eisenhower (*looking at cards*). It'll be a spoiling attack.

Bedell Smith. You ought to take the call, sir.

Bradley. Oh, very well.
Yes. Yes. Listen, you can have the Seventh Armoured
Division of the Ninth Army, and the Tenth Armoured
Division of the Third Army.

(*He rings off.*)

Eisenhower. Everything all right?

Bradley. A captured enemy document speaks of
A pincer attack on Aachen, in the Ninth Army
Area. Hodges has it under control.

Hansen. Sir, do you need me? Hemingway –

Bradley. Go and meet him.

(*Hughes opens his Highland Piper Scotch.*)

Tell him we're drinking a bottle of Scotch
And playing cards in Louis the Sixteenth's palace,
As Louis the Sixteenth did with his courtiers.

Eisenhower (*looking at cards*). Tell him it's like Drake's bowls, we must finish
Our game before we beat off the German Armada.

(*Laughter. The champagne and Scotch are flowing.*)

(*17th December, early morning. Same setting. Bradley and Hansen.*)

Bradley. I didn't sleep well. I was thinking
About the German attack. The main thrust
Is at Liège, our supply line, and the diversion
Is at Luxembourg. I'm sure that von Rundstedt
Is trying to delay Patton's drive to the Saar.
But he's struck where we have not got many troops.

Hansen. I don't like to say it, General, but it's
What Montgomery warned Ike about,
And you replied he should mind his own business.
If it is a big attack, Montgomery will say
"I told you so."

Bradley. And I will have been away
From my post, like Rommel.

Hansen. I hope it's minor.

(*The phone rings.*)

Sir, it's the Commander of 4th Infantry Division.

Bradley. Yes? We might have to evacuate our HQ
At Luxembourg? Never. I will never
Move backwards with a headquarters.

(*17th December. Zonhoven, Montgomery's HQ. Montgomery, Dawnay and Poston.*)

Poston. The enemy gained surprise. The Americans
Have all their troops in the front line and have no
Reserves. The Ninth Army are sending two
Divisions, the First: one. The First Army
Has no idea what to do.

Montgomery. Twenty-eight
German divisions and I argued for forty
In my single thrust. (*Shaking his head.*) I foresaw all this.
We are now in danger. (*To Dawnay.*) Send three British
Divisions –
The 43rd, 53rd and Guards Armoured –
Towards the Meuse to protect our southern flank.
And signal General Whiteley at SHAEF that
The Americans are transferring troops from their
Northern flank, which will set back the crossing
Of the Rhine by months; and that they should draw instead
On their southern flank and cancel Patton's thrust.

(*18th December, evening. Spa, Hodges' HQ. Hodges and Gen. Kean, his Chief of Staff. Breakfast is laid, there is a Christmas tree.*)

Hodges. Three German armies are approaching us.
Panzers are in Stavelot and heading here,
Our headquarters are manning a roadblock,
It's only a matter of time before we are overrun,
The Chief of Intelligence wants us to fly out
In the Cub plane that's waiting. There are four
Million gallons of petrol here, which will fuel
The Germans to Antwerp. We have spoken
Six times with Bradley today, and we're still not sure
If he appreciates the seriousness of
Our position. He's still talking about Patton's
Thrust from Metz to Saar which has weakened us.
Montgomery has urged him to cancel
That thrust, and therefore, out of pride, he won't.
He wants us to survive without weakening Patton.
He's met Patton and there may be token help,
But it is likely to be too late for us.
Bradley isn't interested in coming here.
What should be do?

Kean. We have no alternative
But to move HQ.

Hodges. I agree. We will burn our secret files,
Abandon these buildings for Chaudfontaine.

(*19th December. Verdun. Eisenhower's conference. Eisenhower, Bradley, Patton. Not Montgomery or Hodges.*)

Eisenhower. I'm very worried about the German offensive.
I've reinforced Bastogne to hold the line.
I'm tempted to take field command myself
But am turning to George. Can you go to Luxembourg
And counter-attack with at least six divisions
In three days' time? You will have to turn
Your entire army from eastwards to northwards.

Patton. Sure, I can do it. But three of the six divisions
Have been overrun.

Eisenhower. Oh, yes.

Patton. I've only three divisions.

Eisenhower. So you will abandon the thrust to Saar.

Patton. That's no problem.

Eisenhower (*aside*). He spoke so bitterly
Against Monty's single thrust in August,
Yet he is happy now to support it
Because he has a star role.
(*Aloud.*) I will issue
A directive ordering Devers to
Cease his offensive in the south and relieve
Patton's Third Army so it can move north.
Once this German offensive has been blocked
Bradley's Twelfth Army will mount a single offensive
To the north.

Bradley (*tensely*). That is what Montgomery proposed
At Maastricht, and I opposed.

(*19th December, after lunch. Churchill's Cabinet War Room. Churchill, having had several sherries, marks a map; with Brooke.*)

Churchill. There's no information coming out of SHAEF.
The War Office, Roosevelt and the Combined
Chiefs of Staff all find the same. The only
Person who knows what's going on is Monty.
I'm using his personal signals to you
To mark the Cabinet map. And I can see
A British counterstroke, in the tradition
Of my great warrior ancestor, Marlborough.
I want to order Monty to hurl Horrocks'
30 Corps at the Germans.

Brooke. Prime Minister,
Only Eisenhower can order Monty,
And no one in London can tell a Field Marshal
In the Ardennes how he should act.

Churchill. Oh, well. What can I do to help?

Brooke. Telephone
Eisenhower and say that the northern front

Should be under the command of one General:
Monty.

(*19th December, 5 p.m. Zonhoven, Montgomery's HQ. Montgomery on the telephone to Dempsey.*)

Montgomery. There is no doubt about it, my Liaison Officer
To Bradley, Tom Bigland, went to Hodges' HQ
This morning, and found no one. Breakfast was laid,
The Christmas tree decorated. A German woman
Said they went down the road at 3 a.m. –
Without telling anybody. I have heard nothing
From General Eisenhower, the Commander-in-Chief
In the field, from Versailles; and Bradley's
Out of telephone communication in Luxembourg.
So I have arranged for you to have four divisions
From dawn, to stop the Germans from crossing the Meuse.
My LOs report there are no Americans
Garrisoning the Meuse bridges, so I have sent
Tank patrols fifty miles into the American sectors
Under cover of darkness. I shall tell Mather
To find Hodges and "order" him to block
The Meuse bridges with farm carts. We're ready for
Rundstedt –
Despite the confusion, lack of information
And faulty command we have to operate in,
I have told Whiteley at SHAEF, and Brooke, that I
Should be in operational charge of the northern front.
The question is: will someone now compel
General Eisenhower to accept, three months too late
What he should have accepted three months ago?

(*20th December, 3 a.m. Versailles, Hotel Trianon Palace, Eisenhower's HQ. Bedell Smith in bed in his quarters next to his office. Major-Gen. Strong and Gen. Whiteley, two British SHAEF officers, knock and wake him up.*)

Bedell Smith. For Christ's sake it's three in the morning. Well?

Strong. German forces are beyond Bastogne and near
The Meuse. We know there has been no contact
Between General Bradley and First Army
HQ, Hodges', for two days, and a report
Suggests confusion and disorganisation.
We feel that Monty should command all troops
In the Allies' northern sector.

Bedell Smith. I'll phone Bradley.

(*He rings.*)

Oh, it's Beetle here, sir. Sorry to wake you.
I have Major-General Strong and General Whiteley
Here, they say the Germans are on the Meuse,

That you've lost contact with Hodges, and suggest
That Monty takes over the whole of your front
North of Bastogne. Would you object? Huh huh.
You doubt the situation is serious enough
To warrant such a fundamental change of command,
Especially considering the effect it might have
On opinion in America. Thank you sir, good night.

(*He rings off.*)

You sons of bitches and limey bastards, you've
Put me in the position of questioning
General Bradley's competence, you're sacked.
Because of the view you've taken of the situation
You can no longer be accepted as
Staff officers to General Eisenhower.
You will receive instructions tomorrow
And return to England.

(*20th December, early morning. Versailles, Eisenhower's HQ. Eisenhower and Bedell Smith.*)

Bedell Smith. Sir, this report that German paratroops
Dressed in Allied uniform are out to kill
You, General Bradley and other Allied commanders,
And that the murderous Skorzeny is on his way
To Paris with sixty men to kill you – sir,
Your senior staff members feel you should stay
In your office and not go home at all.
Eisenhower. Are you sure it's necessary?
Bedell Smith. Quite sure.
And you shouldn't go out at all, no conferences,
No visits to any Generals or to the front.
Eisenhower. Very well. I'll remain here in the Trianon Palace.
Tell Kay we're living here now.

(*20th December, 9.55 a.m. Versailles, SHAEF Chiefs of Staff conference. Strong and Whiteley, Bedell Smith, Eisenhower.*)

Strong. I agree with Colonel Lash. The two armoured
Thrusts may now have joined up, and Panzer divisions
Are being pulled back from Italy and Russia
To aid the offensive, and they have captured fuel.
So that concludes my briefing of the enemy
Situation. We're now going to see
General Eisenhower.

(*Strong and Whiteley leave. Bedell Smith takes their arm.*)

Bedell Smith. Listen, I've been thinking.
I'll put your proposals to him as my own.
I'll recommend putting Montgomery
In charge of the north, but you must keep silent.

It's better coming from an American.
You wait here. He'll call you in.

(Bedell Smith knocks on Eisenhower's door. Eisenhower calls in Bedell Smith. Strong and Whitely wait outside.)

(*To Eisenhower.*) I am concerned at the situation in the Ardennes.
The Germans are on the Meuse with many divisions,
Two thrusts may have linked up, and General Bradley
Has lost contact with Hodges, who seems to have left
His HQ. All the details are in this report.
Montgomery is on the spot. Bearing
In mind you can't go out because of the paratroops,
I reluctantly recommend that he is given
Command of the northern forces, two of Bradley's
Three armies.

Eisenhower (*astonished*). I can't go along with that.
The American press would never accept it.

Bedell Smith. The press doesn't know how serious the situation
In the Ardennes is. And there's wartime censorship.
And I remind you again, you and General Bradley
Are targets for Skorzeny's assassins.
If Montgomery takes over, they'll switch to him.

Eisenhower. I'm shocked. I need to question General Strong
And General Whiteley about the latest picture,
And their intelligence and operational reports.

(*Later.*)

Eisenhower. I suppose I'll have to go along with it.
I don't like it, but I've no alternative.
I'll telephone Bradley and Montgomery.

(Later. Bedell Smith emerges from Eisenhower's room. Strong and Whiteley are waiting.)

Bedell Smith. It's done. I'm sorry about last night. You're not sacked.
What made me really mad was I knew you were right.
He's told Bradley, he's phoning Monty now.

Strong. How did Bradley take the news?

Bedell Smith. Not at all well.
He objected, but was overruled by Ike
Who said "Well Brad, those are my orders" and
Put down the phone. He's hurt. Thank you, fellows.

(Exeunt Strong and Whiteley.)

(*Aside.*) I thought Bradley could handle the armies.
I flared up at the suggestion that he couldn't.
But I've solved the situation well for Ike.
The American Generals shouldn't go out until
The assassins have been caught or killed. Till then,

Let British Generals risk assassination,
The most prominent being: Montgomery.

(20th December, 10.30 a.m. Zonhoven, Montgomery's HQ. Montgomery. Dawnay, Montgomery's military assistant, answers the phone.)

Dawnay. It's General Eisenhower.
Montgomery. Hello? Yes. Yes.
You're speaking very fast and it's difficult
To understand what you're talking about. (*To Dawnay.*) I don't know
What he's saying, he's very excited.
(*To Eisenhower.*) It seems we now have two fronts? And I am
To assume command of the northern front.
That's all I want to know. (*Shouting.*) I can't hear you
Properly. I shall take command straight away.

(*He puts down the phone.*)

He's still talking wildly about other things.
I want the largest Union Jack that will go
On the car bonnet and eight motor-cycle outriders.
Dawnay (*quietly*). Congratulations, sir. (*Exit.*)
Montgomery (*aside*). Field Commanders
Are least important to governments when they sense
Victory, most when they start to smell defeat.
I have control, albeit temporarily,
Of Allied forces north of the Ardennes,
Of Hodges' First Army and Simpson's Ninth
North of Bastogne, and Coningham commands
All supporting American air forces.
While the Supreme Commander cowers in his Hotel
And Bradley vacates his bedroom, fearing attack
From Skorzeny's assassination squad,
I will show a commander has no fear,
I will boost the morale and self-confidence
Of the American commanders in the field.
Let them call me a showman. It will work.

(21st December, 11 a.m. Zonhoven, Montgomery's HQ. Montgomery. Dempsey and Crerar. Conference for British and Canadian commanders.)

Montgomery. My strategy is not to attack the Germans –
The thick forests and hills of the Ardennes
Are easy to defend, hard to attack –
But to outflank the Germans and take the Ruhr.
We should hold the Germans with American troops,
And give American ground if necessary,
And thrust to the Ruhr with British and Canadians.

(21st December. Versailles, Eisenhower's HQ. Eisenhower and Bedell Smith.)

Eisenhower This Montgomery crows like a rooster,
I have had to give him command, there's no one else
Up there. But the man is impossible.
I have just received this message: "In a press
Statement Monty is claiming his new command
As a personal vindication." He seems to forget
Who is fighting this war. Tell General Marshall
That either Monty or I will have to go.

(21st December. Verviers. Montgomery arrives, Union Jack on the bonnet of his Rolls Royce, and gets out with Henderson. Hodges and Simpson greet him.)

Henderson (*aside*). He's like Christ come to cleanse the temple.
Hodges. We're sure glad to see you, Commander. We've
Not seen Bradley or any of his staff since
This battle began. We just want someone to
Give us some firm orders.
Montgomery. We'll soon have
A properly organised set-up for command,
The battle will soon be under control.
We're going to win, we're going to push the Germans
Back where they came from.

(22nd December. Zonhoven, Montgomery's HQ. Montgomery and Hodges.)

Montgomery. No, you must withdraw, don't think what Bradley will say.
Bradley and Patton think of counter-attack,
But there are now twice as many German troops
In the Ardennes as we landed on D-Day –
Three hundred and thirty-five thousand – and more
Than nine hundred tanks in the ice and snow,
And Bradley, in his Luxembourg Hotel,
And Eisenhower, locked and shuttered inside
His Versailles Palace, and swashbuckling Patton
Talk of counter-offensives, and do not know
The picture I have from my LOs. They wage
Their war by telephone, I mine by scouts
Who each day visit the entire front line
And bring back sightings of enemy movements.
Bradley underestimates German strength,
And so, therefore, in Versailles does Eisenhower,
And optimistically thinks that Patton
Is about to finish the Germans off completely.
Bradley draws lines on maps with a brown crayon
Which indicate advances to be made
But does not know where the men are who will make them.

Let him call me over-cautious, but I honour
The fighting man, and I say "Hodges' troops" are
Tired, have been under strain and should now withdraw
And become reserves, which will be most useful.
No more American lives should be lost
Than is necessary.

Hodges. I agree to be overruled.
I will order the withdrawal.

(25th December. Zonhoven, Montgomery's HQ. Montgomery in full battledress, Christmas cards.)

Montgomery. Inside the Bulge Hundred and first Airborne,
Encircled at Bastogne, were asked to surrender, their
Commander said "Nuts" and beat the Germans back.
Skies cleared and Allied planes strafed the Germans
And Patton began his thrust towards Bastogne
To lift the siege. And now, having been out of touch
Since December the seventh, almost three weeks,
Bradley has come out of his Hotel, has braved
The assassins, and is flying up here to be briefed.
I have not sent a car.

(Enter Bradley, in an old combat jacket, looking tired.)

Brad, you found the way.

Bradley. In a staff car provided by General Hodges.

Montgomery. I haven't seen you since Maastricht, when I
Proposed one unified command, and you
Preferred to command the American army.
Come up to my study, and I'll brief you.
I know what's going on in the American sector.

(Later.)

Montgomery. So the Germans have given the Americans a bloody nose.
And the Americans deserve this counter-attack,
It's entirely their own fault for trying two thrusts
At the same time, neither being strong enough.
If there'd been a single thrust, none of this
Would have happened. Now we are in a muddle.
I always advised against the right going so far.
You advised in favour of it and General
Eisenhower took your advice. So we must withdraw.
If Patton's counter-attack is not strong enough
Then I'll have to deal unaided with Fifth and Sixth
Panzer armies, in which case General Eisenhower
Will have to give me more American troops.
Do you agree with my summary?

Bradley (*uncomfortably*). I do.

Montgomery. Then what does General Eisenhower propose to do?
He hasn't spoken to me since giving me command

Of the main battle in the Ardennes. The Supreme
Commander has given no orders. So I ask
You, what does he propose to do?

Bradley. I don't know.

Montgomery. Don't know? Don't know? A commander has to know.

Bradley (*uncomfortably*). I have not seen Eisenhower recently.

Montgomery. But you and he agreed a better way
Than a unified command at Maastricht.
Surely he has been in touch?

Bradley. Skorzeny
And his paratroops in Allied uniform
Are trying to kill him and me –

Montgomery. And I have been
Riding round the front line in a Rolls Royce
With a large Union Jack, and I haven't seen them.

Bradley. The security problem has hindered communication,
And my telephone lines were cut.

Montgomery. Because you went
Too far, and in too weak a second thrust.

Bradley (*aside*). He is humiliating me, shaming
Me like a Headmaster shaming a naughty boy.
I shall not forgive him for this. I shall demand
That Ike returns the First and Ninth Armies
To my command.

(*27th December, 8 a.m., Versailles, SHAEF conference. Eisenhower, Tedder and Strong.*)

Eisenhower. I believe the German divisions in the Bulge
Are understrength and pummelled, and that their
Supply lines are poor. I want to hit them
Hard and quickly. The Allies are running late
In their counter-attack.

Tedder. The good weather
Will not last much longer, and we must attack
While our planes can still fly.

(*A message is received.*)

Strong. Montgomery
Has a new plan for attack, involving two corps,
Seventh US and 30th British.
A northern counter-attack, Twenty-first say.

Eisenhower. Praise God from whom all blessings flow.

(*27th December. Zonhoven. Montgomery's HQ. Montgomery and Dawnay.*)

Montgomery. I have no idea where Ike is. I ask Bradley,
He doesn't know. Freddie de Guingand asks
Bedell Smith, who says Ike's locked up, whatever
That means. Perhaps Bedell is fed up with

His indecision and has locked him up
To leave it all to me and Bradley. And then
We hear he's sending Tedder and Bull to Stalin,
To discuss Russian offensive plans. He can't
Get anyone to the Ardennes, but he can to Moscow.
And the visit will be seen as desperate begging.
He's more concerned with the Russians than the Ardennes.
Now we hear he's trying to fly to see me,
And now he's coming by train. I can't wait
Any longer, so I have come up with my
Strategic plan, which I'll put to Hodges,
Dempsey, Crerar and Simpson tomorrow
At our conference. Ultra shows the Germans
Will attack, we must lure them onto our positions.
Collins will feint, and we'll strike at the Ruhr.

(*28th December, early afternoon. A carriage on Hasselt station. Eisenhower's train has arrived. Machine-gunners leap out to guard the carriage. Montgomery, de Guingand and Williams. Subzero temperature.*)

Montgomery (*to Eisenhower*). Having arrived in a mere armoured car,
I feel naked before assassins.

(*He greets Eisenhower on the train.*)

Eisenhower (*uncomfortably*). In due course
There will be an enquiry on the need for all this.

Montgomery. Ike, this meeting I want without any staff
Present. You haven't brought Bedell Smith or
Tedder. De Guingand and Williams can wait
Outside in the corridor.

Eisenhower. Come to my study.
Now, I've heard that your northern counter-attack
Will use two corps in an offensive role.
Bradley came to Versailles yesterday afternoon
And is strengthening the southern flank and then
Attacking. I want to hit the Germans hard.
How soon can you attack?

Montgomery. I can't discuss
Timing. You must understand, we are fighting
A defensive operation in the Ardennes.
You can't attack in thick forests and hills.
Germany will make one last big attack
On the northern shoulder of the Bulge. We must
Receive the attack, and then counter at the tip
Of the Bulge, drive the Germans back to the West Wall.

Eisenhower. The tip? We need to attack their flank and
Cut them off. We can't wait or Rundstedt will
Withdraw from the Bulge or put up infantry divisions,
Pull his tanks back in reserve. You must attack quickly.

Montgomery. But first we must receive the German attack.

Eisenhower. There will be no attack. What if there is no attack
Today or tomorrow? Would you counter-attack
On January the first?

Montgomery. I suppose I'd have to.
But once we've held the Germans here, we can
Invade Germany, take the Ruhr. I have
A master plan for the future conduct
Of the war. It is vital to decide on this
So present action accords with the future plan.
It means allotting all offensive power
To the northern front under one man's command.
Bradley has made a mess of the situation.

Eisenhower. Bradley, Patton and Devers all wanted
The Frankfurt thrust, and I gave way to them.
There are difficulties about the unified command.
I've explained about American public opinion.

Montgomery. I think you will find it difficult to explain
That the true reason for the bloody nose
You have just received from the Germans was
Your division of the unified command.

Eisenhower. You still don't understand that Americans
Cannot be commanded by British as they
Are supplying three quarters of all troops.

Montgomery. I say it again, I will serve under Bradley
If that will see a unified command.

Eisenhower (*aside*). He doesn't understand political
Realities.

(*30th December. Versailles, SHAEF HQ. Eisenhower, Bedell Smith and de Guingand.*)

De Guingand. Montgomery will not attack until January the fourth.

Eisenhower. The fourth? He told me the first.

De Guingand. You must have misunderstood.
He would not have said that.

Bedell Smith. What makes me so mad
Is that Monty won't talk in the presence of
Anyone else.

Eisenhower. Damn it, he agreed. He's lied
To me, he's trying to lead me by the nose.
We have a great opportunity in the Ardennes
Which he is squandering by slowness,
Wanting the optimum conditions for his attack.
The time has come to break with Montgomery.

Bedell Smith. We're all in rebellion at how he's carried on.
You should dictate a letter to him.

Eisenhower. Tell him
That if he doesn't live up to his promises,
He will be sacked.

De Guingand. Please do not send it yet.

I will talk to Monty and straighten things out.

Eisenhower (*aside*). He is an affable man, in contrast to his boss.
I like him, and he may secure an attack.
(*Aloud.*) Very well, I'll hold it back till you've seen him.

(31st December. Versailles, SHAEF HQ. Eisenhower, Bedell Smith and Staff, de Guingand.)

De Guingand. I've spoken with Montgomery, and he confirms
That the proper strategy is to let the Germans
Exhaust themselves with one final attack
Before an offensive.

Eisenhower (*angrily*). But he definitely
Promised to attack on January the first. Tomorrow.

De Guingand. You must have misunderstood.

Eisenhower. And Bradley's attacked
In the belief that Montgomery is attacking then.
If he doesn't, the Germans will move Panzer divisions
From the north to the south. We want an attack now.
Montgomery's timing in military
Operations is seriously flawed.
He's unable to see things from SHAEF's viewpoint. He's welched.

De Guingand. He's written you a personal letter.

(*De Guingand hands over the letter. Eisenhower reads it.*)

Eisenhower. He says my policies are wrong and demands
Control of the land battle. He says there must be
A single thrust to the north to seize the Ruhr,
With Patton held, or else the Allies will fail.
He sends a directive along those lines
For me to sign.

(*General indignation and outrage. "O-o-h."*)

(*Aside.*) I've lost control of him.
But he's gone too far. My credibility
Is at stake. He is insubordinate. I must
Keep my staff together.

Tedder. It's outrageous,
It makes me seethe. Sack him.

Eisenhower. Bedell, cable
General Marshall and the Combined Chiefs of Staff,
Saying it's Monty or me. And if it's me,
Then I want Alexander.

Tedder. I'll help you find
Some appropriate words.

(*Bedell Smith receives a signal.*)

Bedell Smith. A signal from General
Marshall, Chairman of the Combined Chiefs of Staff.

It says you have their complete confidence,
That you're doing a grand job, and are not to pay
Attention to British press reports that call
For a British Deputy Commander – Monty? –
To lighten your task as this would be resented
Back home.

(*He hands Eisenhower a paper.*)

De Guingand (*aside*). If Ike sends his cable, Monty will go.
(*Aloud to Eisenhower.*) Please don't send your cable for a few hours,
Until I've spoken with Monty in Zonhoven.

Eisenhower. All right. But I'm now issuing my directive
Which contradicts Montgomery's on every point.
First Army is back in Bradley's control,
There must be a double thrust into Germany.
We must seize the initiative at once,
We must act quickly, with speed and energy
Before the Germans move in more Panzers.
Now draft a covering letter to Montgomery.
I do not agree there should be a single ground
Commander. I don't want to hear any more
About putting Bradley under his command.
I have planned an advance to the Rhine
On a broad front, and will no longer tolerate
Any debate. Say I don't want to take
Our differences to the CCS, but if necessary I will
Even though it damages the goodwill between
The Allies.

(*31st December, 3 p.m. Zonhoven, Montgomery's HQ. De Guingand is drinking tea with Montgomery in "A" Mess.*)

De Guingand. The fog is really thick.

(*Montgomery rises.*)

Montgomery. I'm going upstairs to my office.
Please come up when you've finished your tea.

(*They go up to Montgomery's study.*)

Well?

De Guingand. The feeling against you at SHAEF is very strong.
Eisenhower has drafted a signal to Marshall
Saying it's him or you. He's set to resign.
Marshall has cabled the CCS's support.
Smith's very worried. They think you'll have to go.

Montgomery. It can't be that serious?

(*De Guingand hands over Eisenhower's letter and directive.*)

De Guingand. The Americans
Now have three-quarters of the war effort.
If the CCS sack you, there is little
That Churchill can now do.

Montgomery. Who would replace me?

De Guingand. Alexander. His name is in the draft signal.

Montgomery. Alexander? He's a weak commander
Who knows nothing about field operations
And is unable to give firm and clear decisions.
He's ineffective in Italy, he'd be a disaster.
What a team: Eisenhower, Bradley and Alexander.
The Germans would push them back to Normandy.

De Guingand. He's in the signal.

Montgomery. What shall I do, Freddie?
What shall I do?

(*De Guingand pulls out a letter from his battledress pocket.*)

Sign this. It's a letter
Of apology to Eisenhower. It says
There are many factors "beyond anything I realise",
That he can rely on you "one hundred per cent",
And that you're "very distressed" your letter
Upset him, and that he should tear it up –
The one about you having sole command.

(*Montgomery signs the letter.*)

Montgomery (*aside*). I humiliated Bradley in this room
And Eisenhower on his train, but now it's me.
I've had to swallow my pride and humble pie
To keep my job.
(*Aloud.*) I shall begin my attack
Twenty-four hours early, at dawn on the third.

De Guingand. I'll take this straight back to SHAEF. Good-bye, sir.
(*Aside.*) He looks nonplussed and so terribly lonely,
I feel sorry for him. He knows he's lost.

(*Exit de Guingand.*)

Montgomery. And yet it hurts my principles to recant.
The single thrust, the sole command, were right.
Marshall and Roosevelt behind him have clipped my wings
Just when the eagle was soaring again.
I will not accept this American interference
Which has taken away my command just when I have
Defeated the Germans in the finest
Defensive Allied battle of the war,
The second time they've removed my command
At the height of victory, four months after

I defeated the Germans in the finest
Offensive Allied battle of the war.
(*Defiantly.*) I will hold a press conference about how I won
The Battle of the Bulge.

(*5th January 1945. Zonhoven, Montgomery's HQ. His study. Churchill arrives with Brooke. Montgomery.*)

Churchill. We've been travelling on Eisenhower's train,
The *Alive*. Your battle seems to be going well.

Montgomery. In three feet of snow in places, which makes
It hard for tanks to advance, and the Germans won't
Withdraw. Collins is fighting hard, but we
May not have the strength to push the Germans out
Of the penetration area. We are fighting
A defensive, not an offensive, battle
No matter how they present it in SHAEF.

Brooke. And the business with Eisenhower was sorted out.

Montgomery. Ike has abandoned the American advance
To Frankfurt via the Saar, and the main effort
Is to be north of the Ruhr, with the US Ninth
Army under my command, in Twenty-first.
I have "power of decision" to plan for the Ruhr,
And Bradley has to move his headquarters
To be nearer to mine. I have most of what I asked.
And Ike has given me a new Dakota
As mine was destroyed in the New Year's Day air raid.

Churchill. But Bradley's not pleased. He's driven to Etain
Airfield to protest to Ike.

Brooke. On the switch to the north.

Montgomery. Bradley wants the Ninth Army back, but Ike
Knows he's been the cause of an American defeat.

Brooke. And the American public will soon know
As SHAEF have held a press conference today.
For the first time, Americans will know
That you have fought the battle of the Ardennes,
Not Bradley.

Churchill. The Anglo-American
Alliance is still strong?

Montgomery. Yes. I am giving
Hodges two hundred British tanks. We're closely knit.
The German breakthrough would have been most serious
But for the unity of the Anglo-American Army.
But we need more fighting troops if we're to advance.

Churchill. I will cable President Roosevelt tonight.
There is a campaign in the British press
To cast doubt on Eisenhower's fitness
To command the Allied Armies in Europe.
Eisenhower has had difficulties with de Gaulle,

He's had to help the French defend Strasbourg
With troops who should be reserves for the Ardennes.
I'm concerned to preserve Allied solidarity.

Montgomery. Could I help Eisenhower and set things straight
By talking frankly to the press? I would
Tell the story of the battle of the Ardennes,
Explain how we have stopped the Germans in
A joint effort, stress the great friendship between
Myself and Ike, and call for more Allies
Solidarity and team spirit.

Churchill. That would be
Invaluable.

SCENE 7. STALIN'S OFFENSIVE

(*6th January. Stalin and Gen. Antonov.*)

Stalin. Churchill has written asking for a Soviet attack
In the east to prevent German troops being switched
To the western front. He wants an attack
Across the Vistula in January. Reply we will attack
Not later than the second half of January. Now phone
The four Marshals involved to start at once for Berlin
Regardless of the bad weather. Koniev first,
He must use artillery without air cover.
One day later, Chernyakhovsky, and one day later
Zhukov and Rokossovsky. Tell them they are all
In a race for glory – Western competition!

(*7th January. The Adlerhorst, or Eagle's Nest, Hitler's western field HQ near Bad Nauheim, in the Taunus mountains outside Frankfurt. Hitler, with his Generals.*)

Hitler. The offensive has ended, you say, and we
Must protect our forces. Very well. I will
Allow a withdrawal from the Ardennes,
But only a limited one.

(*Guderian waves a paper in Hitler's face.*)

Guderian. I have
An intelligence report, there will be
A massive Soviet offensive in the east
At any time now. We must withdraw
Troops from the west and send them to the east –

Hitler (*raging*). The report is incorrect. Who is responsible
For it? He must be mad, he should be locked up
In a lunatic asylum –

Guderian. General Gehlen
Is my intelligence officer in the east,
And if he is mad, then I should be certified

As well –

Hitler. The eastern front has never been
Stronger. It is a concrete wall of men over
Seven hundred and fifty miles in length.
Our reserves have never been greater in the east.

Guderian. The eastern front reserve are twelve divisions.
One breakthrough and the whole front will collapse.

Hitler. What do you think, Himmler?

Himmler. The Russians are
Bluffing, my Führer.

(*Hitler smiles.*)

(*7th January. Montgomery's press conference. Montgomery in a red Airborne Corps beret with two badges. Williams next to him.*)

Montgomery (*jauntily*). As soon as I saw what was happening,
I took certain steps myself to ensure
That if the Germans got to the Meuse they would
Certainly not get over the river.
And I carried out certain movements to meet
The threatened danger, i.e. I was thinking ahead.
Soon General Eisenhower put me in command
Of the northern flank, and I then brought the British
Into the fight and saved the Americans.
And the Germans never reached the Meuse or Antwerp.
You have thus the picture of British troops fighting
On both sides of American forces who
Have suffered a hard blow. This is a fine
Allied picture. It has been a very interesting
Battle, rather like El Alamein. Indeed,
I think it's possibly one of the most
Interesting and tricky battles I have ever handled.
GIs make great fighting men when they are
Given proper leadership.

Williams (*aside*). It's coming across
As if he rescued the Americans,
As if the British won the Battle of the Bulge
When the Americans stopped the Germans
Before he came on the scene. It's appalling,
He's preening himself like a cock on a dunghill.
The Americans will be furious.

(*7th January. Patton and press.*)

Patton. Hardly any British forces were even engaged
In the Bulge and Montgomery didn't direct
The victory but got in everyone's way and botched
The counter-attack so we missed bagging
The whole German army. I wish Ike were
More of a gambler, but he's a lion compared

To Montgomery, and Bradley is better than Ike
As far as nerve is concerned. Monty is a tired
Little fart. War requires the taking of risks.
And he won't take them.

(*8th January. Zonhoven, Montgomery's HQ. Montgomery and Henderson.*)

Montgomery. Goebbels has broadcast an edited version.
And Churchill has heard from Marshall and wants
Me to eat humble pie, and in public I must.
But the truth is, the Germans have given
The Allies a bloody nose. Eighty thousand
American casualties in the battle
Of the Ardennes. This need not have happened.
It would not have happened if we had fought
The campaign properly after our great victory
In Normandy. Now the war will drag on
Another six weeks. And hundreds of thousands
More will die in extermination camps.

(*8th January. London, underground war rooms. Churchill and Colville.*)

Churchill. We must not offend the Americans.
They have borne great losses in the Battle
Of the Bulge, under Monty's leadership. I
Will say there was only a minor British involvement
In the greatest American battle of the war,
A famous American victory.
We need American resolve and troops,
And Monty for reasons of personal vanity
Delights in irritating Eisenhower.
Monty may be a great General, but he is
Still in the kindergarten in diplomacy.

(*8th January, evening. Bradley and Hansen.*)

Bradley. SHAEF have given me a direct order
Not to make an unauthorised statement
To the press. I can't do it.

Hansen. The staff's morale
Is breaking. Montgomery is the symbol
Of the British, you of the American effort.
Ike has to straddle the two, it's for you to speak
To correct the British press and the BBC
Who are saying there was an increase in
Montgomery's command.

Bradley. I'll do it. But
Although I am pleased my Ardennes plans are passed,
Ike still pursues the northern thrust to the Ruhr
And I am still upset that the Ninth Army
Stays with Montgomery. At bottom he's
A British General whose plans have one aim:

To further his own aggrandizement.

(*8th January. Bad Nauheim. Hitler, Göring, Rundstedt, Bormann.*)

Rundstedt. North Wind has failed. The enemy nearly
Evacuated Strasbourg, but sidestepped.
Montgomery's new offensive in the north
And Patton in the south are attacking the Bulge.
We have destroyed one thousand two hundred tanks
And taken twenty-four thousand American prisoners,
But it is now time to cut our losses. Model
Has requested we pull back on our western flank
The 47th Panzer Corps. I ask you
To authorise this move.

Hitler. And also the south
Panzer Army, which should now be in reserve.

Rundstedt (*aside*). He has indirectly admitted that
He has lost his Ardennes gamble.

(*Hitler withdraws. Bormann follows him.*)

Bormann. The war is not lost because we are pulling back.

Hitler. (*depressed*). The war was lost two years ago.
But still the killing must go on. It is a crusade
Which must take precedence over everything,
Including the war effort, so that there are no Jews
Left to worship the Satanic Jehovah,
The demiurge who created the evil world.
So that a New Order can prevail for
The Aryan Sixth Root race, a race of Supermen.
Jodl did not understand this. He said
That in Warsaw the SS were proud of
Their killing, "their murder expedition",
But he did not understand that genocide
Is how we cleanse the earth, change the world.
Genocide can transform the world for good.

(*10th January. Berlin, a courtroom in the Prussian Court of Appeal. Freisler is trying von Moltke, Delp and Sperr.*)

Moltke. This Court's proceedings are secret, I must object.
The others are innocent.

Freisler (*banging the table*). I will not stand
For that sort of thing, I will not listen. They all
Plotted against the Führer, we have heard the evidence.
What do you say about the evidence against you?

(*Moltke is silent.*)

You will speak when the Court speaks to you. The Court
Is now interested in your guilt, as leader
Of the Kreisau Circle of Prussian plotters.

Moltke. My great-great grandfather was the Field Marshal

Who crushed France in 1870 so
Bismarck could unite Germany under
Prussian rule. My grandfather was chief justice
Of South Africa. I am Prussian and
I was brought up with a sense of justice
And I tell you, the six other accused
Are innocent.

Freisler. Enough. I will have no more
Of this.

(*He puts on a black cap.*)

The Court sentences Count Helmuth
James von Moltke, Jesuit Father Alfred
Delp and ex-Colonel Franz Sperr to death by hanging.
Sentence to be carried out in Plotzensee prison.

(*21st January. Eva Braun and her sister Ilse are dining in the Chancellery library, white-gloved servants serving from silver dishes.*)

Eva. The Führer left the Adlerhorst nearly
A week ago. He came into Berlin
Early in the morning with the blinds pulled down
The car windows, because the bomb damage
Upsets him. He was shocked to see how badly
The Chancellery was damaged. Every window
Broken, the west wing with our private apartments
Collapsed. General Rattenhuber of the
SS advised him to move his office
And our residence into the bunker
Under the garden outside. This was his study,
Where he holds his conferences. He has his SS
Guards round him all the time following the
Wicked attempt on his life in July.
Even though we cannot put you up here,
We can still give you dinner in the Chancellery,
And you will find the Adlon Hotel very comfortable.

Ilse. I cannot believe the luxury in Berlin,
When in the countryside, the snowy roads are lined
With fleeing refugees who have nothing.
There was one train at the station, and several
Froze in open wagons, waiting for it to leave.
People are trudging south or west through snow.
I was three nights without sleep travelling here.

Eva. I shall join you in Breslau in two weeks' time.

Ilse. Breslau is lost. Do you not understand?
The Russians have taken Silesia, Germany
Is finished. As I travelled here I saw
Columns of hungry refugees and the Russians
Are burning and plundering and raping all.
Your Führer is responsible for the invasion.

He's destroying our country, and you, and us.

Eva. You're mad. Crazy. How can you say such things
About the Führer who is so generous?
He's invited you to stay at his house at Obersalzberg,
You should be shot.

Ilse. You need to open your eyes.

(Enter Hitler briefly. He is a wreck, his left hand trembles, his left side shakes, he stoops, hunchbacked, with a pot belly. He shuffles. Bormann is with him.)

Eva. My sister will gladly stay at your house.

Hitler *(nodding, to Bormann).* I want
Eva to follow her. She is a distraction here.

Bormann. Jawohl, mein Führer. *(Fade on Eva and Elsa.)*

Hitler *(to Bormann).* I have decided,
In view of the failures of my Generals
In the Ardennes, that every General should inform me
In advance of every movement in his unit,
In time for me to intervene in their decisions
If I think fit, and for my counter-orders
To reach the front-line troops.

(Hitler goes to Führer bunker. Below, conference room or map room and Hitler's office or study/living room in which is Anton Graff's life-sized portrait of Frederick the Great. Hitler sits by dim candlelight and stares at the painting.)

(Alone.) Frederick the Great, you expanded Prussia,
You fought Russia and Austria and France
And your luck turned when Tsarina Elizabeth died.
You are called "Great" because of what you endured.
Your spirit is with me, help me, help me.

(He lights another candle and performs an occult incantation.)

O power that I first contacted when Dietrich
Eckart opened my higher centres, power
Whose Will has carried me from the Munich
Beercellars to the highest point in the world,
Power which has filled me with an electric current
Of dynamic energy when I needed it,
Power which I have summoned through ritual magic,
And human sacrifice as Eckart taught,
Power you knew, Frederick, in your illumined search,
Do not desert me in my hour of need.
I have done your Will, I have speared Jehovah,
Whom there will soon be no Jews left to worship.
I am the chosen spear of the Antichrist,
The man chosen to wield Longinus' spear
Which I took from the Vienna Hofburg

And hid in sacred safety in Nuremburg,
And, inspired by Lucifer, to conquer the world
And lead the Aryan race to glory as
A race of Supermen – do not abandon me,
Your foremost Superman, *your* Overlord,
Fill me with your power, but more importantly
Strike down my enemies, give me a sign
That you are still supporting my world rule.
Strike dead Stalin or Roosevelt, my Overlord.

(*A knock on the door. Enter Burgdorf and Guderian.*)

Burgdorf. Sir, The Chief of the General Staff, Heinz
Guderian, who you summoned.

Hitler. Ah yes.
My Generals continue to defy my orders.
General Hossbach has withdrawn his Fourth Army
From East Prussia after it was overrun
By Rokossovky. Did you know this?

Guderian. No sir, but I know Hossbach wants to save
As many men as possible, and keep a corridor open
For the East Prussians –

Hitler. Pah! The man is a traitor.

Guderian. He cleared the withdrawal with Colonel-General
Reinhardt –

Hitler. Commander of Army Group North,
But not with you – or me. I demand that
You now dismiss Hossbach and Reinhardt and
Their treacherous staffs, and court-martial them.

Guderian. Sir, I'm an East Prussian, born on the Vistula,
And I do not consider these men traitors.

Hitler. I will dismiss Reinhardt immediately.
Replace Reinhardt with Colonel-General Rendulic,
He is a National Socialist.

Guderian. But sir –

Hitler. And Army Group Centre is now in the command
Of Colonel-General Schörner.

(*Guderian leaves and meets Ribbentrop in the corridor.*)

Guderian. Foreign Minister, the war is lost. I urge
You to negotiate an armistice in the west
And transfer troops to face the Russians.

(*Ribbentrop enters Hitler's office or living room, Guderian waits. Then Hitler appears.*)

Hitler (*shouting*). Anyone who tells anyone that the war is lost
Will be treated as a traitor, with consequences
For himself and his family. I will take action
Regardless of rank and reputation.

Guderian. My Führer, I do not mean that the war *is* lost,

Only that it *will* be lost unless we transfer more troops.
Hitler. No.
Guderian. My Führer, we need a new emergency
Army group to support Army Groups North
And Centre and stop Zhukov's advance.
Hitler (*calming*). Yes,
That is good.

(*24th January. The row of eight meat hooks on a girder. Von Moltke, Delp and Sperr are hanged under film lights. The nooses are of rope and are in figure of eight shape.*)

(*24th January. Berlin, the Führer bunker. The conference room. Hitler and Guderian.*)

Guderian. I recommend Field Marshal von Weichs as
This commander.
Hitler (*thinking*). No, I have decided.
The new reserve army will be known as
Army Group Vistula. It should be commanded
By Himmler.
Guderian (*exploding*). But Himmler has had no previous
Military experience, except as an
Army cadet.

(*Bormann has appeared.*)

Bormann. SS leader Himmler is a great
Organiser and a good administrator,
And he is the only man who can immediately
Form such a force.
Himmler (*appearing, enthusiastically*). My Führer, I will be
Honoured to raise a reserve army for
The eastern front, and I will go to Danzig.
Guderian (*alone*). So Bormann is envious of my rapport
With the Führer, and has just clipped my wings.
But the Führer now believes in a non-existent
Force.

(*27th January. Moscow, Stalin's office in the Kremlin. Stalin and Antonov.*)

Stalin. My Generals have now submitted reports and plans.
Where do they all stand? Start with Koniev.
Antonov. Koniev's First Ukrainian Front broke through
The German defences in snow with non-stop shells
And advanced along a two hundred mile line,
And with the sun glistening on snow, took Lodz
And the same day Krakow, the capital
Of Poland's kings and of the Nazi "General
Government", in the rear. The Germans fled
And Hans Frank's city fell without damage.

Koniev has pushed on and taken Silesia
And has crossed the Oder.

Stalin. And Zhukov?

Antonov. Zhukov's
First Belorussian Front, led into battle
By Chuikov, the hero of Stalingrad, bombarded
The Germans and advanced south of Warsaw,
And cut the city off from the west, then
With another artillery barrage, tanks smashed through
The Germans in the south while the 47th
Army crossed the Vistula to the north
And surrounded the city. The Germans destroyed
Warsaw, shooting, hanging and burning thousands
Of Poles, and evacuated the city.
And Posen is now surrounded. Zhukov
Is crossing the Oder.

Stalin. And the defiant Rokossovsky?

Antonov. Rokossovsky's advance to the north of Zhukov
Has been slower because of the Masurian lakes,
And the ice of the River Narcis was not thick
Enough to bear tanks. The Imperial
Russian Army was defeated in that terrain
In the First World War, at Tannenberg. Even so
Rokossovsky is near the Baltic, he has
Advanced along the Vistula towards Danzig
And has cut off Germans in the Baltic
And East Prussia, and forced them to dig up
The remains of Hindenberg and his wife
Who were buried at Tannenberg.

Stalin. Good. But
Rokossovsky has not advanced as fast
As the others who cover fifteen, eighteen,
Twenty-five miles a day. Tell him to turn
Towards East Prussia and support Zhukov.
He will not go down in history as
The Soviet General who took Berlin.
What is Zhukov's plan?

Antonov. In February, a new
Non-stop offensive, smashing across the Oder
And into Berlin with one gigantic thrust.

Stalin. And Koniev's plan?

Antonov. Destroy the German forces
At Breslau, and reach the Elbe, then join Zhukov
And capture Berlin.

Stalin. Both men seek to become
The "conqueror of Berlin". Let them race each other.
The one will spur the other.

(*A message comes in.*)

Antonov. News just arrived. This morning a Soviet scout
In a snowstorm, entered a camp with wooden buildings
At Monowitz near Katowice in
Upper Silesia, and found a slave labour
Factory belonging to I.G. Farben.
Half an hour later, the Hundredth Division
Found six hundred sick, emaciated people
And a pile of corpses. This afternoon
Our men took Oswiecim, Auschwitz-Birkenau
As the camp is known, and found a gas chamber
And crematorium the Germans left
Eleven days ago when they blew up
The barracks with prisoners inside. They have
Found an extermination camp for Jews.

Stalin. The Final Solution Heydrich announced.
For three years we have known they were doing this.

(*27th January. Berlin, the Führer bunker. The conference room. Hitler and Guderian.*)

Guderian. Himmler's defensive line of reserves should be
From North to South. It is from east to west,
From the northern Vistula to the Oder.
It does not protect Berlin, and Zhukov has ignored it.
He has passed it on the south and has reached the Oder.
The eastern front has crumbled.

Hitler. I tell you,
The British and Americans are wary of the Russians.
They will join the Germans to fight in the east.

Guderian. A fantasy –

Hitler. No, there have been reports.

Burgdorf. Sir, Colonel-General Schörner of Army Group Centre.
He has ordered the evacuation of Silesia.

Hitler. But I forbade retreat on pain of death.

Schörner (*on phone*). These troops in Silesia have fought hard
For two weeks and are finished. If we don't relieve
Them, we will lose the Seventeenth Army
And Bavaria. We are moving back to the Oder.

Hitler (*wearily*). Yes. Schörner, if you think that it is right,
I will have to agree.

*(*30th January. Burgdorf to Hitler. He hands Hitler a paper.*)

Burgdorf. Sir, a message from Speer: "The war is lost,
Now Upper Silesia is lost and with it our coal
For sixty per cent of our coal is from Silesia."

Hitler. The war is not lost, Speer is completely wrong.
I am taking afternoon tea with the Goebbels
At their home in Schwanenwerder. Fetch me
A flask of tea and a bag of cakes.

Burgdorf. The Goebbels

Are surely trustworthy, sir?

Hitler. I trust no one. (*Fade on Hitler.*)

Burgdorf (*to a colleague*). A message from Neukölln. Women have charged
A truck of potatoes, police have fired
And killed several. And the Führer is eating cakes.

(*30th January, later.*)

Hitler's voice on radio. Berliners, keep up your morale. Berlin
Is fully armed. Like a vast porcupine
With steel quills it will pierce the heart
Of any attacker or turn him back.
My new secret weapons will soon expel
The enemy from our Fatherland. I
Am with you in this crisis, this emergency,
And our Great German Reich will emerge
Stronger, defending Europe against the east.
Germany will never surrender, will
Fight to the very end. I am with you.

(*Late January. Versailles, Eisenhower's HQ. Eisenhower thinking aloud, to Bedell Smith.*)

Eisenhower. All our armies are fighting towards the Rhine.
Monty will cross north of the Ruhr, Hodges
And Patton to the south. With Monty coming
Down from the north and Bradley coming up from the south,
The two Army Groups can encircle the Ruhr.
How did Hannibal encircle the Romans
At Cannae? Can you find me a book? We can then
Fan out and overrun Germany. I know
Monty and Brooke favour a thrust to Berlin,
But we want it done quickly, so the main effort
Should be given to Brad. Monty would take six months
To prepare. Marshall's happy with that plan,
But Patton wants a larger role, and Brad
Is not happy that Monty has any role.
But that's the plan.

Bedell Smith. That's right.

Eisenhower. But we're not getting
There. American casualties in the Ardennes
Are almost as many as in the entire
Normandy battle. And for what? Brad has Hodges'
First Army, but won't give Simpson's Ninth the
Division he needs for Monty's pincer plan,
Because the Ninth is Monty's and Hitler
Is transferring his Sixth Panzers to Hungary.
We're not making an impact on the Germans.

Bedell Smith. So what do we do?

Eisenhower. End the Ardennes offensive,

Shut down Brad's operations and transfer him
To Monty's flank in the north to capture
The Roer dams.

Bedell Smith. Brad won't like that.

Eisenhower. But it's right.

Bedell Smith. It also smacks of what Monty's been saying.

Eisenhower. It's the way forward to the plan. I've decided
To end the Ardennes offensive. I'll clear it
With the CCS and then ring Brad.

(3rd February. Chorus of Berliners.)

Chorus. The American bombers have filled the sky.
For two hours the ground reverberated.
Craters, fallen trees, roads filled with rubble,
Fragments of walls, no lights or water.
Hitler was unharmed in his bunker,
Freisler the judge was killed by shrapnel.
We queue at standpipes to fill saucepans, pails.
We now have one loaf a week and most shops
Are ruined or boarded up, and money is worthless.
After each air-raid we just carry on
Alas, what will become of us? Alas!

(5th February, early evening. Yalta, the conference. Churchill, Eden, Stalin and Roosevelt.)

Stalin. Germany should be dismembered into five
Separate states, as Roosevelt proposed in Teheran.
We then agreed Poland's borders would be
Between the Oder and the Curzon Line
And that Prussia should be isolated
And we have now agreed the zones the four
Allied powers, including France, will occupy.
We should now dismember occupied Germany.

Churchill (*to Eden*). The only bond of the victors is their common
Hate. To make Britain safe in the future
She must become responsible for the safety
Of a cluster of feeble states.
(*To Stalin.*) I advise caution,
There should not be a too-rapid dismemberment
Of Germany. We must remember the mistakes
Made after the First World War. Twenty-five million
Troops hang on our words.

(Stalin reacts with chagrin.)

(*Aside.*) I can tell he's disgruntled.
I've thwarted him, and I must now watch out
That he does not dismember Germany
In practice with his army or by some other way.
Roosevelt's powers are failing, he is frail,

He could not get out of his car and he
Doesn't say anything and does what his adviser,
Alger Hiss, says, which is generally to
Stalin's liking. I must be doubly vigilant.

Stalin. Well, can we at least reaffirm our policy
Of unconditional surrender. We
Will not make any separate peace with the enemy,
Who therefore cannot divide our unity.

(*Churchill looks at Roosevelt, who looks at Alger Hiss. Hiss nods. Roosevelt nods.*)

Churchill (*to Eden*). We can't object to that? (*Aloud.*) Yes, we agree.

Stalin (*impassively*). And to help our eastern front, we request
A heavy Allied air attack on all
German communications in the Berlin-
Leipzig-Dresden region. The bombing of
These cities is now a matter of urgency.

(*Churchill looks at Roosevelt, who looks at Hiss. Hiss nods. Roosevelt nods.*)

Churchill. We agree.

Stalin (*aside*). They fell for it. They resisted
Dismemberment, and conceded what I
Was really after, unconditional
Surrender, in other words: the assistance
And time for me to conquer eastern Europe
And then dismember Germany through my strength.

(*6th February. Zhukov with his five army commanders and his Chief of Staff, General Malinin.*)

Zhukov. If we are to take Berlin in ten day's time,
We must have new bridgeheads across the Oder
And forward airfields for the Red Air Force
Within four days and all tanks and heavy guns
Must have had their refit and be ready.
It is asking a lot.

Chuikov. But it must be done.
One knock-out punch and the war will be over.

Zhukov. You speak like Montgomery. But if the Germans
Attack us from the north on our right flank
Which Rokossovsky has not yet protected
We will be cut off.

(*The phone rings.*)

Malinin. Comrade, Stalin from
Yalta.

Stalin (*on phone*). Where are you? What are you doing?

Zhukov. At Kolpakchi's headquarters, with the army
Commanders, planning to reach Berlin.

Stalin. You are wasting your time. Consolidate
On the Oder, then join Rokossovsky
And smash the enemy's Army Group Vistula.

(*Zhukov puts down the phone and rises, saying nothing.*)

Chuikov. Berlin is postponed?
Zhukov (*bitterly*). Because Rokossovsky is slow.

(*A few seconds later. Stalin in Yalta, with Molotov and Antonov.*)

Stalin (*putting down phone*). My Generals are in a hurry.
Molotov. Was that wise?
Stalin. I can now tell you, Churchill and Roosevelt
Have confirmed to me that they will not accept
Anything less than unconditional surrender -
No separate peace that transfers troops to the east.
We can take our time, we need not take risks now.
We can build up our forces for the final attack.
Molotov. (*enthusiastically*). You have done well.
Stalin. One good conversation
Is better than a month of ten armies.
And now I need to dictate a memo.
Your wife, please.
Molotov. Yes, of course.

(*Exit Molotov.*)

Stalin (*aside*). I can delay
Taking Berlin until I have overrun
All eastern Europe and unconditional
Surrender gives me the time.

(*Paulina Molotov appears.*)

(*gently*). Come here, my dear.
I have had a trying day outwitting Churchill
And Roosevelt. Lock the door.

(*Paulina locks the door, then sits on his desk.*)

Paulina. You are so clever.

*(*6th February. Hitler dictating his memoirs to Bormann.*)

Hitler. A desperate fight is a shining example.
Leonidas and his three hundred Spartans
Did not accept their desperate situation.
Frederick the Great was in great difficulties
During the Seven Years' War, then the Tsarina died
And the situation was reversed. If Churchill
Were to disappear, everything could change.
We can still snatch victory at the eleventh hour!
Providence will give us a miracle yet.

(8th February. Montgomery and 21st Army Group leaders.)

Montgomery. Winter is now over, and four million Russians
Are only fifty miles from Berlin, thanks
To Hitler's rashness in taking troops from
The east to attack us in the Ardennes.
Now it is our turn. I have agreed with Ike
That we will break through the Siegfried line
Of Hitler's western frontier, and cross the Rhine
To Wesel and the flat country north of the Ruhr.
In Veritable the First Canadian Army
And British Second Army will drive for the Meuse,
While in Grenade, Simpson's U.S. Ninth Army,
Which is under my command for this operation,
Will advance between Venlo and Julich and
Join the British and Canadians on the Rhine.
I wish you good hunting in Germany!

(11th February, noon. Yalta. The Big Three: Stalin, Churchill and Roosevelt, who is very sick.)

Churchill. So here we are at the end of our Yalta talks
To sign a Declaration on Liberated
Europe, which "upholds the right of all peoples
To choose the form of government under which they will live"
And pledges "the restoration of sovereign rights
And self-government to those peoples who have been
Forcibly deprived of them by the aggressor nations".
The Big Three will jointly assist in the holding
Of free elections as soon as possible.
Let us all now sign this Declaration.

(They sign.)

Then there is a communiqué on Poland,
That free elections will be held to establish
A Polish Provisional Government of National Unity.
The Lublin government will be reorganised
On a broader democratic basis, with the inclusion
Of democratic leaders from Poland and Poles abroad.
The London Poles are relegated to "Poles abroad"
And I do warn Marshal Stalin again that I
Will be strongly criticised for this at home as
We have yielded completely to the Russian view.
We went to war for Poland and we expect
A democratic and independent Poland now.

Stalin. But Soviet troops are masters of Warsaw
And stand on the banks of the Oder, and that
Is the reality.

Churchill. Let us sign the communiqué.

(11th February. Yalta. Stalin, Molotov and Antonov.)

Molotov. Koniev has broken out west of the Oder
And smashed a hole in the German defences
Forty miles deep and ninety miles wide,
Surrounding Glogau and Breslau, and he
Is now on the Neisse, the Germans in flight.

Stalin. He must stay there until Rokossovsky
Advances to Zhukov, and blocks an attack
From the north.

Antonov. Rokossovsky has been slowed down
By mud, rain, sleet and snow. His men sink knee-deep.
Roads are like quagmires.

Stalin. The Germans may counter-attack.
We must wait for the gap to the north to close.

(13th February. Berlin, the Chancellery. Guderian, with his Chief of Staff Wenck, his adjutant Loringhoven and ADC Boldt. They surrender their weapons to SS officers and guards outside the ante-room, or refreshment room, to Hitler's office or study. The guards examine their briefcases.)

Guderian. I am Chief of General Staff, and with me are
My Chief of Staff, adjutant and ADC
Am I not above suspicion?

SS guard (*shrugging*). No one is here.

Guderian (*left alone, to Wenck*). Remember, we are staking everything,
Your head and mine, to obtain a counter-attack.
Troops must be moved from Italy, Norway,
The Balkans, East Russia.

Wenck. The last two rows
You had with Hitler were awesome. If we
Had not pulled you back, Hitler would have hit you;
But he would not pull troops from the south,
And sent our best Panzers into Hungary.

Guderian. This time I must argue more strongly.

Wenck. No please –

(The SS guard returns. The four go into the ante-room, or refreshment room, where a group are having coffee and sandwiches: Burgdorf, Bormann, Keitel, Jodl, Dönitz, Himmler, Fegelein, Kaltenbrunner, Göring. Burgdorf, Hitler's adjutant, goes into Hitler's study and returns.)

Burgdorf. The Führer would like you all to come in.

(All enter in strict order of rank: Göring first. Hitler, head and limp left arm trembling, shakes each with a trembling hand. Hitler sits. They all sit.)

Jodl. Under the leadership of our Führer,
The situation is excellent on all fronts.

On the east our defensive line is holding
Thanks to SS Reichsführer, Himmler's
Army Group Vistula. On the west, likewise.

Hitler. Guderian, what do you think?

Guderian. I disagree.
The Russians on the east are tired, we must
Counter-attack them in two days, strike hard.

Himmler (*stammering, taking off his pince-nez and polishing them*).
I-It can't be done. The front line needs more fuel,
More ammunition.

Guderian (*shouting*). We can't wait for
The last can of petrol and the last shell,
The Russians will be too strong.

Hitler. I will not allow
You to accuse me of procrastination.

Guderian. I am not accusing you of anything,
But there is no sense in waiting for supplies
And losing the most favourable moment
To attack.

Hitler. I have just told you, I will not allow
You to accuse me of procrastinating.

Guderian. I want General Wenck as Chief of Staff
At Army Group Vistula or the attack will fail.
Himmler can't attack without help. Look at him.

Hitler (*rising*). The Reichsführer is man enough to lead
The attack without help.

Guderian. He does not have
The experience or the staff. He needs General Wenck.

Hitler. How dare you criticise the Reichsführer!
I won't have you criticise him!

Guderian. I insist,
General Wenck must join Army Group Vistula
To lead the attack.

(*The others have quietly slipped away into the ante-room, leaving Hitler, Himmler, Guderian, Wenck and their adjutants. Hitler explodes with rage, his fists raised, trembling, strutting up and down the carpet, stopping to scream accusations.*)

You come in here and accuse me of delay,
And the Reichsführer of inadequacy –
I will not take any more of your arrogance,
I will not have you criticise us, when
We are the ones who are defending Berlin
Against the Russians. You say there must be
A counter-attack, but….

(*Two hours later.*)

Hitler. Himmler is well able to lead the attack.

Guderian. It must be General Wenck, or it will fail.

Hitler (*suddenly giving up*). Well Himmler, General Wenck will go tonight
To Army Group Vistula as Chief of Staff.
(*To Guderian.*) Now let us continue with the conference.
Today, Colonel-General, the general staff
Has won a battle. Call the others in.

(*Guderian and Wenck go to the ante-room.*)

Keitel. How dare you upset the Führer.

Others. That was not right.

(*Guderian looks at them contemptuously.*)

Guderian. Wenck, give orders for a counter-attack
In two days' time.

(*13th February, night. Chorus of Dresdeners.*)

Chorus. Alas! Dresden is flattened. The Allies
Rained bombs from the night, first the British with
Eight hundred bombers, setting the city on fire
With high explosive bombs and incendiaries,
And then a wave of American bombers when
We were fleeing the firestorm, heading west.
Refugees choked the roads, German reinforcements
Could not get through the burning city to
The eastern front, as Stalin no doubt wanted,
But at what cost! Sixty thousand of us,
Sixty thousand civilians have been killed,
And all to choke the roads and slow down
The German reinforcements, to the Red Army's
Advantage. Alas, we are homeless, widowed, orphaned.
Alas, Dresden is no more, and we've nowhere to go.

(*16th February. Zhukov, and his aide, Malinin.*)

Malinin. News of Wenck.

Zhukov. Ah yes, of the counter-attack.

Malinin. Wenck's troops captured Pyritz and pressed against us,
He drove to Berlin and briefed Hitler all night.
At dawn his driver was sleepy, so Wenck took
The wheel of his staff car – and fell asleep.
The car crashed into the side of a railway bridge,
And burst into flames. Wenck was pulled out
But he has fractured his skull and five ribs,
And the counter-attack is finished.

Zhukov. We are in luck!

*(*1st March. Moscow. Stalin's Kremlin office.*)

Stalin (*on the phone*). Zhukov. I'm glad you're there. Rokossovsky

Has thrust at the Baltic coast and has holed
The German defences near Stettin, cut off
Their forces in Danzig and Gdynia.
He is at the mouth of the Oder, and can
Attack Berlin from the north. Join him there.
Bombard the Germans and when your tanks are ready
And the Germans think you are heading for Berlin,
Go northwards, take Stargard and link up with
Rokossovsky. I want our entire force
On the Oder.

*(*Early March. Versailles, Eisenhower's HQ. Eisenhower and Bedell Smith.*)

Eisenhower. It's March, and a month of fighting through thaws
Has ended in triumph. Monty's two pincer movements,
Veritable and Grenade, have reached the Rhine
Under one plan and a single commander,
The Allies have taken a hundred thousand prisoners.
Simpson's Ninth US Army is on the Rhine,
And now we're preparing to cross: Operation Plunder.
I intend to move Bradley north, and give
Him command of Ninth and First US Armies
Alongside Monty's Second British and First
Canadian Armies. Do you think they can work together?

(*8th March. Eisenhower in his HQ.*)

Eisenhower (*alone*). My broad front in the west is now ready.
Monty has smashed nineteen German divisions
And ninety thousand men, and has occupied
The west bank of the Rhine from Nijmegen
To Düsseldorf. From there Bradley has cleared
Eighty miles on the west bank down to Koblenz,
Southwards and Hodges has captured Cologne,
And taken out forty-nine thousand men
And Collins has crossed the Rhine at Remagen
And established a bridgehead several miles deep.
Patton has reached the Rhine from Moselle.
We are all in place to advance into Germany.
The Ruhr is now within the Allies' reach.
I have told Marshall and Roosevelt, the Red Army
Is fifty miles from Berlin, while we are
Two hundred and eighty-five miles away.
I have asked: do they want us to take Berlin?

(*9th March. Berlin, the Führer bunker. Hitler and Bormann.*)

Bormann. Sir, a message. The US Third Army
Has reached the Rhine and joined the First Army.

(*Silence.*)

Hitler. Cowards! The German soldiers are cowards.
How can my generals allow this to happen?
I am betrayed by my Commander-in-Chief.
Sack von Rundstedt, replace him with Kesselring.
He has more fight in him, that will remove
Him from negotiating surrender in Italy.
And I issue a decree against cowardice:
Anyone captured without being wounded
Or having fought has forfeited his honour.
I will have executions for cowardice.

(13th March. Berlin, Defence Council building near Brandenburg Gate. Lieutenant-General Reymann and Goebbels.)

Reymann. The first I knew of any of this was
After the firebombing of my Dresden.
Burgdorf rang me and said. "The Führer has
Appointed you military commander of Dresden."
I said, "Tell him there is only rubble here."
An hour later he rang again. "The Führer has
Appointed you military commander of Berlin."
I was astonished, then I found my sick
Predecessor von Havenschild had done
Nothing to protect the civilians here
Or evacuate children or the elderly.
And now this thirty-three page document
Which I have never seen bears my signature:
"Order for the defence of the Reich capital."
It details three rings, outer, second and inner.
Did you write it?

Goebbels. I did, and you are wrong
To criticise the lack of evacuation.
There is enough canned milk to last three months,
Enough men, weapons, food and coal to last
For eight weeks under siege.

Reymann. I am a trained soldier
And I can see a lack of ammunition,
And where is the military equipment apparently
Stored in railway sidings? I need men
And materials to build defences. I need
Two hundred thousand men.

Goebbels. You speak like a bourgeois General,
And I remind you of Hübner's court martial
Which executed the General who did not
Blow up the bridge at Remagen, and seven
Senior officers. And that General Fromm,
Executioner of that traitor von Stauffenberg,
Was shot on the ninth for cowardice. Generals
Are not exempted if they are incompetent.
You can have thirty thousand men, there are no more.

(*14th March. Dr. Morell, Hitler's doctor, is visited by Magda Goebbels.*)

Dr. Morell (*concerned*). I hear the Ministry of Propaganda
Was destroyed in last night's heavy air raid.

Magda. It is completely destroyed. When my husband
Heard it had been hit, he drove at once
To the Wilhelmstrasse to see for himself.
It was still blazing, and he was afraid
Five hundred Panzerfaust missiles in the basement
Might explode. That beautiful old palace
Which he restored. At home he was melancholy.
He still says we can win the war, but I know
The end may come soon. When I raise such matters,
He says I should take our six children and
Go westwards, find safety with the British, but I
Cannot leave him. I have not told him I am here.
I must not weaken his will to resist.

Dr. Morell. What would you like me to do?

Magda. For nine years now,
I know, you have given the Führer pills,
And kept him going with amphetamine
Injections I believe. My children....
I see the future, I know in a few weeks' time
I may have to kill them. They are so innocent.
I wonder how I shall do it. I cannot talk
To my husband, undermine his resolve,
And so I turn to you.

Dr. Morell (*giving her two bottles and a syringe*).
I will be happy
To give you what you need to end their lives.
This is a sleeping draught, you inject their
Chocolates, and these are cyanide capsules
You make them bite when they are asleep.
And I hope you will not have to use them.

Magda. I am full of grief but thank you, thank you.

(*18th March. Berlin, the Führer bunker, Speer waiting in the corridor ante-room or reception room. Burgdorf.*)

Burgdorf. The Führer rose at midday, he is on the phone.

(*Enter Hitler.*)

Hitler. To Goebbels about the daylight air raid.

Speer. Two thousand American planes filled the air,
Glinting in the sunny Sunday morning,
There was some opposition, our Messerschmitts
Shot some down, but the Luftwaffe is short of fuel,
Aircraft and pilots, and the bombs thundered down,
Everywhere now there are fires, and the people suffer.

Hitler. The Allies' air raids are assisting our

Scorched earth policy. The Soviets will have nothing.
They will find rubble, as they found Warsaw.
I will destroy Berlin and the whole country –
Its industrial plant, power stations, water and gas works,
All stores, bridges, public buildings, ships, trains –
Rather than hand them over to the Soviets.

Speer. I built your new Berlin and your Third Reich
To last a thousand years, I beg you, please
Do not do this. I have brought a report.
The economy will last one month or two,
Then the war must stop. Please think of the people.
They need electricity, gas, water and bridges
To continue their food supply so they survive.
Führer, on human grounds, do not raze Berlin.

Hitler (*contemptuously*). If the war is lost, the nation will perish.
And the nation will not be the good ones, who will have been killed,
But inferior ones and cowards who did not die.
If the war is lost, Germans do not deserve
To have the essential services, and they will not.
Tomorrow I issue my Nero Order
To destroy all installations and services.

Speer (*quietly*). Nero burned Rome and is now considered mad.
I tell you, German civilians will fight
Kesselring's men as they implement your will.
(*Wearily.*) But Allied air raids will accomplish all
Your order seeks. You and the Allies will leave
A pile of rubble for the advancing Soviet tanks,
The rubble of what I built, of my life's work.

*(*19th March. Himmler's pillared HQ at Birkenhain, Guderian with SS Brigadier-General Lammerding, Himmler's Chief of Staff.*)

Guderian. The Reichsführer?

Lammerding. He is not here. Can I help?
I am his Chief of Staff.

Guderian. Since Wenck's car crash
The general staff have not received one report
From Himmler. We have a huge Soviet build-up
Around our bridgehead at Küstrin and Frankfurt.
We can't wait any longer, we must have news.
On the west we have Kesselring, a soldier
And we have the Weser and Elbe as barriers.
On the east we have Himmler and only fifty miles.

Lammerding. Sir, can't you rid us of our commander?

Guderian. That is a matter for the SS. Where is he?

Lammerding. At a clinic twenty miles away. He has flu.

(*19th March. Hohenlychen. Guderian and Himmler.*)

Himmler. I have a slight cold in my head, that's all.

Guderian. My sympathy. Perhaps you've been overworking.
As well as commander of Army Group Vistula,
You are leader of the SS, chief of police
And the Gestapo, Minister of the Interior,
And commander of the Reserve Army.
It's enough to burden anyone. Why not
Give up one job, such as Army Group Vistula?

Himmler (*eagerly*). It is true, I have too many positions
For my health, but how can I tell the Führer?
He would not like it if I said that.

Guderian. Will you
Authorise me to say it for you?

Himmler. (*nodding*). Thank you.

Guderian. There is a need for an immediate armistice.

Himmler. I will not be drawn on matters such as that.

(*19th March. Berlin, Führer bunker. Hitler and Guderian.*)

Guderian. The Reichsführer is overworked and wants
To be relieved.

Hitler. It is very inconvenient.
This is the wrong time to make a change on the east.
Himmler has knowledge, who can replace him?

Guderian. Colonel-General Heinrici, First Panzer.

Hitler. He is a cousin of von Rundstedt, whom I sacked.

Guderian. He is in eastern Czechoslovakia,
He knows the Russians, they haven't broken through him.

Hitler (*sighing*). Oh very well.

(*20th March. Berlin, the Chancellery. Hitler walking with Himmler. Enter Guderian.*)

Guderian. Can I speak with the Reichsführer a minute.

(*Hitler gestures.*)

(*To Himmler.*) The war cannot now be won, the bombing must end.
You and Ribbentrop alone have contacts
In neutral countries, to arrange an armistice.
Ribbentrop will not approach Hitler, so you
Must go with me to ask him for an armistice.

Himmler. I share your concern, but cannot support you.
Hitler would have me shot for such a proposal.

(*That evening. Berlin, Führer bunker. Guderian and Hitler after the daily conference. Bormann is present in the background.*)

Hitler. Guderian, Himmler has spoken to me.
I understand your heart condition is worse.
You should go to a spa for a cure at once.

Guderian (*taken aback*). My deputy General Krebs has been wounded

In an air raid. I cannot leave my post.
Until I find a replacement. Then I'll go on leave.

(*21st March. Straelen, Montgomery's HQ. Montgomery and General Jock Whiteley.*)

Montgomery. I've been explaining Plunder to the senior
Officers of my three armies, Jock. Now
Eisenhower wants me to share command in the north
With Bradley, once the Allies are across the Rhine.
I have a better plan. Gerow should hold
A defensive front across the western Ruhr.
Bradley should stay south and pincer-attack
From Remagen, join me and encircle the Ruhr.

Whiteley. That sounds a very good idea to me.

Montgomery. One man must be in general command
North of the Ruhr, and that man should not be Bradley.
Can you dress this up as a SHAEF proposal
So it can be put to Ike in Maastricht?

(*21st March. Cannes. Eisenhower and Bradley in conference. Kay and three WAC girls playing bridge. Everett Hughes and Tex Lee.*)

Hughes. Ike's back to himself today. He's slept two days.
Yesterday Kay suggested bridge. He said
"I can't keep my mind on cards at present,
All I want to do is sit here and not think."

Lee. The stress of great men's jobs and lives.

Hughes. You share
An office with Kay. Do you think Ike sleeps with her?

Lee. No, I don't. He's always writing to Mamie.
He's cooling towards Kay. She's fun to be with,
Someone he can talk privately with. That's all.
He knows there's no place for Kay in his life.

Hughes. I disagree. I think he is. But one thing's sure,
There is nothing we can do about it.

(*Fade on Hughes and Lee.*)

Bradley. You ask me about the risks of taking Berlin.
Even if Monty reaches the Elbe before
The Red Army reaches the Oder, fifty
Miles of Lowlands, with lakes, streams and canals
Would still lie between the Elbe and Berlin.
It would cost us a hundred thousand casualties.
For a prestige objective, then we'd have to fall back
Because Yalta gave Berlin to the Russians.

Eisenhower. Brad, you were my friend and classmate at West Point.
I want you to lead the final victorious assault
Against Hitler. A SHAEF directive will
Instruct you to send Third Army over the Rhine
Near Mainz-Frankfurt and advance to Kassel.

Hodges will push east from Remagen and link
First and Third Armies, encircle the Ruhr.
I shall take the Ninth Army from Monty's command,
Remove it from Twenty-first and give it to you,
And shift the main thrust from the north to the centre.
I have decided not to take Berlin
But to leave it entirely to the Russians
And go for Dresden and Leipzig instead.
This is for your ears only at this stage.
We all have our masters, mine are Marshall
And Roosevelt, who agreed at Teheran
And Yalta to draw a line down the map of Europe
And place Berlin on the Russian side.
In the prevailing political climate
Of Yalta, and of those who control
Our President and Stalin, it is wise
To leave Berlin to the Russians. But Brad,
Political considerations aside,
I have been coming round to this view on my own
For military reasons I find sound.
Since January I've wanted to strengthen your front.
I first saw your front as a diversion, then
As a secondary thrust to help Monty,
Then as a major thrust if he gets bogged down
As he did near Caen. But now I see it as
The main thrust, and Monty's as secondary.
I have decided, I will not be lectured
Or dictated to by Monty any more.
He has been so personal, denying the Americans
And me credit, that I have stopped talking to him.
I know Monty wants to lead the armies
Into Berlin, and I know I should explain
This change of strategy to Churchill.
But I shall follow my masters and keep silent.

(*He rises and moves away. Fade on all except Eisenhower.*)

(*Aside.*) General Marshall has pointed out again,
Berlin's in the Russian occupation zone
As agreed at Yalta, and we should not interfere.
Berlin is in the Russian sphere of influence.
There will be a problem if we take Berlin
At a cost of a hundred thousand Allied lives
And then withdraw under the Yalta terms,
Hand it over to the Russians. At home
They'll say, "Why were so many Americans killed
To hand Berlin over to Russian occupation?
Was this what we voted for four months ago?
Let the Russians take the casualties, not us."
I'll secure Marshall's approval to cable

Stalin and suggest the Americans meet up
With the Russians at Dresden, well away from Berlin,
A token meeting-place this side of the Elbe
That will justify the bombing Stalin sought.

(*22nd March. Zossen. Heinrici, a short stocky man with a moustache, with Guderian.*)

Heinrici. I am shocked at how weak we are on the Oder,
How little information Himmler has given.
I have two armies.
Guderian. Manteuffel's and Busse's.
And Busse will soon attack the Russians round Küstrin.
Hitler has ordered five Panzer divisions
To cross the single bridge at Frankfurt where
They will be under Russian artillery fire.
Heinrici. Our troops will be driven back to the Oder.
It will be a disaster.
Guderian (*looking at his watch*). It is time to leave
For the Führer's daily conference. It makes me wild
The way they run this war, their idiocies.
The Führer is surrounded by incompetents,
Hangers-on, flatterers, featherers of their own nest.
Hitler will discuss the Küstrin attack. Come.
Heinrici. No, I am still uninformed, I must stay
With my Army Group. Hitler can wait a few days.

(*22nd March, later. Berlin. Himmler and Heinrici. A stenographer records the conversation.*)

Himmler. And I tell you, my policy was right,
The Army Group Vistula has held back
The Russian attack at each of its strong points.
Heinrici. You have spoken for forty-five minutes
And I still know nothing of the forces
I command, or of the situation.

(*The phone rings. Himmler answers.*)

Himmler. It is Busse. You are the new commander
Of Army Group Vistula. You take this call.
Heinrici. Busse says that the Russians have broken through
And enlarged the bridgehead near Küstrin.
Himmler. You are the commander. Give the right orders.
Heinrici. I do not know a thing about the Army Group,
What troops I have, or who is where or when.

(*Himmler is silent.*)

(*On phone.*) What do you propose? I agree, counter-attack.
I will join you, we'll inspect the front line.
Himmler. My policies, then, have been proved right, and I –
Heinrici. It is imperative that I have your assessment

Of the Küstrin situation and our war aims.

(Himmler leads Heinrici to a couch out of the stenographer's earshot.)

Himmler. I want to tell you something in confidence.
I am negotiating peace with the West.

Heinrici. Fine. Through?

Through a neutral country. Well now
You are in charge, I have to go. I am glad
I will not be in charge if the eastern front breaks.

★*(23rd March, evening. The eastern front. Heinrici and Busse.)*

Heinrici. Today I've driven behind the entire front line,
Looking at the terrain. The Russians will strike
Between Frankfurt and Küstrin. Our defensive line
Will therefore be along the Seelow Heights.
And I will open the sluice gates of the lake,
Empty the Ottmachau into the Oder
And flood the Oderbruck as an obstacle
For Chuikov. Now attack Küstrin again.

(23rd March. Namur, Bradley's HQ. Bradley is on the phone to Eisenhower.)

Bradley. A new SHAEF plan? I wouldn't wait until
Mid-April to command the First and Ninth
North of the Ruhr, I'd have immediate
Command of the First and Third and push south of
The Ruhr into Germany. Whiteley's plan.
And then drive on towards Frankfurt, do you say?
I'm very pleased with it. It keeps me apart
From Montgomery. What was that Marshall said?
"The overdose of Montgomery which is now
Coming into the country."*(Laughing.)* He's right on.
So you've approved this plan and you want me
To hold a press conference now about
Twelfth US Army Group operations.
The Ruhr, north and south, it is. I just wonder.
You don't think Montgomery wants to finish
The war himself, and leave Devers and me
With subordinate roles? Or is he being possessive?
Does he want to command as many American troops
As possible, including the Ninth Army?
You'll come and see me tomorrow? That's good.

(23rd March, just before 9.30 p.m. Straelen, Montgomery's HQ. Montgomery, Churchill and Brooke leave Montgomery's caravan in moonlight by the Rhine. Churchill is in the uniform of 4th Hussars. Sound of artillery barrage.)

Brooke. It's good news that Eisenhower has approved
The Whiteley plan that will put you north of the Ruhr

And Bradley south. You'll be in a good position.

Churchill. That was a good dinner, and now we have
Studied the maps, all that remains is to watch
The boats and pontoons drift to the other side,
Which is, what, five hundred yards, would you say,
As we put a quarter of a million men
Across the Rhine, the first military crossing
Since Napoleon, the first time British troops
Have fought on German soil since the battle
Of Leipzig in eighteen thirteen, against the French.

Montgomery. Have you seen my message to the troops?

Churchill (*reading*). "Over the Rhine then let us go. And good hunting
To you all on the other side. May 'The Lord
Mighty in battle' give us the victory
In this our latest undertaking as He has done
In all our battles since we landed in
Normandy on D-Day." Very eloquent.

Montgomery. There go the first commandos across the river.
Do you see their green berets?

Churchill (*excited*). Yes.

Montgomery. Through the night there will be landings along
A twenty-mile front, in ten places, two
Airborne divisions –

Brooke. They've started.

(*Dawnay approaches.*)

Dawnay. Sir, Patton
Is across.

Montgomery. What?

Dawnay (*handing him a message*). We've just heard, the Americans
Crossed near Mainz at 10 last night. Bradley gave
Patton permission to cross in assault boats
By stealth – no barrage or paratroop drops –
And has put ten divisions into the new bridgehead.
He has given Hodges ten divisions to break out.
The US Twelfth Army Group plan to race
Your Twenty-First Army Group into the Reich.
Patton has said, "I want the world to know
Third Army made it before Monty starts across."

(*Silence. Exit Dawnay.*)

Montgomery. Ike is behind it.

Churchill. And Roosevelt behind Ike.

Montgomery. Even now the Americans are fighting their own war.
But for them, we would be in Berlin now.
It is time I retired to bed.

Churchill. You can't leave this.

Montgomery. Nothing disturbs my routine. Well, good night.

(Exit to caravan.)

Churchill. How can he go to bed at such a time?
Despite the ominous news about the Yanks
I am exhilarated, let us walk
In the moonlight and watch and talk until
I return to my red boxes in my caravan.
What do you think the Americans plan to do?

(Fade on Churchill and Brooke. Montgomery in his caravan, praying.)

Montgomery. O Lord, who helps the righteous in peace and war,
O Lord of Love and Light, O mighty Lord,
I have flung a quarter of a million men
Across the Rhine to thrust towards Berlin
And root out the Nazi evil around Hitler's power.
O Lord of Light, fill me with your wisdom,
O God of Light, come into me now, come.
Purify my thinking, so my decisions are right,
Exonerate me from the deaths I cause.
I submit to you the power I have over men.
Guide me with your power, you ah! bright Light,
Guide me with your Providence. Thy Will, not mine,
Be done. If it is Thy will, let me have
The victory, let the Germans surrender to me
As your chosen instrument doing your will.
Not to the Americans, but to me.
Let me cleanse the earth with the Light you give me.
And after its moral cleansing may the soil
Return to your beauty, devoid of tanks
And guns and shells, the machines of war
Which so disfigure your simple paradise.

THE WARLORDS, PART TWO

SCENE 1. CROSSING THE RHINE: BERLIN OR DRESDEN?

(24th March. Straelen, near the bank of the Rhine. Churchill and Brooke sitting with a hamper near an armoured car, watching the airborne operation and crossing.)

Churchill *(excitedly)*. Monty's missing a treat, he ought to be here,
Not discussing the new plan with Eisenhower
And General Simpson at Rheinberg Castle.
Two thousand aircraft, paratroops in the sky
Assault craft ferrying men, guns and, tanks.
Before our grandstand.

Brooke. You are like a small boy!

Churchill. You know, I have long held an ambition
To urinate in the Rhine. Will you join me?

(Churchill and Brooke stand on the bank of the Rhine with their backs to the audience.)

The British Prime Minister and the Chief
Of the Imperial General Staff, Field Marshal Brooke,
Will now express their opinion of Hitler,
Of the Third Reich and the Nazi movement,
And of American underhandedness.

(They urinate in the Rhine. Enter Jock Colville, Churchill's private secretary, covered in blood. He stares in disbelief.)

Churchill. Jock, what has happened?

Colville (*proudly*). I crossed the river.
German shells fell round us, and our driver
Was hit by shrapnel. This is his blood, not mine.

Churchill. What a lark.

Montgomery (*entering, angrily to Colville).* You had no permission to cross.
You exposed yourself to danger without my permission.

Churchill. I would like to have crossed, I envy him.
Talking of exposing ourselves, we made a gesture.

(He points to the Rhine.)

Montgomery (*understanding*). You didn't.

Churchill, Brooke. We did.

Churchill *(sadly).* But there were no press
Photographers to record the occasion
For posterity. Come on, Monty, your turn.

(24th March, evening. Montgomery questions his last Liaison Officer, who is then replaced by de Guingand. Churchill sits outside with Brooke.)

Churchill. I've been watching Monty and working out
How he conducts a battle on this gigantic scale.
He's questioned his young officers for two hours now.
Each one has been to a different part of the front
With power to question anybody. Each one's
At least a Major, and some have travelled
Hundreds of miles by jeep or plane. Monty
Listens to their reports, then questions each
Searchingly. At the end he gives directions
To de Guingand, which go into the staff
Machine. His Liaison Officers are based
On Wellington, but it was my ancestor,
The Duke of Marlborough, who first stationed look-outs,
Lieutenant-generals, to watch the battle.
We won the war because we broke Hitler's codes.
He's never fathomed that, he blames his Generals.
Wherever he puts his Generals, we are there
And we have told the Russians, until now.
We won the war because a Polish genius, Rejewski,
Cracked the Enigma code, and another
Genius, Turing, invented the world's first
Electronic programmable computer,
The Colossus machine at Bletchley Park,
Which meant we knew Hitler's orders before
They had even reached his Generals. But you know,
If we hadn't broken his codes, I reckon Monty
Would still have beaten him through his LOs.

(Exit de Guingand.)

Montgomery. That's it for tonight. I didn't tell you,
At Rheinberg I discussed with Eisenhower
Enveloping the Ruhr from the north and south,
The new plan, and then racing on to the Elbe
And I drew on a map the boundary I would like
Between Bradley and me, and Ike said Magdeburg
Should be on Bradley's side. No other comment
Was made, and I'm wondering if he has approved
My drive to the Elbe and thence to Berlin.

(25th March, Churchill, Montgomery and Brooke sitting with Eisenhower, Bradley and Simpson, at Rheinberg Castle, Simpson's Ninth Army HQ overlooking the Rhine.)

Churchill. We have come from a Palm Sunday Service.
Eisenhower. I rested in Cannes, then flew to Wesel
And watched Simpson's Ninth Army cross the Rhine
Virtually unopposed. The plan's going well,

Under Monty's leadership.

(He exchanges pointed glances with Bradley.)

(To Brooke.) Do you agree
With the new plan, with going north and south
Of the Ruhr, and in the south, pushing for Frankfurt
And Kassel?

Brooke. I see no danger in it.
The Germans are crumbling and we should push
Them wherever they crumble.

Churchill (*showing a note*). Ike, read this.
I received this note last night from Molotov.
He accuses Britain and America
Of lying, of going "behind the back
Of the Soviet Union, which is bearing
The brunt of the war against Germany," by
Opening negotiations for a separate peace
In Switzerland and in Italy. The accord
Between the three powers at Yalta is strained.

Eisenhower. These are unjust and unfounded charges
About our good faith. They make me angry.
We will accept surrenders in the field
When they are offered. In political matters
We will consult the heads of governments.

Churchill. I think the Allied Expeditionary Force
Should beat the Russians to Berlin and hold
As much of east Germany as possible, until
My doubts about Russia's intention have been cleared away.

(Eisenhower exchanges glances with Bradley.)

Eisenhower. The truth is, we're five times as far from Berlin
As the Russians are. You want me to think
Less about the Germans than the Russians,
But I don't believe the Wehrmacht is finished
Until it has surrendered unconditionally.
It can set up Headquarters in the Austrian Alps,
With Hitler as its guerilla leader.
I want a quick end to the war. That means
Capturing the Alps, moving towards the south:
The Alps are a more important objective
Than Berlin, or racing the Russians there.

(There is a silence with exchanged glances.)

Churchill. The Kremlin has stressed the importance of the Alps
To direct our attention from their goal of Berlin.

Montgomery. But the main thing is, the objective is still Berlin.

Eisenhower. These are political considerations
But our assessment is primarily military.

Churchill. Berlin is our priority objective.
It is a political centre and if we can
Beat the Russians to it, the post-war years
Will be easier for us. We must look ahead.

(There is a silence with exchanged glances.)

Bradley. Political considerations can complicate the war
With political foresight and non-military objectives.
Eisenhower. The Ruhr should be surrounded and mopped up
Before any advance to the east begins.

(25th March. Churchill, Montgomery, Eisenhower and Simpson on the riverbank with others.)

Churchill (*cigar in mouth*). I would like to get in that boat and cross.
Eisenhower. No, Mr. Prime Minister. You might be killed.
I'm the Supreme Commander, I refuse to allow it.
Now I am due at my next appointment. Good-bye. *(Exit.)*
Churchill *(to Montgomery)*. You see that small US Navy launch, there?
Why don't we go across and look at the other side?
Montgomery. Why not?
Simpson. Are you sure?
Montgomery. I'm in charge now Ike's gone,
And the US Navy's under me, including
That tank landing craft just there.
Churchill (*excitedly*). Wesel,
Where the fighting is, let's go down to Wesel.

(Later.)

Simpson. I was so worried, to spite Ike Monty
Drove the PM in his jeep to the Wesel railway bridge.
Churchill scrambled among the wrecked iron girders.
He was under fire from snipers, shells and mortars.
They were landing all round him, he was thrilled,
There were plumes of white spray in the river.
We could not get him away. He was like a boy.

(28th March, late morning. Rheims, Eisenhower's Forward Headquarters. Butcher and Bedell Smith.)

Bedell Smith. He really needed his holiday in Cannes.
He had flu, his back hurt where the cyst was cut out,
His knee was badly swollen, he had bags under
His eyes, his blood pressure was high, I said
To him, "You can hardly walk across the room."
He slept most of the time for a couple of days.
He was really run down, physically. Since Cannes
He's been travelling: to Namur to see Brad,
Then he crossed the Rhine at Remagen with Brad,
Hodges and Patton, then back here to Rheims

Yesterday, then to Paris with you. He's got new zest.
Butcher. His press conference in Paris was a peach,
And then he had some R and R: a preview
Of a D-Day film in the Champs Elysées,
And don't tell anyone, but he spent the night
With Kay at the Raphael Hotel incognito –
I booked them in myself – and I think you'll find
He wasn't impotent for once, he's got
Untired, he's bodily fit. And now back here.

(Enter Eisenhower.)

Bedell Smith. Sir, a signal from Montgomery. You're not
Going to like it sir. He has ordered
His army commanders to go for the River Elbe
"With all possible speed and drive", and then Berlin.
He says he feels SHAEF will be "delighted".
Your Rheinberg directive of yesterday
Laid down that the Ruhr was to be surrounded
And mopped up before any advance to the east.
Eisenhower (*stunned, reading).* He's ordered his British Second Army
And Simpson's US Ninth to Magdeburg.
He ends: "My TAC HQ moves to the north west
Of Bonninghardt on Thursday 29th March.
Thereafter my HQ will move to Wesel,
Munster, Wiedenbruck, Herford, Hanover –
And thence by autobahn to Berlin, I hope."
(Blowing up.) It's open defiance of my orders.
He thinks he's Supreme Commander, not me.
Of all the imperious and tactless things he's done,
This tops the lot. My reply will show my anger.
My message will be clear and uncompromising.
I will think it out while I lunch with Brad.

(Later. Eisenhower and Bedell Smith.)

Eisenhower. Brad says again that capturing Berlin
Would cost us a hundred thousand casualties.
If Brad were to the north, I might say Yes.
But it's Monty, after his slowness in the Ardennes.
The American armies are having great success.
I am determined to do right by Brad
Regardless of the British Chiefs of Staff,
And give him back his three US armies.
I've talked with Brad, it's time to block Monty.
I will be decisive. Say, "There will be no drive
For Berlin." Say, "Simpson's Ninth Army will
Be under Bradley's control once it has joined
With US First Army and encircled the Ruhr."
Say, "Bradley will deliver his main thrust
On the axis Erfurt-Leipzig-Dresden

To join hands with the Russians." Dresden
Is the shortest route to the Red Army, it will
Cut the German forces in half. Say, "Bradley
Will swing well south of Berlin, the mission
Of your army will be to protect Bradley's
Northern flank." Say, "My present plans
Are co-ordinated with Stalin." Cable Stalin,
Tell him of my intentions, ask for Soviet plans
To harmonise the operations of our two armies
Which are advancing from east and west.
Make it a personal message to Stalin
Via the Allied Military Mission
In Moscow. Say I am encircling
The enemy in the Ruhr until late April,
That I'll then seek to divide the enemy
By joining hands with Russian forces on
The axis of Erfurt-Leipzig-Dresden,
The focus of my main effort, and later in
The Regensburg-Linz area to stop
All resistance in a southern redoubt.

(Surprised, Bedell Smith hesitates.)

Bedell Smith. Sir, are you sure –
Eisenhower. It's all right, I know what I'm doing.
Don't question me about this cable. Do it.

(28th March. Moscow, the Kremlin. Stalin's office. Stalin and Antonov.)

Stalin. I have just told the State Defence Committee
I am pleased with Eisenhower's signal
But I am suspicious that the Americans
Are trying to lull me into a false sense of security
And snatch Berlin from my grasp. Send a signal
To Marshall, complaining the information
About the German Sixth Panzer Army is false.
Suggest the Americans misled the Soviet Union.

(Enter Zhukov. Stalin extends a hand.)

Zhukov. Chuikov has taken Küstrin.
Hitler and Guderian ordered Busse to break-out,
Heinrici was against it. We massacred them,
Then entered the fortress at two this afternoon.
Stalin *(nodding)*. The German front in the west has collapsed for good.
The Hitlerites didn't want to halt the Allies.
They are reinforcing the units facing us.
I have a letter from "a foreign well-wisher"
That warns the Germans may be doing a deal
That gives the Allies a clear run to Berlin.
How quickly can we start our Berlin offensive?

Zhukov. In two weeks' time. Koniev will be ready then.
But not Rokossovsky.

Stalin. We shall have to begin without him.
Antonov has the maps, sit with him now.

(28th March. Berlin, the Führer bunker, the daily conference in Hitler's conference room. Hitler; Busse, a large man with spectacles; Guderian; Jodl, Keitel, Loringhoven and Thomale.)

Hitler (*frostily*). You are here to give an account of yourself.

Busse. All three counter-attacks on Küstrin were doomed.
The orders were impossible, given the strength –

Hitler (*shouting*). Why did they fail? Because of incompetence
And negligence. I am the Commander.
I gave the orders you are questioning.
The whole military command is incompetent.
Busse, Guderian, Heinrici. There was not
Sufficient artillery preparation.

Guderian. There was not enough ammunition for a barrage.

Hitler (*shouting*). Then why did you not supply Busse with more?

Guderian (*shouting*). Yesterday I explained that General Busse
Was not to blame for the failure of the Küstrin attack.
He followed orders. He used the ammunition
Allotted to him. Look at the casualties.
The troops did their duty.

Hitler. They failed, they failed.

Guderian. You do not know what you are talking about.
You are an amateur meddling in
Military matters you do not understand.
We professional soldiers are operating within
A context of bungling amaterishism.
And interference and wrong-headedness.

(Hitler has sunk lower in his chair. He jumps up, his face blotchy, his left side and arm trembling. He glares at Guderian.)

Hitler. The whole of the general staff and officer corps
Are responsible for every failure
And disaster of the last few months. They are
Fools and fatheads, cowards, incompetents.
They have misled, misinformed and tricked me.
They are dominated by deceitful aristocrats.

Guderian (*shouting*). The disasters in the Ardennes and the east,
In Hungary and the Baltic have been caused
By your incompetence, your misjudgement,
Your lack of skill as a military commander.
We desperately need divisions; you sent eighteen
To Latvia. When will you bring them back?

Hitler. Never.

(Loringhoven dashes out to the corridor or reception room and phones Krebs.)

Loringhoven. Krebs, Guderian is shouting at the Führer.
Do something before he is taken out and shot.

(Jodl and Thomale pull Guderian away from Hitler. Burgdorf helps Hitler to his chair.)

Krebs has an urgent message for you.
Guderian (*shouting on phone*). Calm down?
Calm down, you say. The man is a lunatic,
We're ruled by an imbecile without military sense.

(15 minutes later, Hitler's conference room, but all are calm.)

Hitler. Everyone leave except Guderian and Keitel.
(*Coldly.*) Colonel-General Guderian, you are
In a poor state of health, you will now take
Six weeks' sick leave immediately.
Guderian (*saluting).* I'll go.
Hitler. Please wait until the conference is over.
Burgdorf. Sir, the conference is finished.
Hitler (*calling him back*). Guderian,
Take good care of yourself. In six weeks' time
The situation will be critical. I'll need you.
Where will you go?
Keitel. The spa at Bad Liebenstein?
Guderian (*caustically*). It's in American hands. (*Leaving, to Loringhoven.*) It's safer not to say.

**(28th March. Berlin, Defence Council building. Goebbels and Reymann and his Chief of Staff, Col. Refior.)*

Reymann. I am worried about the defence of Berlin
Fourteen anti-aircraft batteries have been removed
To the eastern front, and there is no plan
To evacuate children. How will we feed babies?
There is no milk.
Goebbels. We will bring cows into Berlin.
Reymann. Into a battle area where they can't be fed or milked?
We must consider the immediate evacuation
Of women and children before it is too late.
Goebbels. If an evacuation becomes necessary,
I will be the one to make the decision.
But it will create panic if I order it now,
There is plenty of time. Good evening gentlemen.

(Later.)

Refior. Good news. Berlin has been placed under Heinrici,
Whom you know well, and Army Group Vistula.
Reymann. (*gloomily*). Heinrici is holding the Oder front. He will not
Accept the hopeless task of defending Berlin.

(28th March, 9 p.m. Straelen, Montgomery's HQ. Montgomery and Dawnay, his senior staff officer.)

Montgomery *(devastated).* I am stunned by Eisenhower's cable.
I am shocked. "My present plans being co-ordinated
With Stalin." And no mention of Berlin.
I am speechless. "The mission of your army group
Will be to protect Bradley's northern flank."
I am devastated, fuming at his folly.
Why are they so hostile to me at SHAEF?
Who are my enemies? Public opinion?
Simpson's Ninth Army, taken away from me
And reverting to Bradley to mop up the Ruhr.
Bradley having the main role, and to Dresden.
And nothing of this said to us at Rheinberg.
And co-ordinating with Stalin, a Commander-in-Chief
With a Head of State. And did Tedder know?
Not going to Berlin, I can't believe it.
Is he blind, does he realise what he's giving Stalin?
The US and Russians must have made a deal.
There is very dirty work behind the scenes.
Until I know what Eisenhower is doing
With Stalin, the wisest counsel is silence.

(He goes to his caravan.)

(Praying.) O Lord, I do not understand your ways,
But if it is your will that Stalin should have
Berlin, and control free elections there,
Then I'm happy to accept that Bradley should
Lead Simpson to Dresden. Thy will, not mine
Be done. But how, Lord of Light, how, how, how
Is your will served by Stalin having Berlin?
By Communism ruling eastern Europe?
By a regime as bad as Hitler's controlling Poland?
Please give me an answer, for I do not understand.

(28th March. London, underground war rooms. Churchill and Brooke.)

Brooke. A wire from Monty: "I consider we
Are about to make a terrible mistake."
He hopes Eisenhower's order can be rescinded.

Churchill. Ike did not consult his Deputy Supreme Commander,
Tedder, about his change of plan, nor did
He mention it to the Combined Chiefs of Staff.
He said nothing of this to us at Rheinberg,
And for a General to communicate directly
With a Head of State, and so untrustworthy a one
As Stalin, leaves me speechless. It signals
To Stalin that his troops can take great tracts
Of Germany, a danger I foresaw

In Yalta, and tried to prevent. I ask myself,
It must have been premeditated, he
Must have known this when we talked at Rheinberg?
And Stalin. He must have cleared it with Marshall.
Not even Monty would cable Stalin
With a change of plan without contacting us.
But given that he cleared it, the question is,
Did Ike act alone, or was he under orders
From higher up? Let us try to find out.

(Exit Brooke.)

(Aside.) In every time there has been an eruption:
The French Revolution, the guillotine and
Napoleon, which came out of a suppressed
Bavarian movement; the Bolshevik
Revolution, Lenin and firing-squads,
Which have been funded by the Rothschilds' banks;
Now the Nazis, Hitler and extermination camps,
Which came out of Eckart, Rosenberg and the Thule
Society in Munich, Bavaria.
What if this seismic movement against government
And religion which kills in different times
Has one volcanic source which is behind
The hand of Robespierre, Napoleon, Lenin,
Stalin, Hitler – and Roosevelt? What if Eckart,
Lenin, Baruch and Marshall are all connected?
What if there is one single idea behind
All the warlords who have shaken our century?
It's a nightmare I prefer not to think about.

(29th March. Washington. Gen. Marshall, US Chief of Staff, with aide.)

Aide. A protest from the British to Roosevelt.

Marshall. Now the President is sick I have taken charge
Of the conduct of the war. I will reply.
Ike is the most successful field Commander.
It is incredible that the British
Do not trust his military judgement now.
Churchill has phoned Ike at SHAEF to protest,
He's urged our forces to turn north, not east.
It is not clear whether he wants the Ninth
Army back, or the capture of Berlin.
Churchill says the fall of Berlin will send
A signal to the German people and will have
A psychological effect on German resistance.
Ike here denies he has changed his plans.
He says the British have called for one big thrust
Which he gave to Bradley; that his aim
Is to defeat the German forces, not turn aside
With many thousands of troops; that he has one thought:

The early winning of this war. It makes sense to me.
Only Ike is in a position to know
How to fight his battle, and exploit the changing situation.
Montgomery is slow, overcautious.
He wants to be sure before he attacks.
He'll mass hundreds of tanks when thirty will do.
He won't take risks. Eisenhower, for all his faults,
Is the best Commander the Allies have.

(Exit aide.)

(Alone.) The young American civilisation
Like Rome after two Punic wars, is poised
For a world role: involved in Europe and
Controlling the older Russian civilisation
Financially, American money will
Undertake urban reconstruction and spread
American influence and use Moscow
To end the European empires before
Our coming world rule. I wanted to squeeze
Europe, contract it to the east.
I did not want the Allies to take Berlin.
And I made sure, through Ike, they did not, so
The post-war world is America's, not Europe's.
Baruch did well when he identified Ike
And promoted him as the instrument
For our larger long-term, global purpose.

(31st March. Rheims, Eisenhower's HQ. Eisenhower and Bedell Smith.)

Bedell Smith. Sir, a wire from Churchill: "Why should we not
Cross the Elbe and advance as far eastward
As possible?" He says the Russian Army
May take Vienna, that we must not give
The impression the Russians have done everything,
That we must avoid "the relegation
Of His Majesty's Forces to an unexpected
Restricted sphere". He says Britain is being
Relegated to an almost static role
In the north, and that the British cannot now enter
Berlin with the Americans. He says, "I do not
Consider that Berlin has yet lost its
Military and political significance."
He's very critical.

Eisenhower. I am upset by that.
Say, I have not changed my plan. I still intend
To send Monty over the Elbe, but towards
Lübeck, not Berlin, to keep the Russians out
Of Denmark, an important objective.
Say I am disturbed and hurt that he should suggest
I have "relegated" his forces, or "restricted" them.

(31st March. Rheims. Eisenhower's HQ. Eisenhower and Bedell Smith.)

Eisenhower. A further signal to Montgomery:
"You will note that in none of this do I mention Berlin.
That place has become, so far as I am concerned,
Nothing but a geographical location,
And I have never been interested in these. My purpose is
To destroy this enemy's forces and his power to resist."

(1st April. The Kremlin, Stalin's study. Stalin, Antonov and Shtemenko.)

Stalin. Cable Eisenhower that Dresden is the best place
For the AEF and Red Army to meet.

(He chuckles quietly.)

Add, "Berlin has lost its former strategic significance,
The Red Army will allot secondary forces
To capture the German capital in
The second half of May." Do not add that
Berlin is our primary objective,
We have allotted a million and a quarter men.
And aim to take it by mid-April; or that
I want it taken now in frantic haste.

(Enter Molotov, Beria, Malenkov, Mikoyan, Bulganin, Kaganovich and Voznesensky in no order of precedence. Also Zhukov and Koniev. They sit and form the State Defence Committee which runs the Soviet war.)

Stalin. I have received information about the Allies' plans
Which are less than allied. The Little Allies
Intend to get to Berlin ahead of the Red Army.
(*To Shtemenko.*) Read the telegram from the Soviet mission
To Eisenhower's HQ.

Shtemenko. "The Ruhr will be surrounded.
The Allies will advance to Leipzig and Dresden.
British and American forces under Montgomery
Will attack north of the Ruhr and take Berlin
Before the Soviet Army. This is Montgomery's plan."

Stalin. Well, who will take Berlin? We, or the Allies?

Koniev. We will take Berlin, and before the Allies.

Stalin. So that's the sort of fellow you are! But how
Will you do it? Your main forces are to the south.

Koniev. Don't worry, comrade Stalin. We will organise them.

Stalin (*nodding*). Zhukov.

Zhukov. The men of the First Belorussian Front
Are ready now. We are nearest to Berlin.

Stalin (*smiling*). Very well. You will both stay in Moscow
And prepare your plans. You will report them
To the Stavka within forty-eight hours.
We shall pay attention to your starting dates.

(Aside.) He quotes Livy and Pushkin, this Koniev,
But in February at Korsun, he massacred
Thirty thousand trapped Germans, crushed their tanks
While the Cossack cavalry slashed with sabres.
He carries a library of classics
But the mind of a brutal exterminator.

(2nd April. Brunen, Montgomery's HQ. Montgomery and Dawnay.)

Montgomery. There is nothing more to be done. The advance
To the Elbe is off, we have to halt. I must
Hand over the Ninth tomorrow, and without it
I cannot advance to the Elbe between Hamburg
And Magdeburg and must wait near the Ruhr. It's strange
That Eisenhower, who has been impatient for
Reckless advance, should halt us now when I could
Be seizing Holland, Bremen and the North German
Ports, and keeping Denmark from the Russians. Churchill
Has had to accept that I am relegated
To a secondary role. To Roosevelt he
Has expressed his "complete confidence" in Ike,
And his "admiration for his great and shining quality,
Character and personality", adding that
He still feels the AEF should take Berlin.
He has sent Ike a copy of this message.
For the record, write that I consider
It useless to continue to argue with
The American Generals as they cannot see
My point of view, and that I have decided
To make no comments of any kind
On the American plan, and to adopt
A policy of complete silence. They are wrong!

(3rd April. The Kremlin, Stalin's study. Stalin, Zhukov and Koniev.)

Stalin. I have heard you both, and your plans agree.
Zhukov's eight armies are along the Oder,
And on the Neisse from Guben to Schwedt
Koniev's five armies are along the Neisse.
Your two fronts will attack simultaneously.
The starting date, we agree, the sixteenth of April,
One month earlier than I told Eisenhower.
I expect Berlin to fall in twelve to fifteen days.
Koniev. Where will my front boundary be? It affects
Whether I get to Potsdam or Berlin.

(Stalin takes a coloured crayon and draws a line on the map.)

Stalin. The line goes as far as Lubben. If the Germans
Offer heavy resistance to the east of Berlin
And Zhukov is delayed, you can strike from the south.
Whoever breaks in first, let him take Berlin.

SCENE 2. THE DEFENCE OF BERLIN

(4th April. Berlin, the Führer bunker. The conference room. Hitler with Krebs, Guderian's replacement.)

Hitler. The Soviet preparations for an attack
On Berlin are simply a deception,
A secondary thrust. The main attack
Will come round Prague, which we must defend.

Krebs. But Führer –

Hitler. No, Schörner has written:
(*Reading.*) "Remember Bismarck's words 'Whoever holds
Prague holds Europe.'" Schörner is loyal to me,
He is facing Koniev, he has been hanging
Deserters from trees with placards round their necks.
I promote him to Field Marshal, and transfer
Four of Heinrici's divisions from the Oder
To defend the Reich in Czechoslovakia.

(5th April. Berlin, the Führer bunker. The conference room. Heinrici with Krebs.)

Heinrici. Half my armour taken. Now twenty-five
Divisions face one hundred and ninety-two
Russian divisions on a hundred-mile front.

(Krebs takes him in to Hitler who wears tinted green dark glasses, shuffles and shakes his hand limply. Bormann and Krebs sit behind him on a bench, Heinrici stands on Hitler's left, Eismann stands on Hitler's right. Keitel, Himmler and Dönitz sit at the table.)

Krebs. You know Heinrici and Colonel Eismann,
His operations chief. They will now give
Their report on the Oder front, and then return
To their headquarters.

Heinrici. Führer, gentlemen,
The Soviet armies are building for a huge attack.
The main thrust will be against Busse's Ninth Army.
I am doing everything to strengthen
Our defences there. I am taking troops from the left,
Manteuffel's Third Panzer Army, but they
Are of poor quality: Hungarians,
Russian ex-prisoners, young boys. We have no
Artillery or ammunition.

Krebs. There will soon
Be a delivery of artillery.

Heinrici. I need
More than promises. When the spring floods go down,
Rokossovsky, who is heading for Zhukov's right,
Will attack Manteuffel on our left.

We need to strengthen the Ninth Army round
Frankfurt, and I propose that the fortress there
Should be abandoned, releasing thirty thousand
Men who can help with our defence.

Hitler (*harshly*). I refuse to accept this. It is like Küstrin.
I had this argument with Guderian.
There must be no withdrawals from fortresses.

Heinrici (*patiently*). Sir, Eismann has the figures in a paper.

(Eismann lays a paper before Hitler.)

My Führer I feel that it would be wise
To give up the defence of Frankfurt.

Hitler (*nodding*). Krebs, the General is right. Prepare the order.

(The other Generals are astonished. Heinrici is impassive but exchanges glances with Eismann. Enter Göring, noisily. He shakes Hitler's hand.)

Göring. I'm sorry I am late, I've been visiting
My Luftwaffe troops on Heinrici's front.

(Göring sits between Dönitz and Keitel.)

I found everything ready, the men well-armed.

Hitler. No one is doing what I want. Fortresses
Are essential. In Posen and Breslau
We have tied up countless Russians. Fortresses
Should be defended to the last man. History
Has proved me right. The fortress at Frankfurt.
Must not be abandoned.

(Hitler falls back, trembling in his chair.)

Heinrici (*patiently*). My Führer, we need
Troops to strengthen Busse's position, we must
Withdraw troops from the fortress at Frankfurt

Hitler. Six battalions only, I will not allow
Any more.

Heinrici. My Führer, the Oder front
Cannot resist the Russian attack. The transfer
Of the Panzer divisions south has left us men
Without experience like the paratroops
Göring has just visited –

Göring. I will not listen
To scurrilous talk about my paratroops.

Heinrici. I am saying they are untrained. Experience
Has shown that untrained men are shocked by war.

Hitler. Then units must be trained. There is still time
To train them before the battle.

Heinrici. That can be done.
But we have no reserves. All troops must go
Straight to the front line. We will lose a division

Each week, we have no replacements. I need
A hundred thousand men, or in a few days
Our resistance will come to an end.

(There is a silence.)

Göring (*standing*). My Führer,
I will give you a hundred thousand men
From the Luftwaffe.

Dönitz. I will give you twelve thousand men
From the navy.

Himmler. My Führer, the SS will give
Twenty-five thousand men for the Oder front.

Hitler (*to Krebs*). Bring in Buhle.

(Enter Major-General Buhle, Reserve Army, from the ante-room in the corridor, or reception room.)

How many men can you supply
For the Oder front?

Buhle (*drunk on brandy*). Thirteen thousand men.

Hitler. You have a hundred and fifty thousand men

Heinrici. I am grateful for this generosity,
But they are untrained and will be against
The most battle-hardened troops in the world.
They will be massacred.

Hitler. These reserve troops
Can be in a second line eight kilometres
Behind the first. The front line will absorb
The shock, the second line will get used
To battle, and can fight if the Russians break through.

Heinrici. I must have my Panzers back.

Burgdorf (*whispering*). Finish. No more.

Heinrici. My Führer, I must have my Panzers back.

Hitler. I had to take them away. The Russian attack
Will be against Prague, not Berlin, so Schörner
Needs them more than you. You will have to face
A secondary attack.

Heinrici (*staring in amazement*). In that case, I cannot guarantee
To fight off the Soviet drive towards Berlin.

Hitler (*shouting*).You must have faith, you must believe in success.
You must fill every commander with confidence.
You must radiate faith and inspire your troops.

Heinrici. My Führer, faith alone will not defeat
The Russians.

Hitler. Colonel-General, if you believe
This battle can be won, it will be won.
If your troops believe it, you will have victory.
Miracles can happen to those who believe the most.

(Heinrici looks at them all, then leaves. Krebs stops Heinrici in the ante-room or reception room.)

Krebs. Don't count on more than thirty thousand men.

(5th April, evening. Berlin, the Führer bunker. Goebbels to Hitler in his office or study.)

Goebbels. I have brought Carlyle's *History of Frederick the Great.*
Hitler. My favourite book,
Goebbels. I want you to read the turning-point
In the Seven Years War of 1762.
Prussia was at war with Russia, Austria and France.
Frederick said he would commit suicide
If there was no improvement by February 15th.
His greatest enemy, Tsarina Elizabeth, died.
Her successor made peace and became an ally,
Prussia went on to victory.
Hitler *(listening).* Wonderful.
Goebbels. The story told by a British writer, is
Prophetic and it agrees with the horoscope
That was cast the day you became Chancellor.
In the second half of April, all difficulties cease,
And Germany will begin to rise again.
It is in the horoscope.
Hitler (*nodding*). Yes, I believe it.
Goebbels. I have issued this proclamation to the troops:
"The Führer has declared that there will be
A change of fortune in this very year.
The true quality of genius is its awareness
And its certain knowledge of approaching change.
The Führer knows the exact hour of its arrival.
He has been sent to us by destiny,
So that we… shall testify to the miracle."
Good night, my Führer.
Hitler. You alone are loyal.

(Exit Goebbels. Hitler puts down the book and sits before his picture of Frederick the Great.)

I am waiting for a miracle, like you,
Frederick. I believe it is coming.
But it is taking a long time, and I feel
The pressure of my February 15th.
Help my will to manipulate the power.

(8th April. Schönberg. Bonhoeffer dressed as pastor with Vassiliev Kokorin and ex-prisoners.)

Kokorin. That was a wonderful service. I now believe
The war is over, and there will be no more trials.

Bonhoeffer (*smiling*). I am still trying to believe that I
Have been learning Russian from the nephew of Molotov.

Ex-prisoner. Bad news. Dohnanyi was tried on Friday
At Sachsenhausen, lying on a stretcher,
Only semi-conscious. He was then executed.

(Bonhoeffer is silent. He makes the sign of the cross. Two SS men appear.)

SS Man. Dietrich Bonhoeffer?

Bonhoeffer. Yes?

SS Man. Please come with us.

Bonhoeffer. Where to?

SS Man. To Flossenbürg, to join your friends.
Canaris, Oster, Sack, Strünck, Gehre.

Bonhoeffer. A trial?

SS Man *(nodding).* All conspirators have to be dealt with
Before the Red Army reaches Berlin.

Bonhoeffer. I submit myself to the will of God.

(8th April. Hanover, the outskirts. Eisenhower and Bradley.)

Bradley. We encircled the Ruhr a week ago,
And when the Ninth Army was removed from
Monty's control, Simpson's advance units
Were across the Weser. I told him to proceed
East to Magdeburg, seize a bridgehead over the Elbe
And go down the autobahn towards Berlin.
I want to draw off resisting Germans
From east of Berlin, to help the Russians.
I am merely seeking to establish
A diversionary threat, and then go no farther.
I want to keep Hitler out of the Alps,
But Simpson has one thought: to take Berlin.

Eisenhower (*nodding*). I wrote to Marshall yesterday, that we should
Capture Berlin if it is feasible
As we proceed on the general plan,
But that it is militarily unsound
To make Berlin a major objective
As it's only thirty-five miles from the Russian lines.
Marshall approves this strategy,
And has not discussed Berlin with the Chiefs of Staff.

(Enter Major-General Bolling.)

Alex, when you have taken Hanover,
Which you will easily now you have a map
Of the city's defences from a captured German,
Where are you going next?

Bolling. General we are
Going to push on ahead to Berlin, and nothing
Can stop us.

Eisenhower (*holding his arm*). Alex, keep going. I wish
You all the luck in the world. Don't let anyone stop you.

(9th April, 5.30 p.m. Flossenbürg. Bonhoeffer kneels and prays. He rises and takes off his prison garb, and a guard leads him, naked, to a gallows with steps. He again prays, then climbs the steps, composed, and is hanged by another guard. The first guard takes down the body and picks up his possessions.)

Guard (*dragging Bonhoeffer's body*). He's to be burned with all his possessions
Same as Canaris and the other bomb-plotters.

(9th April, 5.30 p.m. Rheine, Montgomery's HQ. Montgomery with Dawnay.)

Montgomery. Write to Ike: "It is quite clear what you want.
I will crack along on the northern flank.
One hundred per cent, and will do all I can
To draw the enemy forces away
From the main effort being made by Bradley."
Dawnay. Right, sir.
Montgomery. We are moving fast, and as we move
I am shocked at the scenes of destruction I see.
Civilisation reduced to rubble, ruin.
At Munster, tank tracks crunched the carved faces
And limbs of medieval stone statues.
Here at Rheine, bombed shells of houses
And a pervading stench of decay and death.
We are driving through a Hell, and though I am pleased
We are liberating the wretched, I feel sad
That American mistakes have prolonged it all,
That we are not now in Berlin, and at the end.

(Silence. Exit Dawnay.)

(Aside.) A civilisation is a gathering
Round an idea that can be found in its new religion.
It grows and expands, it has a style or art
And architecture, maintains an ordered life
In cities, an economy, fine manners.
Civilisation is the highest aspirations
Of the finest minds in a civilisation.
Barbarism is the lowest expression
Of the sickest minds in a civilisation.
Something went wrong in this one. All this rubble.
We caught the illness of barbarism.
A disease had to be cured, and at what cost.
Is the price of civilisation to purge
A civilisation from time to time?
Is the idea it grew round still here, your Church.
O Lord, your cathedrals round which Europe grew?

(13th April. Berlin, the Führer bunker. The conference room. Hitler at his daily conference with his Generals, who include Jodl and Keitel. Ribbentrop is leaving. Krebs has escorted him to the door.)

Ribbentrop. The Führer is in the seventh heaven.

(Exit from ante-room or reception room. Krebs accepts two messages and returns.)

Krebs. The US Ninth Army now have two bridgeheads
Across the Elbe near Magdeburg.
Hitler. The situation is under control, as
The new German Twelfth Army, commanded by
General Wenck is ready to counter-attack.
Krebs. My Führer, there is also a message
That Vienna has fallen to the Red Army.
Hitler. That is of no consequence. The war will be won
In Berlin. When Zhukov's diversionary attack
Begins, our units will fall back from the Oder
And form a magnet that will draw the Soviets
To it. German armies will then attack
From around it and destroy the enemy
In a decisive battle. I will remain
In Berlin to inspire the victory.
Jodl. But, Berlin is not safe.
Keitel. You should leave the city,
My Führer, as you can inspire our forces,
Should you not be in the safety of Berchtesgaden?
Hitler. I will not consider it. I will remain with the troops.

(14th April. Rheims, Eisenhower's HQ. Eisenhower, sombre, with Bedell Smith.)

Bedell Smith. Sir, General Bradley on the phone for you. *(Exit.)*
Eisenhower. Brad, how are you? I'm just recovering.
I've been to the concentration camp near Gotha,
I've never experienced an equal sense of shock.
What? The bridging operation's a success?
I'm glad to hear that. Brad, what do you think
It might cost us to break out from the Elbe
And take Berlin? You could take it fairly easily.
But once there lose a hundred thousand men?
Say that again? A high price to pay
For a prestige objective and then fall back
To let the Russians take over? That's what I think.
But Simpson thinks he can beat the Red Army there.
Huh-huh. Bye Brad.

(He puts down phone.)

Kay. Can I join you, General?
Eisenhower. Not just now Kay. I have a decision to make.

Kay. You always have a decision to make.

Eisenhower. But this
Is some decision. If I get it wrong,
It will return to haunt me. Send Beetle in.

(Exit Kay.)

I am in agony, for I must make a choice
That will have a universal application,
Affect all mankind, and men still unborn,
Shape history, and if I become President,
Tie my wrists with the rope of my own decision.
Should Berlin be American or Russian?
Militarily, I have only fifty thousand men
Who have advanced two hundred and fifty miles
In two weeks, and have already stretched
Their lines of communication. Racing them
Are two and a half million men, who are fresh,
Who have prepared two months, and are twenty miles
Away, and who must surely get there first.
To try and lose is worse than not to try.
Politically, if I win, I present Truman,
A new President, with the choice of rescinding
The Yalta agreement, that Berlin is Soviet,
And, worse, I raise doubts in Stalin's mind
About American good faith over Yalta.
He is anyway quick to say we are misleading him.
Then a hostile Soviet army, like a tidal wave,
Two and a half million men against our small force,
May keep going into Normandy, to the Atlantic
And swallow all that we have won from Hitler.
It is better not to anger the Russians.
It is wiser to stick to our agreement
And not risk what our hard-won efforts have gained.
Politically, I know, since the First World War,
There have been men in Washington, and London,
Who seek to promote Communist world rule,
Who would dearly love Stalin to have Berlin.
They follow their own agenda, not SHAEF's.
I have my suspicions about some men, including
Two who promoted me from nowhere to
This pinnacle from Lieutenant-Colonel
To Supreme Commander within three years,
Two years nine months. My career progressed
When, like Churchill, I wrote to Barney Baruch.
Now I must choose on military grounds,
As the voice of SHAEF, and shut out all interests.
I am in anguish as I must decide
A course I know to be politically wrong,
But militarily right. Judgement is like love,

You weigh everything up, and then choose heart
Or head. I must choose head, but my heart yearns.
Berlin, Kay. A leader reviews, decides,
Communicates, inspires, and then defends,
And I will have a lot of defending to do.

(Enter Bedell Smith.)

Bedell Smith. You sent for me, sir?

Eisenhower. Telegraph the Combined
Chiefs of Staff. I intend to hold a firm front
On the Elbe; to undertake operations
To the Baltic at Lübeck, and to Denmark;
And to thrust in the Danube Valley to join with
The Russians and break up the southern redoubt
So Hitler can't continue the war in the Alps.
As the thrust on Berlin must await the success
Of these three operations, I do not include
It as part of my present plan, the essence of which
Is to stop on the Elbe and clean up my flanks.

(15th April. Wiesbaden, Bradley's HQ. Bradley and Simpson, who has just stepped off a plane.)

Simpson. *(shaking hands)*. You have received my plan to take Berlin?

Bradley. Simp, I have to tell you right now. You have to stop
Right where you are on the Elbe. You are not
To advance any further towards Berlin.

Simpson. I could be in Berlin in twenty-four hours.
Where did this come from?

Bradley. From Ike. My orders
Are to defend the line of the Elbe. The supply
Columns are being attacked with German tanks
And assault guns, round Hanover and elsewhere.
We hold the bridgehead as a *threat* to Berlin.

Simpson *(depressed)*. So this is the end of the war for us. This is
As far as we go. We're not going to Berlin.

(15th April. The Oder front. Heinrici and Eismann, his operations chief.)

Heinrici. Waiting, waiting for the Russians to attack.
The tension is in the atmosphere and every limb.
When will the attack come? Now? Tomorrow?
We are outnumbered ten to one, and no
Intelligence reports contain hard facts.
I can only speculate, among possibilities.
I must imagine that I am Zhukov.
I plan to pull my troops back from the first barrage
So the shells fall on empty trenches and –

Eismann. Sir, Speer is here. *(Exit.)*

Heinrici. I cannot be distracted now.

(*Enter Speer with two chiefs, of roads and state railways.*)

You come when I am deep in thought. The attack.

Speer. I want your support. Hitler has ordered
A scorched earth policy: industrial plant,
Bridges, power stations to be destroyed. Why should
They be destroyed when Germany is already defeated?

Heinrici. I will do what I can to stop the blowing up.

(*Re-enter Eismann.*)

Eismann. Sir, Reymann is here.

Heinrici. Ah Reymann, thanks for coming.
You know these gentlemen? I wanted to explain,
Army Group Vistula cannot take Berlin
Under its command.

Reymann. I cannot defend Berlin.
My position is hopeless.

Heinrici. If the Russians break through,
I will withdraw to the north or south, there will be
No battle within Berlin. Do not count on
Units I may be ordered to send in.

Speer. The Führer has ordered you to destroy
Most of the nine hundred and fifty bridges
Across our waterways, which carry water
Gas or electricity. If you do, Berlin
Will be paralysed for a year and millions
Will catch disease and starve. Do not obey
The Führer's orders, I implore you.

Reymann. In that case
I will be shot.

Heinrici. On this map, I will mark
Bridges that carry no services and can be blown.

(*Later. Heinrici, alone again.*)

Heinrici (*concentrating*). When will it come? What would I do if I
Were Zhukov? (*Suddenly.*) Tomorrow, in the early hours,
Of course. Chief of Staff, an order to Busse.
Move back to the second line of defence.

(*16th April. Chuikov's command post on a hill overlooking Reitwein on the Oder's west bank. Zhukov, Chuikov and officers leave their dugout for observation post. Three red flares.*)

Zhukov (*quietly*). Now, comrades, now.

(*A bombardment.*)

Chuikov. No answer from German guns.

(*Soviet searchlights.*)

Zhukov. Out of the trenches, throw yourselves at the river.

Chuikov. They are launching pontoons. See the assault boats.
Zhukov. Your infantry men are silhouetted.
Chuikov. Dust. I can't see. Visibility zero.
Zhukov. Radio telephones. Where are the messengers?

(He receives a message.)

*(Irate.)*Tank detachments and guns falling behind.
The bridges across the Old Oder and canal
Have been blown. Reports of quagmires and mines.
No air support because of the dust clouds.

(Silence. Sound of guns.)

Heinrici's drawn us into a dust trap.
Gunners are opening fire from the Seelow Heights.

Soldier. We have a bridge.
Chuikov (*to Zhukov*). Our troops are pinned down.
Zhukov. What the hell do you mean?

(16th April, 1 p.m. Moscow, the Kremlin. Stalin's study. The phone rings.)

Stalin. Zhukov. You expect to take the Seelow Heights
This evening? Tanks? I would use bombers as well.
Oh, Koniev is doing well. He has crossed the Neisse
And is pressing forward without too much resistance.

(He chuckles as he rings off.)

(16th April, towards midnight. Moscow. Stalin's study still. Again the phone rings.)

Stalin. Zhukov. You haven't taken the Heights yet?
Three houses on the edge? That's not a breakthrough.
You should not have departed from the plan.
You should have sent in the First Tank Army
Where General Headquarters ordered. What do you mean,
The slower now, the quicker you'll take Berlin?
It's easier to crush the enemy on a battlefield
Than in a city?

(Paulina appears. Stalin loses patience.)

We have been thinking
Of ordering Koniev to take his tank armies
From the south towards Berlin, and Rokossovsky
To cross the river and attack from the north. Good night.

(17th April, just after midnight. Berlin, Ministry of Propaganda. Goebbels returning to his office.)

Goebbels. Ribbentrop has asked diplomats to leave Berlin.
I have visited Busse near Küstrin, and I told
The officers of the miracle that saved
Frederick the Great, and urged them to believe in fate.

What are those fires?

Staff 1. The Adlon Hotel, and
The Chancellery, both hit in the evening raids.

Staff 2 (*calling out*). Herr Reichsminister, Roosevelt is dead. It is true.

(Enter Goebbels' press officer, Rudolf Semmler.)

Semmler. It is confirmed. Truman is the new President
Of the United States.

Goebbels. This is the turning-point.
Is it really true? Open the best champagne.
I must telephone the Führer. *(On phone.)* My Führer,
I congratulate you. Roosevelt is dead.
You recall the horoscope. The stars proclaim
That the second half of April will be our turning-point.
Providence has struck down your greatest enemy
On Friday the thirteenth, it is like the death
Of Tsarina Elizabeth for Frederick the Great.
(Putting down phone.) The Führer is overjoyed. It's the miracle.

★*(17th April, morning. Moscow. Stalin's study. The phone rings.)*

Stalin. Koniev. Where are your headquarters? An old castle
Near Cottbus. Your tanks are rolling forward. Good.
Koniev, Zhukov has not yet broken through.
You can turn your tank armies towards Berlin
At Zossen? What map are you using? The one
To two hundred thousand.

(Stalin searches his map.)

You know the German
General Staff Headquarters is at Zossen?
Very good. Turn your tank armies towards Berlin.

(18th April morning. Zhukov's HQ. Zhukov and his Chief of Staff, Popiel.)

Zhukov. All commanders are to go for the front line
And speed things up. Koniev is heading for Berlin.
I want the Heights taken, whatever the cost.
Then full speed to Berlin. (*Exit.*)

Popiel. He is roaring like a lion.

(18th April, evening. Moscow. Stalin's study.)

Stalin. Zhukov. Chuikov has the Heights and has broken
The Germans' first line of defence? Good, good.
The cost, *thirty* thousand men? They gave their lives
For their motherland.

(He puts down the phone.)

Thirty thousand,

That's war. Hitler attacks me with Barbarossa,
Seeking to eradicate all Soviet Jews.
And fifty million die in repelling him.
Thirty thousand to drive towards Berlin.
This blood will achieve territory, our rule.
I took over from Lenin a divided land,
I killed six million to unify it,
Reshape its borders, rule a vast expanse
From the Baltic to the Pacific from a strong centre,
A union that will now expand westwards,
As far west as the Allies allow my troops.
If they weaken, I am ready to push on
Till the whole continent, from the Atlantic to the Pacific,
All Euro-Asia, will be under Red rule.
The Byzantine Russian civilisation
Is in its greatest extent under my Tsardom.

(He stands before a picture of Ivan the Terrible.)

Ivan the Terrible, I look to you.
You approve of everything that I have done.
You know our Byzantine Russia must expand
At the expense of the Holy Roman Empire
And the Habsburgs, and their successors,
And the British Empire, the non-Orthodox faiths.
You know Russia's Byzantine destiny
To rule the world through a creed that captures minds.
Autocracy, through Communism, is our way.
I keep the tradition of the Russian Tsars,
I unite our lands and cultures with the glue of power,
And keep it stuck together by repelling force.
Thirty thousand is a small price to pay.
A human life is material which the State
Can remould into a peasant or a soldier.
It i*s* while it is alive and then, is nothing.
Death is like a curtain drawn across a window.
It is nothing, it has no significance.
It is the end of life, as evil is the end of good.
There is no sacredness, men have bodies
That can be used like shell cases. There is nothing
Sacred about life, no good. Ivan *you* knew.
We have millions of material units
To sacrifice, to expand our empire.

(20th April, just after 12 noon. Berlin, the Führer bunker. The refreshment room outside Hitler's office. Hitler in greatcoat and peaked cap with Bormann, Goebbels, Ribbentrop, Speer, Himmler and Jodl, all in uniform. Göring arrives in plain olive uniform.)

Burgdorf. The Führer rose at eleven and is greeting
Well-wishers on his fifty-sixth birthday.

Göring. My Führer, congratulations on your birthday.
I passed Goebbel's banners on my way here.
One, stretched across a ruined building, says
"We thank our Führer for everything."

Speer. I was just saying to the Führer, there are posters
On doors, walls, windows, saying "Should Berlin
Share the fate of Aachen and Cologne. No!"
The early morning shelling of Berlin has brought
Out resistance. What news of the air raid?

Göring. A thousand American bombers, silver
Planes glistening in the blue sky, too high for flak.
We have no German fighters to attack them.
They had a clear run and have knocked out
The city's water, gas, electricity and sewage
Supply. There is no power. The bombardment
Ten minutes ago was from Zhukov's long range guns.
The Allies' "happy birthday" to our Führer.

Goebbels (*taking message*). My Führer, the news is bad. Weidling, Heinrici
And Busse have been overrun, as you know.
Reymann says it is no longer possible to defend
The capital. All possible troops must be
Dispatched to the front.

(Hitler nods tiredly.)

Göring. My Führer, you should leave Berlin.
You should fly south and go to Berchtesgaden.

Speer. Führer, he is right, you should leave today.

Hitler. No, I will remain. I must inspect the parade.

(He climbs the stairs to the wrecked Chancellery garden with Burgdorf, Axmann, Krebs, Fegelein and the others. Göring goes to a phone. Speer returns.)

Speer (*to Göring*). I can remember when, for his birthday parade,
Forty thousand men and hundreds of tanks
Took three hours to salute him while he stood
On a dais. On his fiftieth birthday
I rode with him in his car as he stood,
Arm raised in salute; slowly we passed hundreds
Of thousands of soldiers standing silently.
He was like Tamberlaine in a chariot.
The Army had increased sevenfold in four years,
The Rhineland, Austria, Sudeten and Czech lands
Behind, Danzig, East Prussia and the Polish
Corridor ahead, and who could stop him?
Each man had sworn an oath to his Napoleon.
He was magnificent. I knew then it was war.
When he spoke the world trembled, and we were all proud
To follow him. Now a few SS men and

A few boys from the Hitler Youth. He's trembling
Fumbling for their hands, patting their cheeks, pinning
Iron Crosses on those Axmann points out,
He's staggering unsteadily, saying
The enemy will be destroyed outside Berlin.
It's pathetic. I couldn't bear to watch any more.
I know Stauffenberg's bomb began the decline,
And Dr. Morell's syringe has played a part,
But I can't help feeling power festers in the flesh
And infects the blood till the health corrupts.
I've seen it in other leaders. Power ruins
Like a drug an athlete takes to enhance
Performance; soon the body craves for more
And is addicted, and the doses must be increased,
And his health is past its peak. So it is with him.
Amid the trappings of power, he is impotent.
He was the mightiest in the world, and now
He looks like a drug addict who's terminally ill.

Göring. It's finished, you are right. I am leaving Berlin.
This morning I learned that Rokossovsky is
Twelve miles from my estate in north east Berlin,
Karinhall. I have packed my possessions –
Things I brought back from countries we conquered,
Souvenirs, you might say – into twenty-four lorries
And blown up the building. I could hardly bring
Myself to press the plunger, but I did.
That beautiful castle is now rubble.

Speer. And the lorries?

Göring. Parked at the Luftwaffe game park
Near Potsdam. I'm joining them now. We will drive
In convoy to my house at Obersalzberg.
Do not be trapped in Berlin.

Speer. I certainly won't.

(Hitler returns down the steps. The Führer's conference begins in the conference room.)

Krebs. The overall picture shows Berlin is
Half encircled. In the north, Rokossovsky
Has cut Manteuffel from the rest of the army.
Zhukov is in the north-east suburbs and
Will attack to the north-west. On the Oder,
Busse is encircled – but not Weidling's Panzers –
And Koniev has cut it off from the south.
Koniev is attacking the north and at Zossen,
In the south. Four hundred aircraft have been destroyed.
The Americans have trapped Model in the Ruhr pocket
With over three hundred thousand troops, while
Montgomery is attacking Bremen and the Elbe.
The Americans have taken Leipzig and Nuremberg,

The French Stuttgart and the Poles Rothenburg.
Berlin can only survive if Busse's Ninth Army
Is pulled back from the Oder.

Hitler. No withdrawal.
I refuse to allow any withdrawal.

Krebs. Heinrici
Reports that all along the line, men are retreating,
On foot and in vehicles. He is trying
To prevent them, but he now needs more troops.

Hitler. Send the Muller Brigade from Wenck's Twelfth Army.

Krebs. Führer, without transport will they arrive in time?

Hitler. Heinrici must take Reymann and Berlin
Under his command.

Göring. My Führer, I am now convinced
You must leave Berlin. Planes are standing by
At Tempelhof to fly out you, Keitel
And Jodl.

Hitler. If the Russians and Americans
Cut Germany in two, the northern half
Will be under General Admiral Dönitz, and I
Transfer the command to him now. The southern half
Will be under Kesselring, but I retain
The command in case we fight on from the Alps.

(Silence. The Generals all talk among themselves. The conference is over.)

Jodl.

Jodl *(surprised)*. Yes, my Führer?

Hitler. You have been a good
OKW operations chief. I shall fight
As long as the loyal fight beside me,
And then I shall shoot myself.

Göring. Good bye, Führer.

Hitler. Good bye.

(Exit Göring.)

Speer. Where are you going, Himmler?

Himmler. To meet Schellenberg
At Zietten. And you?

Speer. To Hamburg, for a radio speech.

Himmler. We are on the same side. You will call on
The people to stop fighting. I know. While I,
Let me say I am preparing peace.

(All leave except Hitler. Enter four secretaries, Traudl Junge, Gerda Christian, Christa Schröder and Johanna Wolf with schnapps. They toast him in the ante-room or refreshment room outside his office or study.)

Secretaries. Happy birthday.

(Enter Eva Braun. She sits beside him. Silence.)

Eva. Happy birthday.

Hitler. Who else would have come back
To Berlin when they could have gone to the Berghof?

Junge. Can I ask you something, as it's your birthday?

Hitler. Go on.

Junge. We're all wondering, will you leave Berlin?

Secretaries. Yes tell us.

Hitler. I can't leave. Why I would feel
Like a lama turning an empty prayer wheel.

(All laugh.)

I must resolve this war here in Berlin
Or go under. I must stay and see it through.

(Silence. Hitler and Eva rise and go to his office or study.)

Christian. He believes the war is lost.

Schröder. That's clear.

Wolf. She knows it.

Junge. She defied his orders five days ago.
She chose the room next to his bedroom, she made
Soldiers carry down her bed and dressing-table.

Christian. She's here for the end.

Wolf. And we?

Junge. Our clothes are dirty.
We have nowhere to wash, we stink.

(Eva returns.)

Eva. Come on,
We're going upstairs to the old Chancellery
To our private apartment.

(They go up the stairs with Bormann and Dr. Morell who carry champagne and a gramophone which is put on the one circular table. Hitler joins them. Outside Soviet guns.)

Let's drink and dance.

Bormann. We only have one record.

(He plays 'Red Roses Bring You Happiness'. He and Morell dance with two of the secretaries. Hitler and Eva dance, he tiredly, she radiantly. Bormann plays it again, 'Red Roses'. A terrific crash.)

A Red shell.

(A telephone rings. Bormann answers. Another crash. All return to the Führer bunker rapidly, leaving the glasses.)

(21st April, 9 a.m. Zossen HQ. Krebs takes a phone call, with Boldt.)

Krebs. Yes Kränkel. Your attack on Koniev has failed?
Heavy losses? We must evacuate.

(He phones the Führer bunker.)

Burgdorf
It's Krebs, from Zossen. The counter-attack has failed.
Koniev's tanks are advancing, we must evacuate
Headquarters. Please ask the Führer for permission.

(He waits.)

(*To Boldt.*) The answer is no.

(11 a.m. Krebs again with phone. Kränkel stands before him, covered in mud. Tank sound above.)

Krebs. Burgdorf. It's Krebs again.
Kränkel is here, the Russians have taken Baruth.
A Russian tank is passing overhead now.
We again request permission to move out.

(He waits.)

(*To Boldt.*) The answer is again no.

Boldt. A Russian camp for us.

(1 p.m. Krebs again on the phone.)

Krebs. Burgdorf. It's Krebs again. There is a line
Of Russian tanks, unopposed. If we do not move out
There will be no one to direct the war.
Everyone is out of contact – Busse, Weidling.

(He waits.)

All OKW operations staff are to go
To the army barracks at Krampnitz. The Führer
Wants me at his daily conference, half an hour
Earlier than usual, at 2.30? And Loringhoven?
We must leave at once.

(Krebs puts down the phone, shaking his head in disbelief.)

(Chorus of Berliners.)

Chorus. We have extra rations for Hitler's birthday:
A pound of meat, half a pound of rice and beans.
We leave our shelters and queue outside food shops,
At every water pump or standpipe.
The Russian guns are shelling our city.
We live in cellars and come out for food.
When will our misery end? When will Hitler give up?

(21st April, Soltau, Montgomery's new TAC HQ. Montgomery and Earle.)

Montgomery. Dempsey fears he can't cross the Elbe until
May the first after he takes Bremen.
I want you to go forward to Lüneburg
And visit General Barker and obtain his plan
For crossing the Elbe with 53rd Division.
But be careful, there are enemy troops
On the edge of Lüneburg Forest.

Earle. I'll take
The shortest route north of the Forest, I'll
Take John with me, we'll be back by nightfall.

(21st April, 3 p.m. Berlin, the Führer bunker. The conference room. Burgdorf and Wenck. Keitel nearby.)

Burgdorf. The Führer is in good spirits now. He was shocked
To learn how close the Soviet guns have reached,
And by the Russian occupation of Zossen
And its underground rooms. It was bad news that
Model has shot himself in the Ruhr. But Schörner
Has counter-attacked Koniev and held him up –
And has been made Field Marshal. And Dr. Morell
Has given the Führer an amphetamine injection
And the Führer's valet Linge has given him eye drops,
Five times the normal dose. They contain cocaine.

Wenck *(to Hitler)*. Führer, I am about to counter-attack
American forces in the Harz Mountains
And on the Elbe.

Hitler. That's excellent. My maps.
Tell Koller at Werder to send jets from Prague
And attack Soviet forces south of Berlin.

(Burgdorf attempts to ring Prague.)

I will pull back the 56th Panzer Corps
To the edge of the city. They can then link
With Steiner's SS German Panzer Corps.

Burgdorf. Führer, we have no communications with Prague
And anyway, jets cannot fly as the Russians
Control the skies. And 56th Panzer Corps
Are already on the edge of Berlin.

Hitler (*transfixed*). Steiner will be the saviour of Berlin.
Every available man is to be given
To Army Detachment Steiner, to push south
And cut off Zhukov's advance, while Busse goes north.
It's a bold plan which cannot fail to succeed.
Get Steiner.

(Burgdorf dials and hands Hitler the phone.)

(*Excitedly*.) Steiner, all your SS troops

Are to be disbanded at once and sent into battle,
Every man between Berlin and the Baltic
Must join the attack I have ordered.

(He puts down the phone.)

We will mobilise thousands of new troops
And send them against the Russians, while Wenck attacks.

(The phone rings.)

Burgdorf. Steiner? What do you mean, you don't know what's going on?
The Führer has just explained. You have no troops
Or weapons?

Hitler. Let me speak to him. Steiner?
The Russians will suffer their greatest defeat
Before the gates of Berlin, thanks to you.
Officers who do not comply will be shot.
You are answerable with your own head.
The fate of the Reich capital depends on your success.

(He puts down the phone. The phone rings.)

Burgdorf. Koller? You want to know where to send the men
You have raised?

Hitler. Let me speak to him. Are you still
Questioning my orders? I thought I had made myself clear.
All Luftwaffe personnel are to join Steiner
For a ground attack. Any officer who
Keeps back men will forfeit his life within
Five hours. Your own head is answerable.

(The phone rings.)

Burgdorf. Heinrici? Steiner must mount his attack.
You cannot reject the order, it has come from the Führer.

(He rings off.)

Hitler. Heinrici is a good General, but can be defeatist.
I will give him a new Chief of Staff, a Nazi,
General Trotha. He will see Heinrici complies.
Reymann is also defeatist. I will replace him
With Kaether of the Waffen SS, Reymann
Will take over the defence of Potsdam.

(Enter Eva with Junge and Christian, the two secretaries.)

Get changed and fly south, all of you.

Eva (*taking both his hands*). But you know
I am going to stay here with you.

(Hitler kisses her lightly on her lips.)

Christian. We will stay here.

Hitler. I wish my Generals were as brave as you.

(21st April, 6 p.m. Earle and Poston in jeep, Earle driving.)

Earle. This route is nearer the Forest we'll be back by dark.

(Shooting. Poston fires back with a sten.)

Poston. I'm out of ammunition.

(Earle drives the jeep at the machine-gunner, killing him. Poston and Earle are thrown out of the jeep and are surrounded by boys in German uniform. Earle tries to wipe a location map and is shot in the back and falls three yards from Poston, who is lying unarmed, hands above his head.)

N-no. Stop – stop.

(Poston is bayoneted above the heart and is killed. The German boys remove a watch and valuables and go. Earle is still alive and is found by a farmer.)

(22nd April, morning. Berlin, Führer bunker. Hitler and Dr. Morell.)

Hitler. I feel ill, not as I did yesterday.
Dr. Morell. I gave you a huge dose of amphetamine.
Shall I give you an injection of morphine?
Hitler. You want to put me to sleep so I can be
Flown out of Berlin to Berchtesgaden.
As my Generals want. You are plotting with them.
Dr. Morell. My Führer, no.
Hitler. You will move out of your room at once.
I will give it to the Goebbels, who are loyal.
Goebbels knows I will stay in Berlin.

(22nd April. Soltau. Montgomery by his caravan. Dawnay.)

Dawnay. Sir, a signal from Peter Earle.
Montgomery. Ah, he hasn't been captured.
Dawnay. Sir, it's bad news. Earle is alive, but Poston.
(Reading.) "Regret to report John Poston killed at
Eighteen hundred hrs Saturday twenty-one
April." Earle's in 212 Field Ambulance
Station. Poston was last seen in a ditch.
I'm sorry, sir.
Montgomery. Kit, send my physician,
Hunter, to check Earle's condition, and then
Recover Poston's body.

(Montgomery turns on his heel and goes into his caravan.)

(Later. Meadow by trees. Poston's funeral. Montgomery weeps by Poston's grave. Tindale, a Scottish Presbyterian padré. Henderson talks with Hunter, the doctor, away from mourners.)

Henderson. There was a touching message from Churchill.
He's like a father weeping for a son.
John was Monty's youngest LO, and had been
With him longest. Twenty-five, and he had
A Military Cross and bar. Did you know he
Fell in love with a girl in London, and asked
Monty what he should do, as there was competition
And he needed some leave to propose,
And Monty said "Take my plane, fly to London
And keep the plane there till the girl says Yes."

Hunter. He was a vivid fellow with a current
Of energy. He was always up to something.
Monty was very devoted to him, I think
He represented something Monty couldn't be
Because he's so disciplined, on a tight rein.
A meadow on the forest edge, with full
Military honours….

Henderson. He's still weeping openly.

Hunter. It's a kind of breakdown. He's been inconsolable.
He's suffered so many blows and disappointments –
His command being taken away, then given back,
Then taken away again – and he's no family,
And for a long time he's suppressed his hurt feelings
And carried on and let some out in prayer.
"A" Mess has been his family, and I'm sure
You're right, he's looked on Poston as a son,
And his death has brought out what should have come up
Months ago. It's cleansing, healthy, cathartic,
It's good. I predict he'll snap out of it now.

Montgomery *(to the padré)*. He would certainly have sailed with Drake.

(Later. Henderson and Dawnay. De Guingand.)

Dawnay. It's SHAEF at Rheims on the phone. What do I do?

(Montgomery appears at his caravan door. He has "snapped out of it".)

Montgomery. SHAEF? I'll take it. Yes, yes. Of course I realise
The need to get to Lübeck before the Russians.

(He rings off.)

(Expostulating.) This is adding insult to injury.
Freddie, get on to Whiteley and inform him
I've always been well aware of the urgent
Need to reach and cross the Elbe quickly, that
It was SHAEF that stopped this plan a month ago,

And removed the Ninth Army, weakening and
Slowing down Twenty-First Army Group, and
If the Russians get to Lübeck and Denmark
Before we do, SHAEF should accept full blame.

(Later. Montgomery and Dawnay.)

Dawnay. Sir, a cable from General Eisenhower.
It reminds you of the importance of
Lübeck and the Danish Peninsula,
And says SHAEF will do anything to ensure
The speed and success of your operation.

Montgomery *(quietly)*. Justifying themselves, that's all they're doing.
They've sent seven armies to cut off Hitler's
Last stand in the Alps, when he isn't there, leaving
Two armies to clear Holland, North Germany
And the North Sea ports, and secure Denmark from
The Russians who are now on the Oder.
Two armies out of nine, and they want more speed!
It's the planning of nincompoops.

(22nd April, 3 p.m. Berlin, Führer bunker. The conference room. The daily conference. Hitler, Bormann, Krebs, Keitel and Jodl in the ante-room or reception room.)

Keitel. The Führer's face is yellow and expressionless.

Jodl. He's sacked his doctor and has withdrawal symptoms.
He can't concentrate. He needs amphetamine.

(In the conference, Hitler twice gets up and goes to his private office and returns, abstracted.)

Krebs. The situation is grim – Koniev has taken
Our main munitions depot, Busse's army
Is trapped. Weidling has retreated to the Olympic village.
We are trying to arrest him.

Hitler (*not listening*). Where is Steiner?
Steiner's Army Detachment. How is his attack?

Krebs. Führer, Steiner has not yet given the order
For an attack.

(Silence.).

Hitler. Everyone is to leave the room
Except Keitel, Jodl, Burgdorf, Bormann
And you Krebs.

(The others leave. Hitler then raves, trembling.)

I ordered Steiner to attack.
Why has this not happened? I am surrounded
By cowards, traitors, incompetents and Generals
Who are insubordinate and disloyal.
Even the SS cannot be trusted, and tell lies.

Everything is collapsing. The war is lost.
I will stay here and lead the final battle.
I shall not fall into the hands of the enemy.
When the last moment comes, I will shoot myself.

(He crumples into a chair.)

(Sobbing.) It's over. The war is lost. I shall shoot myself.

(Silence. All are embarrassed.)

Bormann. There is still hope. You must remain in charge.
But you should move to Berchtesgaden, and
Continue the war from there.
Hitler. You can all leave
Berlin. I will stay and go down with my troops.
I have taken my decision.
Keitel. This is madness.
You must fly to Berchtesgaden tonight
So there is continuity of command
Which can no longer be guaranteed in Berlin.
Hitler. You go. I order you to go. I stay.
East Prussia held while I was at Rastenburg,
It collapsed when I moved back to Berlin.
Keitel. I will stay with you.
Jodl. And so will I.
Hitler. I want
Keitel, as Commander of the armed forces,
Göring, my deputy, and Bormann to fly
Down south tonight.
Keitel, Bormann. We refuse.
Hitler. If there is negotiating to be done,
Göring is better at that than I am.
I told Schörner, my death may now remove
The last obstacle that prevents the Allies
From making common cause with Germany
Against the Russians. Either I fight and win
Here, or I die here. That is my final
And irrevocable decision.

(22nd April, evening. Berlin, Führer bunker. Hitler's office. Goebbels, Magda and Hitler.)

Goebbels. All afternoon the telephone has been ringing.
And voices have implored you to leave Berlin:
Dönitz, Ribbentrop, Himmler, a visit from Speer.
But I have moved into Morell's room to stay
With you.
Hitler *(quietly).* I know, that's why you have Morell's room.
Goebbels. I will die in Berlin. I told Speer,
My wife and children are not to survive me.
The Americans would brainwash them

	And turn them against me and my memory. They would make propaganda from my death.
Hitler.	Speer told me you felt this. You are loyal. You are the only one I can really trust.
Goebbels.	I am honoured that we have a room so near to yours. Magda has told the children they will soon Be given chocolates so they will not be sick.
Hitler.	I have now sorted my documents. Those not burned Up in the garden, to be kept for posterity, Are being flown to Munich tonight in ten aircraft.
Goebbels	(*quietly*). In the coming days, know that I am with you.

(They clasp hands.)

(22nd April, night. Berlin, Invalidenstrasse, waste ground. It is raining, there is a glow from fires. Sixteen discharged prisoners under SS guards in two groups. The first group consists of Bonhoeffer's two brothers-in-law, Klaus Bonhoeffer and Rüdiger Schleicher, and the poet Albrecht Haushofer. They carry bags with their personal possessions. Herbert Kosney is nearby.)

Haushofer.	Why are we leaving the Invalidenstrasse?
SS Officer.	We're taking you to a new prison, there is A short cut through here. From the Lehrterstrasse Prison, through here.
Bonhoeffer.	This is the ruined Ulap Exhibition hall.
SS Officer.	Wait for the others. If You try to escape, we shoot.
Bonhoeffer.	Look at those fires.

(Haushofer puts down his bag.)

Haushofer.	I'm working on a sonnet. It's just bright Enough to read the opening lines. Listen. Your brother-in-law Dietrich would say yes to this. "There are times when only madness reigns, and then It is the best that hang."

(The other 13 prisoners have caught up. The SS men push them all forward.)

SS Officer.	Stand against the wall.
Bonhoeffer.	They're going to shoot us. Faces towards the wall.

(All sixteen are shot in the back of the neck and fall. One, Herbert Kosney, is only wounded in his neck. The SS guards go. Kosney raises his head. Haushofer's hand still clutches his poems.)

(22nd April, evening. Lübeck, the Swedish consulate. Himmler and Schellenberg with Count Bernadotte.)

Himmler: The Führer's great life is drawing to a close.
I feel released from my oath of loyalty.
I expect to be the new Führer, the Overlord
Of the German peoples, and I authorise you
To convey my offer of surrender to
The Western Allies and General Eisenhower.
The German Army will continue to fight the Soviets.
Till the Allies advance and relieve us.

Bernadotte. I will leave
For Stockholm at once.

(23rd April, morning. Wenck's HQ in the Wiesenburg forest near Magdeburg. Wenck. Keitel arrives.)

Keitel. The Führer orders you to drive east and
Save Berlin and the Führer.

Wenck. Very well.
I will dictate an order to the Army now.

(He goes and returns with a document.)

Your copy to take back to Berlin.

Keitel. Thank you. (*Exit.*)

Wenck (*to aide*). Call my staff to the next room.

(He stands and, just visible, talks off stage.)

Keitel has left
With my order to you to go to Berlin,
Which has been requested by the Führer. I
Have no intention of leading you to Berlin.
We will hold our position on the Elbe
As an escape to the west, and we will drive
Close to Berlin and get out as many men
As we can.

(23rd April, 3.30 p.m. Berlin, the Führer bunker. The conference room. Hitler and Keitel at the end of their conference.)

Keitel. Führer, can I persuade you now to leave Berlin?

Hitler. No.

Keitel. You may find yourself cut off. I need
To know of any peace negotiations.

Hitler. It is too early to talk of surrender.
It is better to negotiate after
A local victory, such as the battle for Berlin.

Keitel. I am not satisfied with that answer.

Hitler (*tiredly*). I have approached Britain through Italy
And Ribbentrop is coming here on this.
I will not lose my nerve, you can rest assured.

(Keitel and Jodl leave the ante-room.)

Keitel. He will die here.
Jodl. Göring is the only hope
I have sent Koller to the Berchtesgaden
To tell Göring of Hitler's collapse and tears
And to ask him to intervene.

(23rd April, 6 p.m. Berlin, the Führer bunker. Krebs and Burgdorf receive Weidling and his intelligence officer, Capt Kafurke.)

Weidling. Why has the Führer ordered my execution?
Krebs (*coldly*). For deserting your position and moving to
The Olympic village.
Weidling. I can prove I have been
Within a mile of the front line for days.
And nowhere near the Olympic village. What
Is going on?
Burgdorf. There has been a misunderstanding.
You will see the Führer now. What is your position?
Weidling. Busse has ordered me to withdraw as Soviet
Tanks are advancing.
Krebs. The order is cancelled.
You will defend Berlin.
Weidling. Kafurke will phone Dufving
And reverse the order.
Krebs. We will speak to the Führer.

(Krebs and Burgdorf leave.)

Weidling. It was irresponsible to relieve me
Of my command.
Krebs. The order will be revoked.
Hitler will speak with you.

(At the door Weidling's revolver and holster are removed. He goes into the ante-room or refreshment room past Ribbentrop and on into the office or study, Hitler rises from a table of maps. His face is bloated, his eyes look feverish, his hands and left leg tremble. He grins.)

Hitler. Have we met before?
Weidling. You decorated me, oak leaves on my
Knight's Cross.
Hitler. I recall the name, but not the face.
Now your position.

(Weidling points it out on the map.)

You will stay in Berlin
And take over the southern and eastern sectors.
Wenck is coming from the west, Busse from the south-east,
Steiner's army detachment from the north.

(Weidling leaves Hitler. To Krebs outside.)

Weidling. Berlin is a graveyard.

(Fade on Weidling.)

(The Führer bunker, Hitler's office. Hitler and Bormann.)

Bormann. A cable from Göring. (*Reads.*) "My Führer, in view
Of your decision to remain in the fortress
Of Berlin, do you agree that I take over
The total leadership of the Reich,
Will full freedom of action at home and abroad,
As your deputy, in accordance with your decree
Of 28th June 1941?
If no reply is received by twenty-two hundred hours
I shall take it for granted that you have lost
Your freedom of action, and shall consider
The conditions of your decree as fulfilled,
And shall act in the best interests of our country...."

(He hands the cable to Hitler.)

Hitler (*stunned*). What do you think of this?
Bormann *(softly).* It is treasonous.
Hitler. Göring?
Bormann. Führer, I have a radio message
From Göring to Ribbentrop, ordering him
To go to Berchtesgaden if nothing
Is heard from you by midnight. Göring wants
To start peace talks at once.
Hitler (*devastated, incredulously).* Göring, Göring
(*Pulling himself together.*) Tell the SS to arrest him. Strip him
Of all offices and titles. Göring. A traitor.

(Bormann's eyes gleam as he leaves Hitler. Fade on Hitler.)

Bormann *(alone).* A word here, a raised eyebrow there, no more.
I do not have to suggest my rivals come down.
Kluge, Rommel, Rundstedt, Model, I've seen them fall.
Göring, Himmler, I have had them in my sights
For months, no years. And others too. Burgdorf,
Guderian, Krebs, Jodl, Keitel, Goebbels.
I remember things and bide my time, put on
An oafish air so they do not suspect
My cunning, my deviousness. The way
Of advancement is to be at hand, of use,
To flatter the confidence of a great man,
And knock out the others one by one, secure
Their confidence by taking their side, suggest
A course of action here, an indiscretion,

Then undermine them by subtle reports
Which parade the misdeed unobtrusively,
Then arrange for them to have a disaster,
Then bring it, reluctantly, to the great man's eyes,
And then dispatch them on his authority,
Until in the end all have gone save you and him.
But what if I have to flee before the prize?
And flee I shall. There will be no trace of me
If the Russians put an end to my grand schemes.

(24th April, 10.45 a.m. Berlin, the Führer bunker. The reception room. Krebs, his adjutant Loringhoven, and Boldt, his ADC.)

Loringhoven. I am not pleased to have moved here last night.
Boldt. Nor me. It is a doomed place. But what
Can we do? We are professional soldiers.
Loringhoven. Hourly reports. You on Berlin, me Germany.
What can we say? The war is finished.
Boldt. This bunker doesn't look very secure.
The concrete roof has fallen in, the floor
Is ankle deep in water with wobbly planks,
The air is unhealthy. I don't like it here.
Krebs. Come in, you two.

(They move into Hitler's office or study. Hitler is with Goebbels and Bormann.)

Führer, our hourly reports.

(He lays two papers before Hitler who reads them and looks at his map.)

Hitler (*shouting at Krebs*). The Oder is a natural barrier.
The Russian success can only be put down
To the incompetence of Manteuffel
And the other army Generals.
Krebs. Their men are untrained,
And reserves have been transferred
For the attack to the north of Berlin.
Hitler. It must take place
Tomorrow, no later. Pass that on now.

(Krebs signals to Loringhoven, who leaves the room.)

Krebs. Steiner will lead the attack.
Hitler. The Waffen SS
Are arrogant and incompetent. I will not have
Steiner in command there. Weidling is the man.
Krebs. We nearly had him shot.
Hitler. He will save Berlin.
Appoint him commandant of the Berlin
Defence Region, responsible to me.

(25th April. Chorus of Berliners.)

Chorus. Germany is cut in two, Koniev and Hodges
Have met on the Elbe. At dawn this morning
As we cowered in cellars, the Russian attack began.
A barrage of artillery, pounding
Our houses into rubble, starting fires,
Raining shells onto our squares and gardens.
Then the tanks, crushing barricades, blowing
Apart any building which had a sniper.
Then the infantry, not down open streets
But under cover of ruins, creeping
To cellar doors with grenades and flamethrowers.
Half a million Russian troops, and hundreds
Of tanks against sixty thousand of us,
Pounding our city to a pile of rubble,
And a thousand fires and columns of thick smoke.
We are frightened of what the Russians will do to us.

(25th April, afternoon. Berlin, the Führer bunker, which receives a direct hit from a shell. Bits of concrete fall from the ceiling.)

Krebs (*coughing*). Turn off the ventilators, they are sucking
In fumes and smoke and dust instead of fresh air.
Loringhoven. The telephone's not working.
Boldt. We are cut off.
To the north Steiner attacked and advanced for miles,
But has been forced back.
Hitler (*tiredly*). Under Steiner's leadership
The attack was bound to fail.

(25th April, 10 p.m. Berlin, the Führer bunker. The conference room. Weidling arrives for a conference. Hitler with Goebbels, Bormann, Krebs and Burgdorf. Also Mohnke and Axmann. Weidling shows a map with a ring on it.)

Weidling. This is the Soviet ring. We are being forced
Inwards to the centre of Berlin.
Hitler. Berlin
Must be defended to the end.
Goebbels. Yes.
Bormann. Yes.
Hitler. The East-West road can be a landing strip.
Axmann, five thousand boys on bicycles
Can hold the bridges.
Weidling (*disgusted*). Yes, Führer.
Hitler. Jodl,
Speed up relief. Steiner must attack south-west.
Busse must link up with Schörner and with Wenck.

(26th April, evening. Berlin, the Führer bunker. The conference room. The daily conference.)

Krebs. We had some good news yesterday, the disunity
Between the Americans and Soviets
About the sectors to be occupied.
And now Wenck has launched his attack
And Busse is fighting towards him.

(Hitler is holding a torn map.)

Hitler. And Steiner?
Krebs. He has not started his attack.
Hitler. He is useless.
Krebs. And there is a report that Soviet troops
Are using the U- and S- Bahn tunnels.
Hitler (*in a rage*). The tunnels must be flooded immediately.
Krebs. But Führer, our own troops use them, and trains
Take the sick and wounded to hospitals,
And thousands of refugees –
Hitler. Blow up what keeps
Out the Landwehr canal and flood the tunnels.
Krebs. It will be a human disaster. A wall of water
Will pour through the tunnels, many will be killed.
Hitler. Flood the tunnels. They do not deserve to live.

(Chorus of Berliners.)

Chorus. Misery, there is no end to it. We crouched
In our underground command posts in the stations,
A cascade of water swept through, people fought
Round the ladders, many were trampled. The
Torrent rose a foot then dropped. Many had drowned.
There were floating bodies, screams, cries in the dark.
Where can we shelter if not underground?
Who has done this to us? Who flooded us?

(27th April, evening. Berlin, the Führer bunker. Hitler's office. Eva Braun and Hitler.)

Eva. You were looking for Hermann.
Hitler. Fegelein. He
Cannot be found. Besides being your brother-in-law
He is Himmler's representative here.
Eva. He has rung me this evening. He said that you
Must leave Berlin, and that if you will not,
I must leave alone.
Hitler. What did you reply?
Eva. I said
He should not antagonise you, and that Gretl
Is about to give birth to his child in Bavaria.
Hitler. He has an apartment.

Eva. Off the Kurfürstendamm.
At 10 to 11 Bleibtreustrasse.

(27th April, later that night. Berlin, the Führer bunker. The social room next to the adjutants' room. Bormann, Krebs and Burgdorf, drunk.)

Burgdorf. I tried to bring the army and party
Closer, but my officer friends despise me,
And say I am a traitor to the officer code,
That my idealism is wrong.

Krebs. May I remind you,
We are with Bormann.

Burgdorf. The party leaders have sent
Hundreds of thousands of young officers
To their deaths, not for the Fatherland but for
Their own megalomania and high living.
You have trampled our ideals in the dirt,
Our morality, our souls. Human beings
To you are nothing but uses for your power.
Our culture goes back hundreds of years.
You have destroyed it, and the German people.
That is your guilt.

Krebs. Remember who you are with.

Bormann. There's no need to be personal. Others
Have got rich, but not me, I swear.

Burgdorf. What about
Your estates? Your, your....

(He passes out. Bormann laughs and pours himself another drink.)

(28th April, 5.30 a.m. Berlin, the Führer bunker. Hitler's office. Bombardment in progress. Hitler and Boldt. Bormann, Krebs and Burgdorf slumped asleep.)

Boldt. The ventilation system has been off too long.
I have a headache and am short of breath.

(A crash brings part of the ceiling down. Hitler puts a hand on Boldt's arm.)

Hitler. What gun was that? Could it penetrate here?

Boldt. A hundred and seventy-five millimetre
Heavy artillery. In my view, it
Cannot destroy this bunker.

(Hitler is relieved.)

There is no telephone.
Reports are brought by runners braving shells.

**(28th April, 6.30 a.m. Crossroads near New Brandenburg. Keitel with Heinrici and Manteuffel.)*

Keitel. You did not tell me yesterday that Manteuffel's
Units would retreat, contrary to Hitler's
Orders, and mine.

Heinrici. I cannot hold the Oder,
And I do not intend to sacrifice the lives
Of my soldiers.

Manteuffel. I shall withdraw further
When I have reinforcements.

Keitel. There aren't any.
The Führer's order is you will hold your position.

Heinrici. I shall not give that order.

Manteuffel. My army
Only takes orders from me.

Keitel. It is outrageous
That you should defy the Führer's orders,
And mine. You will have to bear responsibility
For your defiance before history.

Manteuffel. The Manteuffels
Have served Prussia for over two hundred years,
And have always accepted responsibility
For their actions.

Keitel (*to Heinrici*). If you shoot a few thousand men,
There will be no retreat.

Heinrici. Look, thousands of exhausted men.
Why don't you shoot them. Go on.

Keitel. From now on
Follow OKW orders.

Heinrici. How can I follow your orders
When you are out of touch with the situation?

Keitel. You will hear more of this. (*Exit.*)

(Manteuffel's men emerge from behind trees with machine pistols. They had Keitel covered.)

(28th April, 7 p.m. Berlin, the Führer bunker. The conference room. Hitler and Krebs.)

Krebs. The Russians have appointed a commandant
Of Berlin. Orders by Berzarin have
Appeared in Alexanderplatz. The Russians
Have started raping German women.

(Bormann ushers in Lorenz, press officer. Enter Goebbels.)

Bormann. Führer,
Something that you should know.

Lorenz. The BBC
Have reported that Himmler has offered the Allies

An unconditional surrender in
The name of all our troops.

Hitler. Himmler? *Himmler?*
Can it be? First Göring, and now Himmler?
I always thought him trustworthy and loyal.
Has he gone behind my back on so important
A matter? It is the most shameful betrayal
In history. Bormann, Goebbels, come with me.

(Hitler takes Bormann and Goebbels to his conference room, leaving Krebs and Lorenz in the ante-room or reception room.)

Bormann. Führer, we have Himmler's representative,
Fegelein. We found him with his mistress
In his apartment, drunk. He has betrayed
Eva's sister, and his master has betrayed you.

Goebbels. Bring Fegelein.

(Bormann snaps his fingers in the reception room. Enter Fegelein under guard.)

Did you know Himmler would offer
The Allies unconditional surrender?

Fegelein. No, I swear I didn't.

Bormann *(wheedling).* Someone must pay.
For Himmler's treachery.

Hitler. You are close to him.
You knew.

Fegelein. No, Führer, I implore you, as
The husband of Eva's sister.

Hitler. Shoot him.

Fegelein. No.

Hitler. Take him upstairs into the garden
And shoot him.

Fegelein. No, please. I am innocent.

(He is taken away, protesting his innocence. A shot is heard. Then another. Hitler goes out to the sickroom, where Greim sits.)

Hitler. Greim, you are to leave for Plön and arrest Himmler.
A traitor must not succeed me as Führer.
You will take letters with you.

SCENE 3. THE FALL OF HITLER

(28th April, evening. Berlin, the Führer bunker. The conference room. Traudl Junge, who has been asleep for an hour, goes to Hitler with her secretary's dictation pad. Burgdorf is outside.)

Burgdorf *(to Junge).* He's been sitting in his private quarters,

Not moving, his face quite expressionless.
He's thinking about Himmler's betrayal.

(The table in his study has a white cloth with AH on it. Silver dinner service, eight champagne glasses.)

Hitler *(alone).* I made European civilisation
Replace its weak, impure, democratic way
With a stronger, purer stance. But Churchill and
Montgomery stopped me, calling in two
Outside civilisations like starving wolves –
America and Russia – to feed on
The sides of Europe's dying carcass. Both
Have torn off lumps of flesh: Paris, Warsaw.
Europe will now be weak, and as she bleeds
Her wounds will be impure, perhaps gangrenous.

(Enter Junge. Hitler winks at her. He stands at the map table.)

Hitler. I will now dictate my last political testament.
More than thirty years have passed since I made
My modest contribution as a volunteer
In the First World War, which was forced upon the Reich.
In these three decades, love and loyalty
To my people alone guided me in all my thoughts,
Actions and life. I never wanted war,
But it was forced upon the world by the machinations
Of international Jewry. The sole responsibility
For all the subsequent death and horror, including
The death of many Jews, lies with the Jews themselves.
But now the end has come I have decided
To remain in Berlin. I die with a joyful heart
In the knowledge of the immeasurable deeds
And achievements of our peasants and workers
And of a contribution unique in history
By our youth which bears my name.
I cannot, however, speak admiringly
Of the German officer corps which unlike me,
Has failed to set a shining example
Of faithful devotion to duty, till death.
Two of my most trusted Generals have let me down.
I expel Göring and Himmler from the party
And strip them of all office. They have brought
Irreparable shame on the whole nation
By negotiating with the enemy
Without my knowledge and against my will.
When I am dead, Grand Admiral Dönitz
Will be President of the Reich, and Supreme Commander
Of the Wehrmacht. Goebbels will be Reich Chancellor.
Bormann party Chancellor.

(He hands Junge a paper.)

Traudl, I have written
Who will hold the other offices of state.
I urge my successors to uphold the racial laws
To the limit and to resist mercilessly
The poisoner of all nations, international Jewry.
During the years of conflict, I was unable
To commit myself to a contract of marriage
So I have decided the day before the end
Of my earthly life to take as my wife the young
Woman who, after many years of faithful friendship,
Has of her own free will come to the besieged capital
To link her fate with my own. She will, according
To her wishes, go to her death as my wife.
For us, this will take the place of all that was
Denied us by my devotion to the service
Of my people. My wife and I choose to die
To escape the shame of flight or capitulation.
It is our wish that our bodies be burned at once,
Here, where I have performed the greater part
Of my daily work during the twelve years I
Served my people. That is all. Now type it, please.

(Junge looks at him, rises and goes through to her office and starts typing. Enter Goebbels, tears running down his cheeks.)

Goebbels *(to Junge).* Hitler has ordered me to leave Berlin
But I don't want to leave the Führer. My place
Is here, if he dies my life has no meaning.
He said to me, "Goebbels, I didn't expect
You to refuse to obey my last order."
I want to dictate my own will, which should
Be attached to Hitler's as an appendix.

(28th April, later. Berlin, the Führer bunker. The conference room. Hitler and Goebbels.)

Goebbels. No one in the bunker is legally
Empowered to hold a marriage ceremony.
Hitler. I must have a legal authority. I have been
Married to Germany. She is not worthy
Of me, she has failed me, and so I have divorced
Her, and by marrying Eva I will demonstrate
That I have rejected Germany for good.
Goebbels. I know a registrar who is in Berlin.
His name is Wagner.
Hitler. That is appropriate
We are approaching the Götterdämmerung.
Goebbels. I will send SS men to find Wagner.

(28th April, later. Berlin, the Führer bunker. In the conference room, or map room, Eva in a long black silk dress; Hitler in uniform; Wagner, Bormann, Goebbels, Gerde Christian, now senior secretary, Constanze Manziarly, Hitler's vegetarian dietician, Krebs, Burgdorf, Axmann.)

Wagner. I shall not ask the usual questions about
Aryan origins and hereditary disease.
Goebbels *(impatiently).* That's quite all right.
Wagner. And after the ceremony,
Two witnesses must sign.
Goebbels. Bormann and me.
Wagner. *(nodding).* Do you Adolf Hitler, take Eva Braun,
To be your wife?
Hitler. I do.
Wagner. Do you, Eva Braun,
Take Adolf Hitler to be your husband?
Eva. I do.
Wagner. I have the pleasure to pronounce you at law
Man and wife. Please sign the wedding contract.

(Hitler and Eva sign, followed by Bormann and Goebbels. Arm in arm, Hitler and Eva go to the refreshment room before the office or study and offer the guests champagne and sandwiches.)

Eva. *(chatting happily).* It's so good of you to witness our marriage.
I am so honoured to be the Führer's wife,
And so pleased that our long association
Has ended like this, I am so happy my Führer.
O look, Bormann has the gramophone.
I am afraid there is only one record, you know it.
(*The gramophone plays 'Red Roses'*.)
I must go outside to greet the others who
Have not been invited to our private party.

(She appears in the corridor outside, or reception room, and greets Junge, Wolf, Schroder, Boldt, Loringhoven and others who say "Congratulations".)

(29th April, 8 a.m. Berlin, the Führer bunker. The reception room. Burgdorf and Johannmeier.)

Burgdorf. You will now undertake a very important
Secret mission. You will take the Führer's
Last will and political testament out of Berlin
And give it to Field Marshal Schörner, who
Is now Commander-in-Chief of the army.
Zander, Bormann's personal assistant, will take
A copy to Dönitz, the new Head of State,
And Lorenz will take a copy to Munich,

Where National Socialism was born.

**(29th April, 12 noon. Berlin, the Führer bunker. The conference room. The bombardment stops. Silence. Conference conducted by Krebs. Boldt, Loringhoven, Weiss and Bormann.)*

Boldt. Soviet tanks are heading towards the Wilhelmplatz.
And have stopped five hundred yards from the Chancellery.
Wenck is out of contact at Werder.
Loringhoven. It
Would make sense if Boldt and I go to Wenck
And brief him direct.
Krebs. The Führer might not like that.
Bormann. I think it is a good idea.
Burgdorf. So do I.
Weiss. I'll go with them.
Krebs. I'll ask the Führer.

(He goes into Hitler.)

Führer, three officers
Want to break out of Berlin to brief Wenck about
The situation round the Chancellery.

(Hitler stares at his map.)

Hitler. Who are these officers?

(The three step forward.)

How will you leave Berlin?
Loringhoven. By boat down the Havel, at night.
Hitler. Yes, that is
The best way. I know where there is a boat
With an electric motor.
Loringhoven. We can find a boat.

(Hitler nods, rises and shakes hands with each.)

Hitler. Give my regards to Wenck. Tell him to hurry,
Or it will be too late.

(Outside the door the three men smile.)

Loringhoven. We have escaped.

(29th April, afternoon. Belsen. Montgomery. Henderson and Ernie, a private.)

Henderson. The Chief's upset. He ordered cameramen
To record "German bestiality" and he's made
The people in the neighbouring villages
Parade through the camp so they can see what was done
By their own countrymen.
Ernie. Yesterday we saw
Some Canadians so incensed that they took

The women guards to the edge of the camp where there
Are supple trees, they pulled two down and tied
A woman's legs to each and then let go
So she flew into the air and was torn apart.
They did several. I cocked my Browning, but
My commanding officer said, "Don't interfere
Or they'll turn on us."

(Enter Montgomery. Ernie withdraws saluting. Henderson is at hand.)

Montgomery. I don't like to see
The realities of war, the blood and bone.
It upsets me. I avoid seeing wounds.
A commander deals in fit soldiers, and this
Makes me ashamed to be European.

(Three Belsen figures have tottered near him.)

We knew the Final Solution was happening,
Ever since D-Day we've hurried the best we can.
But this was worse than I ever imagined.
If I had had sole command, the war would have
Been over last September, and those corpses would be
Alive. Their deaths are a German responsibility,
Of course, but if Eisenhower, Bradley and SHAEF
Had made better decisions, hundreds of thousands
Who are now dead would now be fully alive.

(Exit Henderson. More Belsen figures gather.)

(Aside.) War is the Devil's game. He inflates egos,
Urges land-grabbing, feeds envy and hate,
Delighting in the ruin that follows,
The destruction and sense of injustice
Smiling at a Paradise on earth destroyed,
At rubble and these puny, thin-armed men
Who resemble walking skeletons in Hell,
More cadaverous skulls with sunken eyes than what
I think of as starving human beings.
The Devil's onslaughts must be repelled, rebuffed
And my skills do this, but my skills, such as they are,
Are of a diabolical order, and for that
I feel self-disgust. The only cleanness
Is in my caravan after nine o'clock,
When I can be pure, and open my self, my heart
And be filled with the health-giving Light of God
And I do not know how it can help you now.
Poor wretch, you tear my heart with your cupped hand.

(The Belsen men kneel at his feet.)

(Aloud.) Get up.

Belsen man. Thank you, Montgomery, thank you.
Belsen men. Montgomery, thank you, Montgomery.

(Montgomery turns away, his eyes filled with tears.)

Montgomery. *(aside, moved).* Not a cupped hand, he's blessing me. He wants
Nothing, only to give his thanks – and I,
Six months late, am not worthy of his gratitude.
I would like to embrace him to demonstrate to all
Our common humanity, but a commander can't.
He is isolated from his fellow men
By the barrier of his command and decorum.

(Re-enter Henderson holding a jug and a chipped mug. He offers it to Montgomery.)

(Aloud.) Give each of these men a drink.

(29th April, later. Berlin, the Führer bunker. Hitler fondles his sheep dog.)

Hitler. Haase, Himmler has given me cyanide capsules.
He is not to be trusted, I want to know
If they work, or if they are to drug me
So he can hand me over to the Bolsheviks, alive.
Take Blondi, with Tornov. In the toilet. Now.

(Hitler fondles Blondi. Haase and Tornov take Blondi. Off stage a dog's whimpering is heard. Hitler winces. Haase returns.)

Haase (*quietly*). Instantly, my Führer.

(Hitler goes out to look. He returns and encounters Traudl Junge and Gerda Christian.)

Hitler (*handing them cyanide capsules*). I am sorry to reward your loyalty
And courage with such a parting gift.

(29th April, 7 p.m. Berlin, the Führer bunker. Bauer, Hitler's pilot at Hitler's office.)

Bauer. My Führer, you can still escape. I can
Fly you out. In a Junkers bomber with
A range of six thousand miles. I can fly
You to the Middle East or South America.
Hitler (*shaking his head*). You have carried Frederick the Great to all
My headquarters, now he is yours. Take him.
Bauer (*stunned*). Thank you, my Führer.
Hitler. I want my epitaph to be:
"He was the victim of his Generals."

(29th April, evening. Berlin, the Führer bunker. The conference room. Hitler's last conference.)

Burgdorf. My Führer, a report. Mussolini and his mistress –
Hitler. Dead?
Burgdorf. Shot by Italian partisans.
Hitler (*sombre after a silence*). How?
Burgdorf. He bared his chest and said, "Shoot me here."
They were left for dead, then hanged upside down.
Hitler *(after a silence).* No one will hang Eva or me upside down.
Weidling, tell me, what hope can you offer?
Weidling. Sir, there is no more ammunition, there are
No tanks, no Panzerfausts and no repairs,
Nothing. Everything must finish tomorrow.

(A long silence.)

Hitler. (*tiredly*). Mohnke, what do you think?
Mohnke. I agree with Weidling.
Hitler. Krebs.

(Hitler and Krebs confer.)

Troops may attempt to break out, but I
Absolutely forbid the surrender of Berlin.

(29th April, evening. Berlin, the Führer bunker. Hitler alone with his Lorenz coding machine.)

Hitler. Keitel, where are the advance units of
Wenck, Busse and Holste?

(30th April, 1 a.m.)

Burgdorf. Sir, Keitel's reply.
Hitler (*eagerly*). Yes, go on, go on.
Burgdorf. Wenck's Twelfth Army cannot attack Berlin,
Busse's North Army is encircled, and
To the north Holste is on the defensive.
Hitler (*after a silence*). The end. I shall not be hanged upside down.

(30th April, 3 a.m. Eva's sitting-room/bedroom. Hitler sitting alone on the settee, Eva asleep on her bed.)

Hitler. In 1940 I offered the British peace
On generous terms. I ruled from Norway to Spain.
I still don't understand why the British
Used up their imperial resources
By fighting a power that did not threaten them.
I said in July, only the US and Japan
Would profit from the end of the British Empire.
I was depressed when Japan took Singapore.
As we approached defeat, I became more
Ruthless, to make our soldiers fight harder.

Someone sitting watching me now, as if
I were talking in a doctor's waiting-room,
Must think I am pitiless, without remorse,
But Britain made me snarl like a wolf at bay,
That intransigent Churchill who threw away
The British Empire to corner me, when I
Did not want to threaten the British Isles
For which I, as a German, have a deep respect.
What did Britain do mostly in the war?
Killed Italians in North Africa and
Bombed German civilians. Why? I know why.
Bankers were behind us all, Churchill, Roosevelt,
Stalin and me, and wanted our cities destroyed
So they could lend their billions to rebuild.
Bankers and Zionists rejected my peace.

Eva *(stirring).* Adolf, my husband, my lord, my Overlord,
I love you very much. I adore you.

(Hitler embraces her.)

(30th April, 5 a.m. Hitler sitting, Eva sleeping.)

It is the Feast of Beltane, the thirtieth,
Walpurgisnacht, when witches meet on the Brocken
And revel with the Devil, the pagan day
Most suited to favourable reincarnation.
And now I must face my own fate. It was
Not supposed to end like this. Many times
I stood in the Hofburg Treasury and gazed
At the spear of Longinus, which pierced the side of Christ,
And called me to war and to rule the world,
And when I took Vienna, I went there
With Himmler, and held it in my hand, certain
That my destiny was to rule the world;
And to be crowned Kaiser Adolf the First,
Of a Third Reich that would last a thousand years;
And to destroy Jehovah by liquidating
The Jewish millions who worship him, so that
The power I serve could fill the vacuum.
It seems only yesterday that Eckart
And I discussed the Final Solution,
How we'd be on the side of divine good
Against the Jewish Satan, the demiurge
Jehovah who is responsible for all
The ills in the world, how we'd be
On the side of a power that opposes
The Jewish Satan and its Christian mask,
And do its work in this impure, tainted world.
My work's incomplete, three million more must die.
But the power that has vitalised my great will

And made me more feared than Napoleon
Is still abroad and still possesses me
And rejoices in universal destruction.
In Vienna I read Nietzsche and Schopenhauer,
And I have tried to bring in the Superman.
My will to power has dominated the will
Of my people and has possessed them all,
And I have left mankind more pure through it.
My power, I know, is a power of darkness, which
Has pierced Christendom and Jewry with its spear.
Lord of Darkness, I am ready for you.

Eva *(stirring).* Adolf, I love you, adore you, my husband.
Come to bed now, you have shed your burden.
You can be virile now you've put down your cares.
Now you have been released from your bond with
Germany, by the betrayal of your Generals,
You can love me without any sense of betrayal.

(30th April, 3 p.m. Hitler has finished lunching with his secretaries in the bunker's refreshment room.)

Traudl Junge (*smoking*). Look what Eva has given me. This coat.

Gerda Christian (*smoking*). Her silver fox coat with four-leaf clover
Entwined with her initials, E.B. It's beautiful.

Gunsche. The Führer wants to say goodbye to all his staff.

(Junge and Christian put down the coat. In the corridor, or reception room, outside the refreshment room Hitler walks down the line and murmurs a few inaudible words to each. Eva is with him, her hair done up and in black with pink roses on either side of a square neckline.)

Eva. Traudl, try to get out of here, you might
Make it. Give my love to Bavaria.

(Hitler and Eva go through the refreshment room into Hitler's office. Gunsche stands outside the door. Hitler sits on the left of the settee, picks up his gun and cyanide capsule and stares into space. He speaks more to himself than to Eva, who is more concerned about the practical business of dying.)

Hitler. And yet, and yet, now that the time has come,
Now that the time has come for me to die,
To release the vapour some call the soul,
What if I find, on the other side, millions
I have put before a wall, waiting to judge me?
I blew up Warsaw – only two houses
Remained standing – and so many places,
And all the extermination camps. Auschwitz-Birkenau,
In one month alone two hundred thousand Jews
From Hungary, one month alone.... The vision I had

In the First World War, of eliminating Jews –
And five out of eight million are now dead,
European Jews, that is, not the world's –
What if Jews too have an immortal *soul*
That comes from a divine web, a *good* whole?
Was I wrong? Will history judge me adversely?
For thirty years, I believed in power over men,
The Thule Society, Ariosophy.
I saw men as unclean souls, to be crushed
So that the world could be cleansed and transformed
For the pure souls who will channel the power.
And now that I must die, I wonder if
When I am the vaporous body in this flesh
I must pay for all I have done on this lower plane.
Why did I not think more about these things
When I heard the applause echo my words
In the Munich beer cellar, the Hofbrauhaus,
As I first announced the name "National Socialism",
When my mentor Dietrich Eckart urged me
To give myself to the occult for power?
Lord, fill me now with your power. Nothing.

Eva. *(summoning him back to the situation).* Adolf.

Hitler. I had a vision of a new Europe
Led by Germany, and in every state free peoples
Going about their business, living free.
There had to be a transitional phase –
Extermination camps and the rule of the gun –
But at the end, under one Overlord,
A great *union* of free democratic peoples
Who are anti-Communist, with a strong centre.
This may still come to pass, people may come to see
That even though my racial ideas are
Repudiated, I brought it into being,
It came out of my anti-Communist vision.
Every leader must keep things developing,
Must have something ahead to aim for, some goal,
To keep the support of his followers. If
There is nothing ahead, or a contradiction,
Then he is lost. My death is necessary
To release all German soldiers from their oath to me,
And so that Dönitz can negotiate a peace
And win the Allies over to oppose the Russians.
By this sacrifice, I will make possible
A German-Allied front against the Bolsheviks.
My sacrifice will turn the war around,
Will save Germany, wrest victory from defeat.
I had a vision and I improvised.
Nothing ahead. Nothing.

Eva *(holding him).* What are you thinking?

Hitler. I am remembering
How clean the air is in Berchtesgaden
And you reclining like a beauty queen
On the stone veranda in the sun, knee up,
Your bikini on, the mountains behind you,
Smiling above the green slopes while I loll,
My head on a cushion, and gaze at Paradise,
And there is nothing you could not make me do.
I, the master of the world, am bewitched by you,
I am your obedient and devoted slave.

Eva. You will do as I say, you will be my slave.
I will bite to commit suttee like an Indian's wife.
Then you will bite and fire. We will be together.

(Eva embraces Hitler. Fade on Hitler and Eva. Outside Magda Goebbels rushes down the corridor into the refreshment room and pushes past Gunsche into Hitler's office.)

Magda. Please leave Berlin, I don't want my children
To die beside me in this bunker.

Hitler. No.
Leave us.

Magda (*weeping*). He will not speak to me.

Gunsche. Too late.

Junge. Have your children had lunch? No? I will make
Ham sandwiches. There is fruit.

(A shot is heard. Gunsche waits and enters, arm raised in the Nazi salute. Hitler is on the sofa, left, leaning over the arm, his head hung down, blood dripping on the carpet. He has shot himself in his right temple with his 7.65 mm. Eva is curled up on the sofa, right.)

Gunsche. Cyanide.
He shot himself in the head to make sure.

Magda (*picking up a capsule like a tube, to Junge, of Eva*).
Cyanide.

(Gunsche picks up a knocked over vase of flowers. He examines Hitler and Eva quickly.)

Gunsche (*shouting*). Orderly, Linge. Bormann.

(Bormann, Goebbels and Axmann enter, arms raised in the Nazi salute, and view Hitler.)

Goebbels. My Führer dead. I want to go out on
Wilhelmplatz and stay there till I am hit.

(Goebbels, Bormann and Axmann follow as an orderly and Hitler's valet, Heinz Linge, wrap the bodies in blankets and carry them out. Junge follows Gunsche.

Magda stands and stares until Junge returns.)

Magda. So. Our world has ended. Well?

Junge. They carried them
Up the stairs and out into the garden above,
And laid them in a shallow trench. Then Kempka,
Hitler's chauffeur, came with three soldiers,
And sprinkled petrol on them from jerry cans.
Shells were falling round them, some very close.
And they tried to set fire to it, but it would not light.
Kempka made a spill from paper and set it alight
And threw it into the trench, and up it blazed
And black smoke rose above the funeral pyre.
All put out their arms in a Nazi salute,
Then ran back inside. They are still up there.

Magda. So died the man who would be Overlord
Of the whole world, feeling betrayed
By all he had trusted, doubting Göring and Himmler,
Save the noble woman who died at his side
And instead of a State funeral through Berlin
This Napoleon received a hurried bonfire
On a patch of waste ground under exploding shells.
A pitiful end.

(Fade on Magda. Krebs and Burgdorf have appeared at opposite ends of the bunker.)

Krebs (*alone*). He was a chancer. He restored German pride
After the humiliation of the First World War.
He took power by fairly constitutional means.
He did not plan war with Britain and the U.S.,
It somehow happened as a consequence of what he did.
His name is terror, under him there was terror
But at the centre was a fumbling man
Who lived from event to event, reacting mostly,
Blaming his Generals for the inadequacy of his plans.
His name is terror, he was responsible
For terror on a colossal scale, but
For all the amphetamine injections there was
Something indecisive at the heart of his vision.

Burgdorf *(alone, scathingly)*. So ended the life of a man who shamed
Germany, and its noble Prussian tradition,
Who dabbled in the occult, mixed weird ideas
From the drunkard drug addict "poet" Eckart,
The crazy anti-Semitic Rosenberg
And the "root race" nonsense of Theosophy,
And thought his foul butchery was doing good.
He never grasped that as all are from the One,
Souls are droplets from the divine thundercloud
Which veils the radiant oft-hidden sun,

And return to it as raindrops evaporate.
His racist philosophy conflicts with the One
And how the universe in practice works,
And can now be reduced to ashes, like himself.
I speak from a noble German tradition,
I think all Fascists and racists are to be pitied
For they are separated from the One
And therefore have a false view of the world,
Which they infect with their odious inadequacy.
I despise myself for having joined the army
And been caught up in such a foul episode,
And I am filled with self-disgust that I
Did not join Stauffenberg's plot and rid the earth
Of a creature who was a disgrace to humanity.

(Chorus of Berliners.)

Chorus. We have heard the good news. Our trials are over.
The dictator is dead, by his own hand,
Leaving a ruined Germany, ruined buildings,
Smashed plant and services, a heap of rubble.
We are overjoyed, the Russians and Allies
Will liberate us from all senseless war.
The Jews are safe, no more the killing wall.
Gone the extermination camp, gas chambers
And chimneys. We are free once more.
We can come out of our cellars and breathe the air.

(30th April, 11.30 p.m. Berlin. Chuikov is finishing supper with music and army guests.)

Glazunov. Sir, a German Lieutenant-Colonel Seifert
Has crossed the Landwehr Canal suspension bridge
With a white flag and news that General Krebs
Chief of German Staff, a senior officer,
Wants to talk to senior Red Army officers.
Sir, he may surrender Berlin to you.
Chuikov (*calmly*). We are ready to receive the envoys.
Cease all firing around the suspension bridge.

(1st May, 3.50 a.m. Berlin, Chuikov's HQ. Krebs, Dufving, Weidling's Chief of Staff, and Nailandis, a Russian interpreter, with Chuikov and Kleber, a Jewish German interpreter.)

Krebs. I will tell you something secret. You are
The first foreigners to know, Hitler has
Committed suicide.
Chuikov (*hiding surprise*). We know. But when?
Krebs *(handing over documents)*. Around 15.30 hours, yesterday.
In his testament he left all his power
To Dönitz, Goebbels and Bormann,
Who has empowered Goebbels to contact Marshal Stalin,

Leader of the Russian troops. I represent
The German army and now seek peace talks.

Chuikov. Do these documents relate to Berlin or
To the whole of Germany?

Krebs. Goebbels has empowered
Me to speak in the name of the whole German army.

Chuikov. You are here to surrender, or for peace talks,
Not both. Goebbels and you must now lay down
Your arms. I will telephone Zhukov. Wait here.

(He phones.)

Krebs (*to Dufving and Nailandis*). I am buying time, so Bormann and Dönitz
Can open talks with the Allies, who mistrust Stalin.

(1st May, 4 a.m. Kuntsevo, near Moscow. Stalin's dacha. Stalin in bed takes a call from Zhukov. His telephone system allows him to hear the caller as he lies in bed.)

Stalin. Zhukov, I was asleep, it's four o'clock.

Zhukov's voice. The Red Flag is flying over the Reichstag.
We cannot clear Berlin by the May Day parade,
But Hitler is dead. Suicide.

Stalin. So that's the end
Of the bastard. Too bad we could not take
Him alive! But where is Hitler's body?

Zhukov's voice. Burnt.

Stalin. Hmm. You have Krebs, you say, at Chuikov's place.
Relay this to Krebs. Ask him directly now,
Is your mission to achieve a surrender?

Zhukov's voice. The interpreter will interpret Krebs' reply.

Interpreter. No, there are other possibilities.
Permit us to form a new government
In accordance with the Führer's will, and
We will decide everything to your advantage.

Stalin (*angry*). There can be no negotiations, only
Unconditional surrender. No talks with Krebs
Or any Hitlerites.

(1st May, 5 a.m. Chuikov's HQ.)

Chuikov. General, we are waiting for you to surrender.
Unconditionally.

Krebs. No, we shall then
Cease to exist as a legal government.

Chuikov. You insist on an armistice and want
Peace talks, but your troops are surrendering
Everywhere. Our men are now advancing.

(He picks up a Russian newspaper.)

Listen. "Himmler offers peace to the Allies."

"Göring seeks a separate peace with the West."

Krebs. I can do nothing more without direct orders
From Goebbels.

(Sokolovsky arrives.)

Sokolovsky (*after conferring*). I will lay a telephone
Line from Chuikov's military HQ
To the Führer bunker. (*Points to Dufving.*) This officer
Will lay it across no-man's-land. I will
Speak to Goebbels. Take him to Prinz-Albrechtstrasse,
To the Gestapo HQ. (*Exit Dufving.*) Comrades, come
For tea and sandwiches.

(Krebs, Sokolovsky and others follow.)

(1st May, 6 a.m. The Führer bunker. Dufving arrives after being under fire. Goebbels, Bormann, Weidling.)

Dufving. The Russians are demanding unconditional surrender.
Goebbels. I shall never, never agree to that.
Is it possible still to break out of Berlin?
Dufving. Only singly and in civilian clothes.
Goebbels. I will speak to Krebs.

(A few minutes later.)

Krebs' voice. I have been talking to Chuikov, the Russians
Are demanding unconditional surrender.
Goebbels. The Führer forbade capitulation.
Bormann. We must reject it.
Weidling. But the Führer is dead.
Goebbels. The Führer insisted we continue the struggle
To the end. I don't want to surrender.
Weidling. It is too late now for further resistance.
Are you coming with me, Krebs?
Krebs' voice. I shall stay
Till the end, then put a bullet through my brain.

(1st May, 6.15 p.m. Magda Goebbels has got five of her six children into bed. Heidi is the youngest.)

Heidi. They are all in bed, mama. I have a sore throat.
Magda. I will put a scarf round your throat. There, there.
And now I will brush all my darlings' hair
And give you a chocolate, for you are going
To Berchtesgaden, with uncle Adolf.
And you will not be air sick if you have your chocolate.
(*Aside.*) A sleeping potion and then a capsule
Of poison, a gentle and painless death.
Finodin to make them drowsy, then cyanide.
Heidi *(seeing Sgt. Misch, laughing)*. Misch, Misch, you are a fish!

(Magda goes into the bedroom. Silence from the room, then sounds of a struggle.)

Magda's voice. Your chocolate.
Helga's voice. No, no, no.
Magda's voice. Helga, have your chocolate.

(Magda comes out and sits in Goebbels' study and plays solitaire. She is pale and smokes. Fade.)

(1st May, 7.15 p.m. Light on Goebbels and Magda sitting in the conference room with others. Enter Artur Axmann.)

Axmann. I have come to say goodbye.
Goebbels. We had good times
In Wedding, fighting in the streets, punching
Communists and socialists, converting workers
To National Socialism. I remember our Führer
Speaking in a Munich beer cellar one
August, on how the enemy was the Jews.

(1st May, 8.15 p.m. Goebbels and the SS guards, who include Sgt. Misch.)

Misch. Up there is yellow dust and smoke, yet it
Is better than down here. Reich Chancellor,
How long must I operate the switchboard?
I would like to be away before the Red Army come.
Goebbels. Try and break out to the west with Rauch's men.

(Pause.)

(*Aside.*) I am sick at heart. My darlings all dead.
And she, a Medea, without asking me.
And yet, it was my intention all along
That it should be this way, so I should be relieved.

(Pause.)

(*To the guard.*) My wife and I will commit suicide
The same way as the Führer, with cyanide
And my Walther P-38 revolver,
But out in the garden, in the open air.
Not down here in this airless bunker. You
Will not have to carry our bodies upstairs.

(Goebbels puts on his hat, scarf, uniform greatcoat and kid gloves, and offers his arm to his wife. Arm in arm they mount the stairs, watched by Traudl Junge. Fade. Two shots are heard. Light on Krebs as Junge returns.)

Krebs. Well?
Junge. Outside they stood together. Magda
Bit her capsule and slumped to the ground.
Goebbels shot her in the back of her head
As she knelt, then fell on the pitted earth.

Then he bit his capsule and put his gun
To his temple and fired. The SS guards
Have sprinkled petrol on their bodies. They
Are now on fire.

(Bormann, Weidling, others make haste to leave.)

Gerda and I will reach
Wenck's troops with Gunsche and Mohnke. Will you come?

Krebs. No, I will shoot myself with Burgdorf and Schedle.

Bormann. I shall vanish, no one will know if I
Am alive or dead.
(Aside.) But I have planned my escape
And have a fortune on the plane that will
Fly me out.

SCENE 4. UNCONDITIONAL SURRENDER

(1st May, 10.20 p.m. Chuikov tries to sleep with a blanket over his head. Distant noise of merriment. An officer, Lt. Col. Matusov,enters.)

Matusov. Sir, a message received by 79th Guards division
In Russian language.

Chuikov (*sitting up*). What are they doing up there?

Matusov. Roasting an ox,
And dancing, the poet Dolmatovsky
Is reciting patriotic verse.

Chuikov *(scoffing).* Dolmatovsky!
Poets meddle in wars and use their horrors
To scan their lines as Homer did. But how
Did poets change the world? It is Generals who
Change it by smashing armies.

Matusov. Poems outlast
Empires, and poets understand their Age
And fix it in the pattern of history
And the universe, and make the world aware
For all time, in all places, universally
Of the horrors of wars, so men think twice
Before starting what we've finished.

Chuikov. Pah! There are
Always wars.

Matusov *(sadly).* The world does not listen to poets,
And resists being changed. Sir, the message.
(*Handing it over.*) German envoys are on their way to Potsdamer Bridge.

Chuikov. Ceasefire around Potsdamer Bridge.

(2nd May, 5 a.m. A cellar. Kiselyov is waiting to attack.)

Kiselyov *(shouting into the darkness).* Who is asking for a Soviet officer?

Voice. Truce envoys. We have a statement of the

Berlin garrison commander, addressed to
Marshal Zhukov.

Kiselyov. Come over with your hands up.

(Germans appear under a white truce flag, holding a brown folder, with a Hitler Youth boy in a steel helmet. Abyzov covers them with submachine guns. Kiselyov takes out two papers.)

German. One is in German, the other is in Russian.
Kiselyov. The light is too dim.

(He hands the Russian text to his comrade.)

Abyzov (*reading, choking with emotion*).
The German command
Is prepared to negotiate an immediate
Ceasefire. Weidling.

(Silence. Kiselyov puts the papers back in the folder. A Young Communist League organiser arrives.)

Kiselyov. Take the envoys at once
To Potsdamer Bridge.

(They leave.)

Abyzov. I can smell lilacs.

(2nd May, 5.50 a.m. Chuikov is still trying to sleep.)

Matusov. There has been a call from Dr. Goebbels.

(Chuikov jumps up and splashes his face with cold water. Three delegates appear, one with a pink folder.)

Heinersdorf. I am Senior Executive Officer Heinersdorf
Of the Ministry of Propaganda.
This letter is from the Director, Dr. Frische.
Chuikov (*reading*). "Former Reichsmarschall Göring cannot be reached.
Dr. Goebbels is no longer alive.
As one of the few remaining alive, I request
You to take Berlin under your protection."

(The phone rings.)

Yes, yes, I see. Weidling has just surrendered
In person. Berlin has fallen to the forces
Of Marshal Zhukov. Our war is over!

(3rd May, 8 a.m. Lüneburg Heath, Montgomery's last TAC HQ. Flagpole without a flag. Montgomery and Henderson before breakfast.)

Montgomery *(with satisfaction)*. We beat the Russians to Lübeck by twelve hours

And sealed off the Schleswig peninsula and Denmark.
I was just thinking, TAC HQ has done well
As the nerve centre of four Allied armies
In Normandy, and then three, and now two.
Yet we've doubled in size: from twenty-seven
Officers to fifty, from a hundred and fifty
Other ranks to six hundred, and two hundred
Vehicles. We're not so much gypsy nomads now
As an army within an army.

(Enter Dawnay.)

Dawnay. A phone call
From Colonel Murphy, Dempsey's Intelligence Officer.
He's received four German officers who wish
To negotiate surrender terms.

Montgomery. Tell Dempsey to send
Them here, then report back.

(Exit Dawnay. Montgomery pushes a buzzer in his caravan.)

(Aside.) If they come to seek
Unconditional surrender, they must be made
To believe in my personal authority
And command, and my determination
To fight the war relentlessly to the end
Unless they obey me. I must be on a pedestal.
They must see me as the Montgomery who
Took on Rommel in the Egyptian sands
Near the pyramids that marked the limit of
Napoleon's power, and fought him to Tripoli,
Invaded Sicily and southern Italy,
Threatening Rome, and then, as Overlord,
Swept through Normandy, France, Belgium, Holland
And Germany, to the Baltic and the Elbe
Without losing a battle. I must be
The invincible Montgomery they fear,
A man as awesome as Napoleon.
I must be Overlord.

(Enter Trumbell Warren with Dawnay.)

Four German officers
Are coming and may have power to surrender.
I want you to get the Union Jack up,
And when they arrive, line them up under it, facing
The office caravan. Get everyone else
Out of sight, get your side arms and stand at ease
To the side about here and don't move till I say.
Get Colonel Ewart and his interpreter.

(Dawnay and Warren raise the Union flag, and, with rifles, escort in four German officers, two from the Navy in long black leather greatcoats, and two from the Army in grey greatcoats, one – a General – with red lapels. From right to left: General Admiral von Friedeburg, Commander-in-Chief of the Fleet; Gen. Kinzel, Chief of Staff of the German Army, North, who is in his late forties, 6 foot 5 inches and wears a monocle; Rear Admiral Wagner, Flag Officer to the Admiral of the Fleet; Major Friedl, Gestapo, 6 foot 2 inches, 28, with a very cruel face. They represent Dönitz and Keitel. They wait a long time facing closed doors of the three caravans. They are uncomfortably hot in their greatcoats. The door of the centre caravan opens and Montgomery appears, dressed in battledress and black beret. The four Germans immediately salute, Friedl keeping his arm down until Montgomery has finished his salute, which takes a long time and is then nonchalant and casual.)

Montgomery *(bellowing austerely).* Who are you?

Friedeburg. General Admiral von Friedeburg,
Commander-in-Chief the German Navy, sir.

Montgomery. I have never heard of you. Who are you?

Kinzel. General
Kinzel, Chief of Staff of the German Army,
North, sir.

Montgomery. Who are you?

Wagner. Rear Admiral Wagner, Flag
Officer to the Admiral of the Fleet, sir.

Montgomery. Who are you?

Friedl. Major Friedl.

Montgomery. Major? How dare you bring
A major into my Headquarters.

Warren *(whispering).* The Chief's putting on
A pretty good act.

Dawnay. He's rehearsed this all his life.

Montgomery *(barking).* What do you want?

Friedeburg We have come from Field Marshal Busch,
Commander-in-Chief, North, to offer the surrender
Of the three German armies facing the Russians
In Mecklenburg, withdrawing between Rostock
And Berlin.

(Col. Ewart interprets Montgomery's words into German.)

Montgomery. Certainly not. The armies concerned
Are fighting the Russians. If they surrender
To anybody, it must be to the Russians.
Nothing to do with me. But I will naturally
Take prisoner all German soldiers who come

Into my area with their hands up.
I demand that you and Field Marshal Busch
Surrender to me all German forces on
My western and northern flanks, from Holland to
Denmark.

Friedeburg. We refuse to agree as we are anxious
About the civil population there.
We wish to reach an agreement to look after it.
Then we can withdraw our forces as you advance.

Montgomery. You talk about your concern for civilian life.
Six years ago you bombed Coventry and
Wiped out women, children, old men. Your women
And children get no sympathy from me,
You should have thought of them six years ago
Before you Nazis blitzkrieged England. You
Have mistreated your own civilians appallingly.
Near here in Belsen there are Germans like skeletons.
You caused their suffering. There are concentration camps
All over Germany, you have systematically
Killed millions of Jews who were civilians.
Don't talk to me about your Nazi concern
For your German civil population.
I reject any agreement regarding civilians.
Unless you surrender unconditionally
Now, I will order the fighting and the bombing
To continue, and German civilians will die.

(Montgomery turns his back on them. The Germans salute. Montgomery goes to Dawnay.)

Montgomery. They need to reflect on what I've said. Put on
The best possible lunch in the Visitors' Mess
And supply all the drink they want.

(Later. "A" Mess dining-marquee. Two mess tables together. Army blankets over tables. Two maps. The four Germans are led in by Dawnay and Warren. They sit on four chairs at the end of the table while Dawnay and Warren sit on either side. Montgomery comes in and sits at the other end of the table, wearing his Field Marshal's tunic. Col. Ewart interprets.)

Montgomery *(abruptly, quietly)*. First. You must surrender all forces to me
Unconditionally. Second. When I have these
I'll discuss with you the best way of occupying
The area and dealing with civilians.
Third. If you refuse to agree I will go on
Fighting, and a great many soldiers and civilians
Will be killed. The map shows the western front.
Your front line is marked in blue, ours in red.
We have tremendous strength pouring into Germany
On the ground, and sufficient aircraft to have
Ten thousand bombers in the air, day and night.

(The Germans study the maps.)

(Aside.) The strength is untrue, we have no more troops
Or bombers, but they have believed me. They
Have no idea of the front lines. One look
At the maps, and they are giving in.

Friedeburg. We have no power
To agree with your demands. We came about
The civilians. I am prepared to recommend
To Dönitz and to Field Marshal Keitel,
The Chief of Staff at OKW, that they
Offer you unconditional surrender in the north
To save further loss of life. I will go
To them now with Friedl, and return in forty-eight hours.

Montgomery. Twenty-four, and there will be day-and-night
Allied bombing if there is no surrender.
And ask Keitel about the surrender of
Other areas, for example Norway.
I can send you on to SHAEF. I will draw up
An account of this meeting which you will sign
And take a copy to Keitel.

(4th May. Führer bunker. The conference room. Dönitz and von Friedeburg.)

Dönitz. Now that Hitler is dead, the last obstacle
Has been removed for an Allied-German alliance
Against the Soviet Union. The Allies may
Now regard Germany as a bulwark against
Communism in Europe and may choose
A new policy of an East-West split,
Which will also split the Alliance. Truman's terms are
Unconditional surrender of all German armies
To the Big Three. Eisenhower and Churchill
Support this. They say they will not accept
A general surrender in the West
Only. While we pursue an Allied-German
Alliance, our policy should be piecemeal
Surrender to the Western Allies, to SHAEF,
While fighting on in the East, and resisting
Capture by the Red Army, which is to be feared;
And delaying surrenders as long as possible
So our troops in the East can escape to the West.
You have done well with Montgomery. Delay
Him this afternoon, and then go to SHAEF,
To Eisenhower, and seek to surrender
The remaining German forces in the West.

(4th May, 5 p.m. Lüneburg Heath. Montgomery in his caravan.)

Montgomery. Warlords expand into their neighbours' land
As pain expands into a healthy limb,

Sending waves of troops like bacteria.
They unify their civilisations through hurt,
Or defend them against a spreading sore
Like inoculations that control disease.
Warlords are aggressors or defenders,
Attackers of civilisations or preservers
Like germs or antibodies which cause pain
Or bring relief. I cauterised the wound,
I acted to preserve the whole body.
Civilisation swells into barbarism
As a healthy body erupts into a boil
That infects the circulation of the blood
And turns septic with putrefying matter,
The squeezing out of which restores its health
So the limb can move as freely as before.
Is not all mankind one body with many limbs?
Warlords, stern men whose authority controls
Front lines on wall-maps without pity, and moves
Armies and orders thousands to their death,
Embody their nation's ego in their own,
Harangue the people forward to their whim
Or just defence. The worst poison the whole
Until they are lanced by the best. I, a jousting
Knight and preserver, have pierced the German boil
And now squeeze out the puss that oozes from
The inflamed mound, plaster it back to health,
Immunise the diseased flesh so it's free from germs.

(Enter the four Germans with a fifth, Col. Pollok. Von Friedeburg climbs the steps and enters the caravan.)

Montgomery. Will you sign the full surrender terms as
I demanded?

Friedeburg. Yes.

Montgomery. In that case, come with me.

(They go into a newly erected surrender tent where there are Allied photographers, soldiers and war correspondents, all very excited. A trestle table covered with an army blanket, an inkpot and army pen. Two BBC microphones. The German delegation salute Montgomery, who salutes back.)

I shall now read the *Instrument of Surrender.*

(He puts on tortoiseshell-rimmed reading spectacles.)

"The German Command agrees to the surrender
Of all German armed forces in Holland,
In Northwest Germany including the
Frisian Islands and Heligoland, and all
Other islands, in Schleswig-Holstein, and

In Denmark, to the C-in-C 21 Army Group."
Unless the German delegation sign
The document in front of me, I will order
Hostilities to resume at once.

(Col. Ewart translates. The German delegates nod.)

(Rising.) The German officers will sign in order
Of seniority.

(Von Friedeburg, Keisel, Wagner, then Pollok sign.)

And Major Friedl
Will sign last. *(Pause.)* Now I will sign on behalf of
The Supreme Allied Commander, General
Eisenhower. That concludes the surrender.
(Aside.) The war is over, and they surrendered to *me*.
I have appeared a ruthless commander
Who will not be disobeyed. I took a million
Prisoners in April, making three million since D-Day,
And I have just saved two million civilians in
Schleswig-Holstein from starvation, while Bradley,
In Wiesbaden, has said we may be fighting
A year from now. I have just saved millions
From suffering and have ended the war
And I bluffed to further your will, O Lord.

(4th May, later. Rheims, SHAEF's HQ. Bedell Smith, Strong who interprets, and von Friedeburg.)

Bedell Smith. General Eisenhower insists that there must be
A general surrender on eastern
And western fronts simultaneously.
General Eisenhower will not see any
German officers until the document
Of unconditional surrender has been signed.
No bargaining, sign it now.
Friedeburg. I have no power
To sign.
Bedell Smith. I insist. Look at these maps. The might
Of the AEF makes your position hopeless.
Friedeburg. I will cable Dönitz.

(6th May, evening. Rheims. Jodl, a Prussian with a monocle, is with Smith and Strong.)

Jodl. General Jodl, the German Chief of Staff.
Bedell Smith. We've been waiting for von Friedeburg for two days.
Jodl. Admiral Dönitz did not give von Friedeburg
Permission to sign. He is willing to surrender
To the Allies, but not to the Red Army.
He will order a ceasefire on the western front
No matter what SHAEF do about the surrender.

Bedell Smith. The surrender has to be a general one
To all the Allies.

Jodl. I'll need forty-eight hours
To get the instructions to outlying units.

Bedell Smith. That's impossible. I'll ask General Eisenhower.

(He knocks and goes into Eisenhower's room next door.)

Eisenhower. I heard it. I think he's trying to gain time
So Germans can escape across the Elbe
From the Russians. Tell Jodl I'll break off
All negotiations and seal the western front,
Preventing any westward movement by
German soldiers and civilians, unless he signs.
But I can grant a forty-eight hour delay
Before announcing the surrender, as he requests.

(Smith returns to Jodl who is with Strong.)

(7th May, 1 a.m. Führer bunker. The conference room. Dönitz.)

Dönitz *(angrily)*. Eisenhower's demands are sheer extortion.
I will have to accept them, and at least
Many troops can escape from the Russians
During the forty-eight hour delay. Cable
Jodl: "Full power to sign in accordance
With conditions."

(7th May, 2.41 a.m. Rheims, SHAEF. Eisenhower's office. Strong enters with Jodl. Eisenhower sits behind his desk, Jodl bows and then stands to attention.)

Strong. All the signatures are here. Jodl, Friedeburg.

Eisenhower. Do you understand the terms? Are you ready to
Execute them?

Jodl. Yes.

Eisenhower. If the terms are violated
You will be held personally responsible.

(Jodl bows and leaves.)

I'm dead beat.

(He rises and goes outside. Photographers appear. Newsreel camera.)

(Later.)

Eisenhower. Message to the CCS. "The mission of
This Allied force was fulfilled at 02.41
May 7 1945."

(Champagne is opened.)

I haven't been
To sleep for three days. The war's ended.

(Everyone cheers and shouts "Hurrah".)

(7th May, 8 a.m. Lüneburg Heath, TAC HQ. Dawnay to Montgomery.)

Dawnay. The surrender to Eisenhower has been signed at Rheims.
The Russian one will be signed in Berlin
Tomorrow by Jodl and Keitel.

Montgomery. Not before time.
If Eisenhower had seen the emissaries,
And not left Bedell Smith to negotiate
While he waited in the next room, three days
Would not have slipped by, allowing German units
Facing the Russians to escape westwards.
True to the end in his incompetence.

SCENE 5. VICTORY IN EUROPE

(8th May, V.E. Day. Chorus of Londoners.)

Chorus. Victory in Europe Day. Huge crowds in New
York, where ticker tape and confetti snowed
Through the air; in Paris, where citizens cheered
From their balconies as Allied planes flew past;
And in Moscow where crowds hoisted Russian soldiers
High above their heads. And here in London,
Standing, leaning from windows, hanging from lampposts,
Crowds filled the streets waiting for the expected news,
Silent as the official announcement came.
In London we heard Churchill speak at three:
"The German war is therefore at an end."
There was a gasp as he spoke of "the evil-doers
Who are now prostrate before us".
The war against Japan has yet to be won
But Japan is far away, the threat is over,
No more will V-1s and V-2s rain down
From the skies, bringing death and destruction to our cities.
We heard the words, he ended "Advance Britannia,
Long live the cause of freedom. God save the King."
We cheered with relief and hope and renewal.
We massed in front of Buckingham Palace and sang
"We want the King" and he came out with the Queen
And his two daughters and we waved and sang
"For he's a jolly good fellow", and they waved back.
Churchill came out with the King and Queen;
The King, bare-headed in naval uniform,
Churchill in a civilian, parliamentary suit.
We cheered and waved, and crushed into Whitehall
And Churchill came out on the balcony
Of the Ministry of Health and we all sang
"Land of Hope and Glory", he too. Then he spoke.
"This is your victory," he told us. "No, it's yours,"

We roared back. He said, "In all our long history,
We have never seen a greater day than this."
He gave the V-sign, and that night we danced
In the streets and drank and embraced strangers,
London was floodlit, searchlight beams played
In the sky, ships' sirens sounded from the Thames,
There were bonfires, fireworks, and we drank and laughed,
We revelled and sang and danced and cheered till late,
We were joyful, for danger had passed, we had
Survived the Blitz and the flying rocket bombs.
Europe was free from Nazi tyranny,
There was a great hope, a new world had been born!

(5th June. Berlin. Eisenhower, Zhukov, de Tassigny and Montgomery at the riverside club which is the Soviet delegation's HQ.)

Eisenhower. I'm worried about Churchill. In his first election
Broadcast he said a Labour government
"Would have to fall back on some form of Gestapo
No doubt very humanely directed
In the first place." He's said Socialism is
"Interwoven with Totalitarianism
And the abject worship of the State".
He's presenting Labour – Attlee – as Nazi.
Montgomery *(shrugging).* He's overexcitable and larger than life,
He must have been carried away when he said it.

(Eisenhower turns to Zhukov.)

(Aside). Here I am in Berlin to divide it into four zones,
And to divide Germany into four zones too,
And I, a soldier, will command the British
Sector of Berlin and of occupied Germany,
Military Governor of a quarter of each.
If I'd got here in November, Yalta
Would not have happened, I would have dictated zones,
I would have told the Russians where they stopped.
Instead the Soviet army controls Poland.
My TAC family's broken up. Sweeney
And Ewart dead like Poston, Warren in the law,
Dawnay and Henderson in the city,
Williams a don, BonDurant US Army.
Many of us have been together since Alamein.
I shall live alone at Ostenwalde and rule
Sectors of Germany, like a Viceroy,
Without any sense of revenge at all
And now that the war is over, sink into
Lassitude, boredom, disillusionment.
I have little interest in the occupation.
I am a man of action and contemplation,
Not a man of administration and red tape.

(21st July. Berlin, Charlottenburgerstrasse. Victory parade, the British saluting base. Churchill and Montgomery beside Alexander, Eden, Attlee.)

Churchill. You must have felt strange, acting for the King
And investing Zhukov and Rokossovsky
With the Order of the Bath under the Brandenburg Gate
For conquering Berlin.

Montgomery. The Berliners cheered.

Churchill. The day after I arrived and you greeted me
I visited the ruins of Hitler's
Chancellery, went down into the bunker
With Eden and Sarah, saw the settee,
And when I came out a crowd of Germans gathered
And they all began to cheer, except for one old man
Who shook his head. Berliners regard us as
Their liberators. My hate died with the surrender.
The next day at Potsdam I lunched with Truman
And Stimson put a piece of paper in front
Of me saying "Babies satisfactorily born".
I didn't know what he meant. He explained:
The test in the American desert has worked.
The atomic bomb is a reality.
Next day I told Truman I wanted to continue
The reciprocal relationship between
Britain and the US. The reply came back,
Eventually, that the US Chiefs of Staff
Will be willing to consult with their British
Opposite numbers, but in the event of
Disagreement the final decision
On the action to be taken will lie with
The US Chiefs of Staff. And Britain will
Have to accept American strategic
Direction in the war against Japan.
We're in a new era, Monty. The US
Is a superpower above the rest. Stalin
Doesn't know yet. I had dinner with Stalin,
He was very friendly, told me I would have
A majority of eighty. He assured
Me he is "against Sovietisation" of
The eastern European countries, which "will have
Free elections". The question is, is he lying?
And if so will the atomic bomb make him back down?
Oh look, here comes the Victory parade.

(24th July. Potsdam, the Cecilienhof Castle. End of plenary session of the Potsdam conference. Round table. Truman, Stalin and Churchill.)

Churchill. Mr President, we British went to war
To stop Hitler from having the atomic
Bomb before anyone else and using it

To wipe out every Jew, till none were left.
Two German scientists got the formula,
Niels Bohr confirmed the equations with Einstein.
Admiral Canaris confirmed it all to us.
If Hitler had got nuclear weapons first,
He would have ruled the world. Roosevelt and I
Rebuffed Bohr when he tried to persuade us
To hand nuclear knowledge to Stalin.
Is it really wise to tell him now he rules
Eastern Europe?

Truman. But Stalin has to know.
In view of what we propose to do in Japan.
I must tell him, I'm going to tell him now
In a way he will not wholly understand.

(Truman and Stalin talk.)

Churchill *(to Eden)*. Can you see what Stalin's saying? "A new bomb?
Of extraordinary power? Probably decisive
On the whole Japanese war. What a bit of luck!"
Now Stalin knows about the atomic bomb,
As he had to, he will want one for himself.
I have an ominous feeling that we
Are facing a new order that is insecure,
That we'll need to strengthen the United Nations
In the coming post-war world.

(27th July. Downing Street. Brooke and Capt. Pim.)

Pim. Outwardly he's taken it on the chin
Without flinching. I brought him the early returns
Yesterday morning, the loss of ten seats.
He was in his bath. He appeared surprised, asked me
To get him a towel. He spent all day in his
Blue siren suit in the Map Room, when it was clear
There would be a Labour landslide. After all
He's done for them.

(Pim shakes his head in disbelief).

Brooke. He has been wrongly advised.
He said that Labour would need "a Gestapo"
To rule, a comment so obviously untrue
It suggested to the electorate
He is out of touch.

(Enter Churchill.)

Churchill. I'm saying goodbye to my
Chiefs of Staff. We've been through a lot, you and I.
We came through, to be shot down not by Hitler
But by the British people.

Brooke. I'm so dreadfully –

(He chokes back tears and cannot speak.)

Churchill. They are perfectly entitled to vote as they please.
This is democracy, this is what we've been fighting for.
Attlee's flown to Potsdam this morning. He asked
If I'd continue there as he's inexperienced,
But I said No, the British people want you,
You go and deal with Stalin on their behalf
And make sure he keeps his word and holds elections
In Poland and the Eastern European countries.
You and Stalin are both socialists, you go
And sort out Russia's misinterpretation
Of the Yalta decisions. The Potsdam meeting
Grew out of what I told Truman on May the twelfth,
That an iron curtain is drawn on the Russian front
From Lübeck to Trieste, including Poland,
And we don't know what is going on behind it.
Still, it's not my problem now. But it grieves me,
Because of Roosevelt's illness and death, and now this
Popular hankering for a form of social reform
We can't afford in our post-war bankruptcy,
Two inexperienced men who were not at Yalta,
Truman and Attlee, will give Stalin what he wants,
He will get away with a military empire.
The Victory in Europe was a partial victory.
In eastern Europe we've all been defeated.
What galls me most is, I have been denied
The power to shape the future of the post-war world.
It's like Monty. You give them victory and
They demote you. They are as fickle as
A woman with several lovers. In May
They shout "It's *your* victory", in July you're out,
They depose you.

(Brooke places a reassuring hand on his shoulder. Pim and Brooke leave.)

(Slumping, alone.) Hitler offered me peace, I rejected it.
I was not chosen to follow Chamberlain's line.
We went to war to stop Hitler's research
So he would not explode an atomic bomb over London.
Two German scientists had discovered
Uranium fission in Berlin in
December thirty-eight. Hahn and Strassmann.
Frisch and Meitner confirmed it that February,
When Bohr isolated isotope 235
Before he and Fermi went to Washington.
On August 2nd Einstein wrote to
Roosevelt about the military implications

Of atomic energy, and the same day
Roosevelt appointed a three-man Advisory
Committee on Uranium, and though U.S.
Atomic weapons development did not begin
Until October forty-one, that is when
We knew we had to fight Hitler, for he
Could threaten London with an atomic bomb
If Heisenberg were to build it fast enough,
And all Jews in the world could be put in
One territory and wiped out in a flash.
The high curve of my Prime Ministership
Was to stand alone against the evil might
Of the barbarous Nazis. I advanced the stature
Of my nation by measuring it against a giant,
I took it on and beat it before an admiring
World. Like Bismarck, I showed that the British Empire
Was the main great power and could not be challenged
By a German rule that threatened its interests.
I acted to perpetuate the strength
Of the British Empire, I drew on our reserves,
Confident that we would get them back by
Advancing our position, securing goodwill
Contracts and trade. Instead, our American allies
Ensured that Stalin took our position;
An ungrateful nation replaced me with socialism,
Which will not cash in the goodwill, and will
Bankrupt us; and now, looking back I wonder,
Should I have staked our empire when I could
Have reached an accommodation with Hitler
As Chamberlain tried? I sometimes think politics
Is persuading people to believe fantasies,
And that politicians are convincing preachers
Of dreams the public would like to believe.

(Silence.)

Now that I am in the wilderness again
I ponder that had I remained Prime Minister
I would have persuaded the Americans to use
Their new power, which is drawn from victory and
The atomic bomb, to confront Stalin,
To make him behave decently in Europe;
And I cannot help wondering, Truman has been weak
Towards Stalin, was this deliberate,
Has Marshall an understanding with him,
Is that why Eisenhower sent Stalin that cable?
I am better placed to judge than most,
And I see the hand of Zionism in the war.
At Yalta Roosevelt told Stalin he was a Zionist
And Stalin said he was one "in principle".

The Jews will have a new state in Palestine
For which I spoke in 1939,
In accordance with the Balfour Declaration
Which was made in exchange for Rothschild's guarantee
He'd bring America into the First World War
On the British side and save us from defeat.
So America entered the First World War
In return for Balfour's promise to a Rothschild
That there would be a homeland for the Jews
In the British mandate of Palestine,
And now the German Jewish Rothschild family
Have seen the Nazis fall and will have their state,
And if I were suspicious I might think
That Hitler was lured into war with Zionist money
Through House, Baruch, Schacht, Wall Street and I. G.
  Farben,
Vast sums that reached the Nazis through Warburg banks
So that Nazis could massacre Jews and swing
International opinion behind this new state.
But I cannot be suspicious. That way madness lies.
That way history is not what it seems, and leaders
Who appear to do their best for their nations
In fact work to another agenda, luring
The unsuspecting into catastrophic wars
That suit their own interests that remain hidden
From view. And what the history books describe
Is wrong, for history is what a cabal intrigued.
I do not want to believe that, I prefer
The view that leaders do their best for their peoples
Without pressures they know nothing of.

(Silence.)

I want to believe that Eisenhower chose
On military grounds not to go to Berlin –
Not that there has since Lenin been
A Zionist-American-Communist joint front
Which engineered the rise of Roosevelt
And, also, the succession of Stalin,
And that Eisenhower was under orders
To make sure that Russia's post-war position
In Europe will be the dominant one,
That he therefore had a political objective
In making sure that Stalin was first to Berlin
By vetoing my wish to attack the soft
Underbelly of the Reich, and then Monty.
I rose after writing to Baruch in thirty-nine,
And after speaking in the House of Commons
In favour of setting up a Zionist state
In Palestine. I fell at the hands of

Public opinion, which can be manipulated.
I do not want to think I fell through a plot,
Because I tried to stand up to Stalin
And was felt to thwart a hidden alliance
Between Zionists, Americans and Russians
Who influenced public opinion against me.
I prefer not to believe that Zionism
Was behind my rise and engineered my fall.
I want to accept the surface of history
And not stir the muddy depths which cloud the reflection.
I prefer not to know "groups" that would run the world.
I stood up to the two most terrible tyrants
Mankind has ever suffered; and I fell.
I am full of questions that will echo
To the end of this century and beyond,
As we regroup in a United States of Europe
And eventually in a United States of the World.

(End of July. Potsdam. Stalin speaks through an interpreter at the conference.)

Stalin. You were not at Teheran where we agreed
That I would co-ordinate my offensive
With Overlord in return for a new
Western Soviet frontier that will make sure
Germany can never again invade Russia,
A defensive barricade; and at Yalta
We agreed that the Oder-Neisse line should be
The western boundary of Poland and that all
East German territory to the western side
Of the Neisse should be under provisional
Polish administration, which will organise
Free elections, as I discussed with Churchill
Before he left for England.

Truman. I think Poland's
Western boundary should be deferred to another
Conference.

Stalin *(casually).* The rest is acceptable?

(Truman and Attlee look at each other uncertainly and nod.)

(6th August. The cruiser Augusta returning from Potsdam. Truman and Aide.)

Aide. I have an eye-witness report from Hiroshima.
The uranium bomb was two thousand times the blast
Of the heaviest bomb ever used before.

Truman. Describe what happened.

Aide. A flash and with a roar
A yellow and orange fireball rolled and shot
Eight thousand feet into the sunny air

And turned into a ten-mile high column
Of black smoke, a mushroom cloud rose and hung,
And as the great wind dropped, on the ground
A flat desert where there had been a city,
The roads like tracks across endless waste ground:
Hiroshima has disappeared, and in its place
Rubble, ruin, twisted metal and people
Horribly burned, lying still, stirring or
Groaning and crawling or just sitting dazed.
Over ten square miles a thousand fires blazed,
And a hundred thousand may have died at once.
Birds had burnt up in mid-air, and people's brains,
Eyes, intestines burst, their skin peeled, and some
Burned to cinders as they stood. Others had
The print of their clothes burnt onto their naked backs.
It was awesome. Sir, this new weapon which
Makes a thousand-bomber firebomb raid look
Insignificant, has in one blast outmoded
Six years of war, which must now be strikes like this
That can wipe out half a country without warning.
A new terror has arrived, that makes one yearn
For the sort of world war we have just seen
Where hatred has a limited radius,
That of a conventional high explosive bomb.

Truman (*with awe*). This is the greatest thing in history. We had
To drop the bomb, I had a report that
Half a million Americans would be killed
If we were to invade Japan. General
Marshall and I are quite clear it will stop
The Pacific war before the Russians reach
Japan, which we can occupy alone.
We have learned from Berlin, where the Russians
Occupy half to our quarter. The hope is that
This bomb will abolish war because no one will
Invade another's territory and risk its use.

Aide. So long as Stalin doesn't steal it from us.

(Silence. They exchange glances.)

(6th August. Moscow, the Kremlin. Stalin, Zhukov and Eisenhower, with the US Ambassador to Moscow, Averell Harriman. Interpreter. Stalin speaks in Russian.)

Stalin. Have you and Zhukov had a good time in Moscow?

Eisenhower. Very good, thank you.

Stalin. Tomorrow there is a Sports
Parade in Red Square. You will stand with me
On Lenin's Tomb.

Harriman. A unique honour for
A non-Communist.

Stalin. And I wish to apologise
For the actions of the Red Army in April.
I told you it would advance towards Dresden,
The place you proposed in your cable to me.
There was a last-minute change to Berlin,
I would like to explain the military reasons
In detail later. You have the right to accuse
Me of lack of frankness, and I would not want
You to believe this of me.

Eisenhower. We were expecting Dresden
But what's done is done. I appreciate your apology
And your frankness.

Stalin. The Soviet Union needs
American help to recover from the war;
Not just money but technicians and science.
(To Harriman.) General Eisenhower is a very great man
Not only because of his military accomplishments
But because of his human, friendly, kind and frank
Nature. He is not a coarse man like most military.

Eisenhower. Marshal Stalin impresses me as benign
And fatherly. There's a genuine atmosphere
Of hospitality.

Stalin *(laughing).* Eh, Zhukov.

Eisenhower. And,
I see nothing in the future that would prevent
Russia and the United States from being the closest
Possible friends.

(A message has arrived which Stalin reads.)

Stalin *(to Eisenhower).* Your Government has dropped
An atomic bomb on Japan, at Hiroshima.
The city is devastated, hundreds
Of thousands are dead.

(Silence.)

Eisenhower. Before this, I could see
No danger to friendly relations between our countries.
Now I am not so sure. I had hoped that
This bomb would not figure in this war. People
Will feel insecure again.

Stalin *(laughing).* The Soviet Union
Can now declare war on Japan as I promised
At Yalta.

(15th August. Washington, The White House. Truman and Gen. Marshall.)

Marshall. Now that Japan has surrendered, the post-war
Arrangements need to be made. For four years
We have supplied the British with food imports
Without any cash payment: Lend-Lease should stop.

The British people have voted out Churchill
For a crowd that want Beveridge's Welfare State
With universal health care we haven't got here.
They're financing something they can't afford
On the back of our subsidy, which should now be stopped.

Truman. They've virtually bankrupted their Empire fighting the war.
There will be austerity if we cancel our aid.

Marshall. There should be no consultation, just cancel it.
If they want to give things to their people that ours
Haven't got, fine, but not on our subsidy.
Let them do it out of their Empire or
Their own wealth-creation, as we do here.
We should not be paying for their socialism.

Truman. Cancel it. It was a war-time arrangement,
And the Japanese war has come to an end.

(November. Frankfurt, the office of I. G. Farben. Eisenhower alone. He studies a tea-mug.)

Eisenhower. This mug has all life on it. A town at war,
At peace; bodies, lovers; a ruin, a church;
A storm, sun; disease, health; a wolf, a dove;
Fields, tanks. It's a work of art, and it holds my tea.

(He puts down his mug.)

America won the war and rules the world
As the only power to have the atomic bomb,
Having fought in Europe and the Pacific.
I led America to victory and
Like Octavius see greater things ahead.
As Commander I found life exciting,
I had an appetite for each day's news.
I find administering Germany tedious,
Here in the office of I. G. Farben.
Marshall is going to China to sort out
The civil war, the Communist threat to Peking,
And I can succeed him as Chief of Staff
And judging from the cheering as I rode
In triumph in an open car, and waved,
I could then become Augustus in the White House.
I long for the States. But what do I do about Kay?
In June I wanted to divorce Mamie,
But Marshall told me it would ruin my career
And refused permission, and I now want to live
With Mamie and not with Kay. Away from war
And exhausting hours and tension, I can be myself,
Vital, virile again, with my natural flow,
Which power has blocked, restored. Kay feels alone
And deserted. And I know I've failed her.
I've got her a job in Berlin with General Clay.

Now I will dictate a business-like letter
Explaining she cannot work for me any more,
And go to Paris at once, and then the States.

(He picks up the mug.)

I do not want to visit the ruins
Of our relationship, like a smashed city,
And wander in the rubble of our streets
Where once there were avenues and green parks,
And say goodbye amid broken memories
Of when it was sunlit and magical,
I would rather slip away without despair.
There is a waste in my heart, a devastation.
I am as shattered as this Germany.

(November. Stalin's Kremlin HQ. Stalin and Beria.)

Beria. Our agents Vasilevsky and Terletsky
Received answers to their questions from Niels Bohr
At two meetings with him in Copenhagen
On the fourteenth and sixteenth of November.
The twenty-two questions were put by Kurchatov.
Bohr had the blessing of the Americans
Oppenheimer, Fermi and Szilard for
This leak of the American atom bomb.
He said there must be international control
Over atomic weapons, hence their leak.
Kurchatov, Khariton and Sakharov
Are now confident that there will be a
Soviet uranium and plutonium bomb.

Stalin. Good. We want our well-wishers in the US
And Britain to find out the technology
To make comrade Sakharov's task easier.

(Exit Beria. Stalin is alone.)

(Satisfied.) I did it. All along I had my own agenda
To transform the Soviet Union from a nation
Of backward peasants with horses and carts
Into a major world power all would fear.
I terrified them into the twentieth century,
Then I allied with Hitler to carve up part
Of Poland. I made overtures to Britain to
Keep pressure on Hitler from the western side.
I counted on Hitler to attack me.
He fell into my trap, he readily obliged.
Then my main thought was a Soviet empire
In eastern Europe and the Balkans. I delayed
Taking Berlin until I had overrun
Eastern Europe. At Yalta, I used their fear
Of Hitler, who was already finished, to redraw

Occupation zones and Poland's borders,
Knowing my stooges would seize power, invite
Russian troops in and give me indirect control.
The Allies were too trusting, they believed my words.
I made them honour their mistake, and took
Berlin. If I were Montgomery I would feel
Aggrieved, but imperial diplomacy
Is about power and achieving your interests.
The Russian civilisation is in a stage
Of union, of reunifying its own lands.
It has expanded to control its parts,
All its territories. It has always claimed
Poland and Eastern Europe, there has been no conquest
Of the European civilisation, which is younger than ours,
Merely a readjustment of our borders.
I secured the Soviet Union's interests –
I needed less than a week to invade
Japanese-held China and secure our
Interests at Port Arthur and at Dairen –
And will go down in history as the ruler
Who, like Ivan the Terrible, held the union
Together and expanded it to its greatest extent.
I have been a Genghis Khan, a Tamburlaine
Over a greater area than they conquered.
Berlin was the key, for with it came Poland,
Czechoslovakia, Hungary, and all the rest.
Occupation is nine points of the law.
And now, thanks to Niels Bohr, though he barely
Knows it, I am about to have the atomic bomb.
I shall challenge America and spread
Soviet influence throughout the rest of the world.
Man is material, which can be raised
Like clay a potter shapes on a turning wheel.

(December. Lüneburg Heath. Montgomery standing alone on the heath.)

Montgomery. So many times during the last eight months
I have longed to feel this heather under my feet.
Travelling around Germany on my train,
Which I captured from Hitler, I longed to see
Lüneburg Heath again, the place where I
Ended my long campaign from the Egyptian sands
And my command of the Americans
By receiving the German surrender.

(He falls silent and looks around.)

Marginalised, I was marginalised,
And with me Britain, and as a result
It's an American-Russian world now.
Did the Americans do it deliberately

To advance their power, or were they just blind?
In not going to Berlin, was Eisenhower
Just being fair, too trusting and naive?
Or honouring a deal that Roosevelt made
At Teheran with Stalin, to secure
A Russian offensive that would coincide
With my Overlord: Berlin in return for attack?
If I had led the Allies into Berlin
Before Churchill met Stalin at Yalta,
I could have held back the Communist tide,
All Europe would be Anglo-American.
Now the Soviet Union surrounds Berlin
And controls Poland. If my way had prevailed,
This would not be so. Does it matter now?
Yes, for many millions will not be free.
Or is there a stability I don't know about,
Is there now a secret east-west accord?
I can't believe that. Once again, I have been proved right.

(Silence.)

I sometimes question what my battles were for.
Was the world a better place for what I did?
Yes. I pushed back Fascism in North Africa
And Italy and North Europe. But as fast
As I rolled it back, Communism took its place.
Hitler was Overlord of Europe till
I invaded Normandy. Who's Overlord now?
Not Eisenhower; not Churchill, nor me, we
Were marginalised. Europe is now divided
Between Truman, all-powerful with his new bomb,
And Stalin, whose huge Red Army has occupied
The east and who cannot be dislodged by
An atomic bomb. Stalin is Overlord –
Apparently, for the real Overlord is you,
My guiding, Providential, loving Light
Without whom Hitler would have won this war.

(Silence.)

Now America is an atomic power
Thanks to German scientific insight,
And Russia will soon be one too, warfare
As I have known it is of the past, finished:
Operating from mobile caravans through scouts
Close to the battle front, like Marlborough
Or Wellington or Napoleon. War
Is now a distant nuclear missile threat.
And where does that leave Great Britain? Not great.
The body of our European civilisation
Has suffered a malignant cancer, which has been cut out

With our consent by the surgery of two other
Civilisations: the American and the Russian.
Now, after our civil war, we are convalescing
And our health will be restored.
But no more have we the energy for empire,
No more is our role in Africa or Asia.
Empire is at an end. We have ended
An imperial phase in our long history.
If that had to happen, then the civil war had to too.
Now the British Empire will collapse for we've
Bankrupted ourselves to recover from Hitler,
And a new Europe will grow out of this ruin.
I, who rule a quarter of Germany, consent
That German people should be in our new Europe
In which Britain, an island, will be different.

(Silence.)

Now, hearing the birds, watching the butterflies,
I know Nature's content. Rabbits, flowers, bees,
Birds, fish, grass, leafy trees, the universe
Just grows despite titanic wars like storms,
Which wreak havoc and uproot. After a storm
The air is so sweet, the earth is so pure,
Unsullied by the blot of tanks and guns.
I love the earth, the trees, the sky, the sun,
And you, my Overlord, who manifests
Into bud and blossom and lambs in the spring
And copper leaves, hips, haws, berries in the autumn.
I love the clear blue sky, the vast seas
The green hills and forests and mountain streams
And valleys and pure rivers. Your storms
Serve a purpose, they shake what is dead,
Blow off crinkled leaves, smash down the old
To prepare for the new. Lord, may there be
No more war. But I know, there must always be
Renewing storms. I would gladly live
In my caravan to be near your world,
At one with your will, in union with Oneness.

(Silence.)

Civilisations go through seasons, we are
In a new season now, a season of winter,
A bleakness and clearing up of devastation,
And then a new growth. I can feel it ahead.
A cold time as we recover, and then,
Though I may not live to see it, spring.
I accept your universe, with its storms and growth.
Through contradictions harmony prevails.
Life is an endless gush of opposites.

A tussle between darkness and light,
Pain and joy, hate and love, and war and peace.
All are manifestations of the One Light
You are, which I know at nine each night,
Which guided me to this point. And now I see
That evil swells like a dark thundercloud
That must grow darker for the rain to burst,
But it is always temporary in your scheme.
Hitler laid waste like a great hurricane;
Now Stalin is gathering like a tornado.
Of his own accord he will blow himself out.

(Silence.)

I see I was not meant to reach Berlin.
That was the will of the one Great Harmony,
And, Providence, with Ike as its instrument
(And Patton and his "niece", who are both now dead),
Blocked me, and in my self-will, egotism,
Vanity and national pique, I did not see this,
And complained, not understanding. But now I see.
The earth is made leprous by volcanic wars,
Happy is the place that does not erupt,
Where opposites live at peace, in harmony,
Which is not disfigured by the disorder of war.
Lord, your ways are magnificently strange,
And the loving spirit in your universe
Endlessly brings new shoots from desolation.
And reconciles all diverging views in
A latent harmony that is often obscured.

(He pauses.)

I said goodbye to the other kind of love
When an insect bite took my wife from me.
I sat with her, she looked so calm, peaceful.
I rose and gently kissed her serene face.
Then the men came in and screwed down the coffin lid.
Since then I've had no use for that kind of love.
I've preferred the cheering of crowds, as when I rode
In an open horse-drawn State landau, and waved.
As a German bomb had destroyed my flat.
I asked the King for a grace and favour home,
But gratitude did not extend that far.
And so I must live in a "borrowed" home, alone.

(Silence.)

For over a year I implemented a plan.
Now there is no need for it any more
I feel slightly lost, a warlord without a war.
I must live again without a plan, I must find

My meaning in God's world, beneath reason.
I must look for the plan in the universe,
Rather than Rommel's, and there is as much
Deception and subterfuge, God is a General
Who guards his secrets from his troops' eyes.

(Silence.)

Under the atomic bomb the world will draw together.
There is a need for a new philosophy
Which embraces all mankind, all religions,
A metaphysic for the United Nations.
The only way I can live without a plan
Is to piece the potsherds of the universe
Into the tessellated urn from which they came
And, like an archaeologist, know its pattern
In the fresh air of the universal sunshine.

(He pauses.)

I understand that Brooke and I will be
Made peers in the New Year Honours, and I will be
Viscount Montgomery of Alamein.
But I have moved beyond war and conflict,
I look for opposites being reconciled.
I hope my son and Rommel's become friends.
And I ask of future generations
Not glorification or triumphalism,
But sober assessment, and credit where due.
More than Lawrence of Arabia, like the moon I drew
Tides of men, and flung them like a stormy sea
Up the beaches across the Channel, towards here.
Like Marlborough, I never lost a battle.
I stood for a Britain that had greatness.
I was a potsherd in the larger pattern,
A fragment, an episode, a chain of events
In the unfolding process of our history;
But I am proud of what our deeds achieved,
How our courage transformed our time, our Age,
And in the stillness of the trees, round this heather,
In the ghostly moaning of the winter wind
Which sounds as if the dead are gathering,
I hear the million men of Overlord
Roar their approval for a job well done.